THE ANSWERS TO CANCER

Glycoscience, Newly-discovered Codes to Health & Well-being and How DNA Therapy Works to Kill Cancer Cells

GARRY ESTRADA, M.S.

Copyright ©2019 Garry Estrada | Garry Estrada Publishing

ALL RIGHTS RESERVED. This book contains material protected under International and Federal Laws and Treaties. Any unauthorized reprint or use of this material is prohibited. No portion of this book may be reproduced, stored in a retrieval system, or transmitted in any form or by any means — electronic, mechanical, photocopy, recording, scanning, or other — without express written permission from the authors or publisher, except for brief quotation in critical reviews or articles. It is illegal to copy this book, post it to a website, or distribute it by any other means without permission from the authors and publisher.

All rights reserved. No part of this book shall be reproduced or transmitted in any form or by any means, electronic, mechanical, magnetic, and photographic including photocopying, recording or by any information storage and retrieval system, without prior written permission of the publisher. No patent liability is assumed with respect to the use of the information contained herein. Although every precaution has been taken in the preparation of this book, the publisher and author assume no responsibility for errors or omissions. Neither is Garry Estrada responsible for any policy changes such as those that occur from time to time and are a necessary part of the evolution of our service. Neither is any liability assumed for damages resulting from the use of the information contained herein. Note that this material is subject to change without notice.

Published by Garry Estrada Publishing
Author Garry Estrada's email: GarryEstradaPublishing@gmail.com

Limits of Liability and Disclaimer of Warranty

The authors and publisher shall not be liable for the reader's misuse of this material. This book is for strictly informational and educational purposes.

Disclaimer

The views expressed are those of the author and do not reflect the official policy or position of the publisher or Business Success Factors.

Copyright Use and Public Information

Unless otherwise noted, images have been used according to public information laws.

Unless otherwise indicated, all Scripture quotations are taken from the NEW AMERICAN STANDARD BIBLE®, copyright© 1960, 1962, 1963, 1968, 1971, 1972, 1973, 1975, 1977, 1995 by The Lockman Foundation. Used by permission.

ISBN: 978-0-578-64042-6   Paperback

PRAISE FOR "THE ANSWERS TO CANCER"

Cancer is no longer a death sentence. Unprecedented progress in medical research brought the cure for not only early stage, but also for terminal cancer. Surprisingly, this truth remains hidden from the public. Cancer became a separate industry in which competitors are fought and destroyed and a possible cure is covered up by a campaign of 'fake news.' **"The Answers to Cancer"** *provides up-to-date scientific information for the general public and removes the shroud of ignorance covering important discoveries. This is a well written and very important book which could save the lives of many cancer patients. It gives me great pleasure to recommend it.*
Stanislaw R. Burzynski, M.D., Ph.D. www.burzynskiclinic.com www.burzynskiclinic.com/dr-stanislaw-r-burzynski/

Dr. Stanislaw R. Burzynski, M.D., PhD., is a nationally and internationally recognized physician and research scientist, who pioneered the use of biologically active peptides for the treatment of cancer. In 1967 He identified naturally occurring human peptides, which were deficient in cancer patients. He concluded that these peptides played a role in preventing the growth of cancer cells.

Between 1970 and 1977, he received funding from the National Cancer Institute (NCI) for his work as a Principal investigator and Assistant Professor at the Baylor College of Medicine in Houston, TX. During this time he authored/coauthored numerous publications, including those detailing his work on naturally occurring human peptides and their effect on cancer – some of which were co-authored by investigators associated with the M.D. Anderson Cancer Center or the Baylor College School of Medicine.

In 1977 the Burzynski Clinic was established in Houston, TX. Since then, more than 10,000 patients have received treatment at the clinic, including more than 2,300 cancer patients who have been treated in FDA reviewed and Institutional Review Board (IRB) approved clinical trials program of Antineoplastons, investigational agents that derived from Dr. Burzynski's early investigations of naturally occurring human peptides. Currently, new FDA-reviewed Phase II and III clinical studies utilizing Antineoplastons are awaiting funding approval prior to patient enrollment.

MORE PRAISE FOR
"THE ANSWERS TO CANCER"

An exhaustive range and depth of information has been assembled in this tome by Garry Estrada on the subject of cancer. In his book, **"The Answers to Cancer"**, *the reader progresses from the ancient history of cancer, to modern theory for causation, treatment and current statistics the lay person and many professional will find more answers than they expected.*

An update on the current trends in cancer and opinions for the increasing incidents of this devastating disease are provided. For the lay "information junky" seeking all they can find about cancer, this encyclopedic effort should represent an informational feast to be devoured robustly by the author's pleasant and communicative style. For the person presented with the sudden and unwanted diagnosis of a malignancy, in need of information of what this entity is, how it may have developed and what can be done for it – such a need is fully answered. For the person who only wants the answer for two questions; "Is it benign or cancer", from their primary physician? "Did you get it all?" from their surgeon, more information than they want is supplied.

In short this is a smooth and informative collection of information on cancer that approaches an exhaustive source of knowledge that offers hope for how cancer is being treated and is improving.

H. Reg McDaniel, M.D. www.wellnessquest.org

Dr. Reg McDaniel was the Chief of Pathology for Dallas-Ft. Worth Medical Center for 3 decades and served as Director of Medical Education. He was a medical consultant for Carrington Laboratories starting in 1985 where extensive research on the active principle in Aloe Vera leaf gel was investigated. He has traveled lecturing on glyconutrients and their support of good health in 15 countries. Dr. McDaniel continues to be active in developing formulations using oligosaccharides from the Aloe plant, combined with other phytonutrients that support normal biochemistry and physiology of the human body.

Note:

I am not a qualified oncologist.

I have no expertise or qualifications to advise you on how to get healed from cancer.

The views expressed in this book are not to be taken as professional advice on treating cancer.

I cannot be held responsible for the decisions and consequences of any cancer-related treatments, procedures or healing modalities you make based on the views shared in this book or any other information contained herein.

~Garry Estrada, M.S.

ACKNOWLEDGEMENTS AND DEDICATION

This book has been a labor of love that began in 2005. I would like to extend my appreciation and dedication of this book to Dr. Reg McDaniel and Dr. Burzynski, PhD., two world-renowned doctors, who took the time out of their busy schedules to assist me in getting their message out. I could not have done it without their input and assistance.

I also want to dedicate this book to my four children – Jenny, Christina, Katerina, and Michael.

Last, but not least, I want to thank, acknowledge, and dedicate this book to The Lord Jesus Christ, who whispered in my ear, *"Don't give up"* and who gave me the endurance, faith, and fortitude to complete this daunting manuscript.

PREFACE

"All truths are easy to understand once they are discovered; the point is to discover them." ~ Galileo Galilei

If you have picked up this book, I assume you are interested in the topic of cancer, so let me ask you a **very** important question:

What would you give if you could change the course of someone's life who has cancer – a family member, a sibling, a mother or father, a close friend? Seriously, what would you give if you could make a substantial contribution in the life of a cancer patient? If you are like me or millions of other Americans, you would give your life for that special someone. I am just like you, I have had many friends die of cancer and I have some friends with cancer, and I am sure I will have many friends who will get cancer. So, how can I, or you make a difference?

You can begin by reading this book and buying one for your friend or friends.

Why?

Because it is filled with the most up-to-date scientific information available on the planet when it comes to cancer.

Why?

Because ignorance is **not** bliss. Historically, ignorance has killed millions.

Why do I want you to read this book?

Because you or someone you love who has cancer is going to make a life and death decision(s) regarding the type of therapy they take and without this knowledge it will be impossible to make a completely informed decision.

Why do I want you to read this book?

Because I sincerely want to help you. I wrote this book just for you.

Let me begin with a story:

> There was a father who had young twin girls, and one of them was diagnosed with a deadly malignant tumor. It was considered one of the deadliest type(s) of tumor. After the initial diagnosis the doctors immediately recommended an aggressive chemotherapy and radiation treatment. After agreeing to the treatment, he went home with his girls and all he could do was cry. All he could do was think that one of his girls was going to die, and she had not even started high school.
>
> He loved his girls so much and being twins they did everything together. He could not imagine life without his twin girls and now one of them will most probably die. He was heartbroken and devastated. No matter what he decided to do, the outcome, according to the doctors, was not promising. All they could promise was to extend the life of his daughter, but that her condition was severe and there was no positive outcome.
>
> As they proceeded to the hospital, his daughter would undergo extensive radiation and chemo treatment. The first thing he noticed was that her beautiful hair was beginning to fall out, then she could no longer keep food down without throwing up. Then there was the severe pain that radiated throughout her body. This would go on for weeks and months.
>
> And as he went through this, being by her side, he remained helpless. He wanted so much to take her pain away. He wanted so much to comfort her, but there were times that even to touch her in the slightest way would seem to create enormous pain.
>
> Finally, the treatments were over, but the news was bad, they could no longer do anything for her. She had completed her treatment and suffered immensely but the latest MRI indicated that the cancer had spread through the brain and spinal cord with over 30 malignant nodules and death was imminent.

The doctors recommended taking her home and prepare for the worst. As he carried his daughter to her room his silent tears fell from his face onto her chest. He was heartbroken. His daughter was dying, and he stood helpless.

One day as he was researching cancer books, he came across a book that talked about Dr. Burzynski. He was amazed at what this doctor had accomplished. He had been successfully treating stage four brain tumors since the late 70s after other doctors had given up hope.

He thought to himself, "why haven't I heard of him? Why didn't I know about him?" He immediately got on the phone with the Burzynski Clinic, went through a consulting process, and on August 24, 1993 his daughter was admitted to the Burzynski Clinic and underwent a Phase 2 clinical trial program of Antineoplastons under the supervision of the FDA.

After a series of treatments at the Burzynski clinic, the brain tumors began to shrink, and after five weeks of Antineoplaston treatment, ALL of the tumors disappeared, with no side effects, and she was eventually diagnosed cancer free. It is estimated that she had up to 650 mutated genes.

But their story doesn't end there because his daughter would soon pass away, but not from the tumor or the cancer but from the extensive doses of chemo and radiation that literally broke apart her brain. She was the only patient in medical history who died tumor free (with this type of tumor) but from the toxicity of chemotherapy and radiation. Her tumor free status and cause of death was confirmed two years later, by autopsy (July 31, 1995).

When she died, he closed his eyes as the silent tears began to flow and the only thing he could think of at that moment in time, was, why didn't someone tell me about the Burzynski Clinic? Why didn't I investigate further? Why? Why? Why?

All he could do was scream. His scream was so intense and painful that it bounced back from the other side of the universe. But his daughter was still dead, and he would still have to live life without her beautiful voice resonating throughout the house and his other daughter would have to go through life without her best friend.

I don't want this to be your story

I don't want you, or a loved one, to make a life and death decision without first knowing what science has discovered over the past 70 years, or even over the last 10 years.

I don't want you, or a loved one, to make a life changing choice without first knowing all your options…without first knowing what advances science has made in effectively dealing with the cancer dilemma.

Before you can fully understand your choices, you will need to read this book. I have taken special care to document every science, so that you can review and validate these phenomenal scientific discoveries.

These phenomenal discoveries will help you to make an informed decision. After all, if you, or a loved one, has been diagnosed with cancer, the next decisions will be life-altering.

If you have decided to continue reading, I want you to stop reading and buy two of these books, one for you and one for a friend. Go to the nearest café shop, sit down, relax and continue reading.

I also want to thank you for allowing me to help you.

I would love to hear from you after you have read my book. If I can help in any way, you can email me at: srmsenior@gmail.com. My heart and prayers go out to you and your family.

TABLE OF CONTENTS

Preface i

Chapter 1: The Greatest Weapon in Fighting Cancer 5
Chapter 2: My Story 9
Chapter 3: Introduction 13
Chapter 4: Understanding Cancer 21
    The History of Cancer 21
    Types of Cancer 24
    Four Key Factors for Cancer Proliferation 25
    Spontaneous Cancers 27
    Characteristics of a Cancer Cell 28
    A Revised Definition of Cancer 35
Chapter 5: The Primary Cause of Cancer 41
    The Basics – Understanding Normal Cellular Function 44
    Normal Cellular Respiration (Aerobic Respiration) 46
    Abnormal-Cellular Function (Anaerobic Respiration) 47
    The Cause of Cancer on a Cellular Level 48
    A Paradigm Shift on Cancer 49
Chapter 6: The Secondary Causes of Cancer 55
Chapter 7: The Biology of Life - Foods 59

Chapter 8: Biological Repercussions 71

Chapter 9: Water 85

Chapter 10: Aging 99

Chapter 11: Electro-Magnetic Pollution 101

Chapter 12: Stress 103

Chapter 13: Toxins 111

Chapter 14: Dr. Burzynski – Genetics and DNA Therapy 119

Chapter 15: Dr. Reg McDaniel and The Science of
Glycobiology 127

Chapter 16: Commercialism - Confronting an Old
Adversary 143

Chapter 17: The Problem with Current Treatments 151

    Chemotherapy 151

    Radiation Treatments 158

Chapter 18: 21st Century Strategies in Dealing with Cancer 161

    Battling Cancer 161

    pH 164

    Cancer Immunotherapy 168

    Duke University & the Polio Vaccine 169

    Foods 171

    Dr. Reg McDaniel - Glyconutrients and the Science of
    Glycobiology 175

Chapter 19: Pulsating Electro- Magnetic Field Therapy 179

Chapter 20: Two Key Organs – The Liver and The Colon 183

Chapter 21: Acerogenin Therapy 187

Chapter 22: Oxygen Therapies: Photodynamic Therapy (PDT), or Blue Light Therapy **189**

    Hydrogen Peroxide Therapy (HPT) 190

    Hypobaric Therapy 190

    Testosterone Replacement Therapy 191

    Gene Targeted Therapy 192

    Immunotherapy 192

    Targeting T-Cells 193

    What to Avoid 194

Chapter 23: Organizations **197**

    Educational Videos 198

Chapter 24: The Great Physician **199**

    The Gospel According to God's Divine Teachings 202

Chapter 25: Summary **207**

    The Primary Cause of Cancer 208

    Secondary Causes 209

Chapter 26: The Cancer Paradigm Shift **215**

    The Cure Requires Knowledge 216

Chapter 27: Breast Cancer **225**

Chapter 28: Prostate Cancer **251**

Why I Wrote This Book **257**

Appendix **259**

References **261**

About the Author **287**

Please Rate My Book **289**

CHAPTER 1

THE GREATEST WEAPON IN FIGHTING CANCER

"My people perish for a lack of knowledge…" (Hosea 4:6)

The greatest weapon in fighting cancer is knowledge and understanding.

Regarding cancer, the lack of knowledge and understanding is not only deadly, it can lead to catastrophic consequences. The greater your knowledge and understanding the greater the power, and knowledge has the power to defeat the greatest of foes.

This book is based on over 14 years of empirical research. Literally, tens of thousands of hours have been devoted to exhaustive research and the documentation of information on cancer.

Based on this information, it is possible to avoid becoming a victim of cancer. Millions of people live their entire life without falling victim to cancer and based on the information I'll be sharing in this book; you could be one of those millions.

But understanding cancer involves more than just a brief introduction. It involves a comprehensive review of cancer from all known angles. This includes an understanding of what cancer is, where it comes from, how we get cancer, and if you have cancer, understanding entails, a complete knowledge of your treatment options, and their side effects.

Because, what you do not know can kill you or, at the very least, alter your way of life, forever.

In the battle against cancer it is NOT enough to simply agree with the knowledge and direction of your primary care physician.

There is a very good chance your primary care physician may not be current with all the recent discoveries in cancer research and of the possible alternatives that are now available.

What your primary care physician does *not* know could kill you or debilitate you for life.

If you are to survive, you will need to dig deeper, you will need to take the bull by the horns and do much of the research yourself. This is where I can help, because I have done most of the research for you.

As you will discover, treatments vary dramatically, and conventional treatments, if you survive, often, alter your way of life, forever. The side effects of conventional treatments are often debilitating.

When diagnosed with cancer the first thing doctors prescribe are one of three choices, surgery, chemotherapy, or radiation therapy. Often doctors will prescribe a combination of treatments.

All three options maintain a series of side effects that vary from individual to individual, but there are precautions, or tests that can determine, before the fact, if, indeed, current chemotherapy treatments will be effective.

But, in America, these precautionary protocols are almost never taken into consideration, and the results can be devastating, and often result in death, if not shortly thereafter, within the following five years.

Today, with the advances in research, you will begin to hear about several, scientifically validated forms of treatment. Indeed, these viable alternatives show phenomenal promise, but it is imperative that you, again, gain a complete understanding of the methods of treatment.

There are some advanced treatments that use drugs, which, by definition, are toxic and, as a result, maintain a series of side effects that vary from individual to individual. Then there are advanced scientifically sound treatments that avoid the use of drugs and the devastating side effects.

The following chapters in this book will provide you with this understanding and assist you in your quest for answers. I am confident that the contents of this book will help you to avoid the pitfalls and assist you in your quest for answers.

May God bless you and your loved ones...

CHAPTER 2

MY STORY

"The Watchman has been examining the truth and declares, 'My people perish for a lack of knowledge.'" Hosea 4: 6

I began my journey into the world of cancer research in 2005, when I became deathly ill. What culminated in a near death experience, had its origins fifteen years earlier as I began a journey within the financial markets and became an independent investment advisor.

I worked hard to attain my professional credentials, often working 12 hours a day. Living life at such a high stressful pace, conducting 40 seminars a year, I often suffered chest pains and anxiety attacks. In 1999 I experienced my first heart attack.

In 2000 the unthinkable happened, the stock market crashed, and I lost most of my life savings. Over the following two years, I continued to lose large sums of money and eventually two-thirds of my clients walked away from a falling stock market. To make matters worse the IRS came knocking at my door, claiming that I owed them additional taxes!

The ordeal with the IRS lasted three and a half years, but they would continue to haunt me for another decade.

In 2002, my wife, who argued that I was gone too often, decided to walk out the door, initially, leaving me with my two children to care for. After insisting on a divorce, and refusing to come home and reconcile, I relented, and three months later we were divorced.

In 2005, depressed over my financial losses, battling the IRS, my wife leaving, the stock market crash, and being alone, I found myself coughing up blood and unable to stop.

At that time, I decided, it was time to drive myself to the emergency room. I remained hospitalized for one week, while steroids were intravenously administered, allowing me to breathe.

The emergency doctor said that my body was having difficulty starting, and they needed to help it along.

After leaving the hospital, I continued my medication for several months. It was at this time that I would battle bouts of depression that continued off and on over the next ten years.

To make matters worse, I soon developed what seemed to be benign tumors. They continued to grow over the next three years, at which time I became very concerned.

After mentioning this to a friend, he introduced me to some organic nutrients, a powdered substance that I knew little about. Because it was recommended by a man, I had the highest regard for, I decided to take it.

I soon discovered that my tumors, which had been growing slowly for several years, were getting smaller. Eventually they disappeared!

It was during this period that I began my investigation into cancer. After my tumors disappeared, I no longer took the nutrients and continued to investigate the science behind cancer growth.

Three years later, I noticed a lump had reappeared. After I noticed that it was growing larger, I began to take the organic nutrients, and again the tumor began to shrink, and eventually they disappeared. Ten years later, they have not reappeared.

What I did not realize, at the time, was that this inquisitive journey into the "What, Why, and How" of cancer, which began back in 2005, would become a passion. An obsession.

MY STORY

As I began to conduct peer-reviewed research, one scientific discovery led to another, and the amount of scientific information and discoveries was so overwhelming that I often became frustrated.

I could not document these discoveries fast enough. Even now, I continue to edit and add to this peer-reviewed book.

What is even more frustrating, is the lack of public awareness.

It seems as if this phenomenal amount of recent scientific information on cancer should be on the front pages of every newspaper and magazine worldwide.

I soon realized that the doors of commercialism often take precedent. If I were to make a difference, it would have to be one voice speaking out and presenting what is so readily available over the Internet.

I often feel like "One crying out in the wilderness," hoping that I can gain the attention of someone who would listen.

People all over the world are dying out of ignorance ("the people perish for a lack of knowledge" – Hosea 4:6). I believe people desperately long to know the truth, to be led along a path filled with current scientific discoveries and knowledge, lest they be deceived by well-crafted commercialism, whose only interest is profit.

The trials of my life have opened a new door for me, gaining new knowledge, purpose, and passion. Stripped of my past ambitions I find solace in knowing that I have gained a new respect for life, money, family, friends, and the simple things life has to offer.

Thirteen years later my life goal is to help as many people as possible. I have become a firm believer in making a difference, one life at a time. I have learned that knowledge is truly powerful and liberating.

Today, I continue to research, write, and lecture whenever possible.

CHAPTER 3

INTRODUCTION

"The truth shall set you free." John 8:32

Cancer, cancer, cancer!

It seems that Americans have become too familiar with these words. When I hear these words I often think of death, dying, pain and suffering.

Unfortunately, no one was around at the turn of the 20th century when cancer only accounted for 4% of all deaths in America. For tens of thousands of years, throughout the world, the cause of death by cancer remained nominal.

Today, that figure is closer to 30%, which is over a 500% increase in less than 100 years.

In a recent publication in the journal, Cancer (2014), Anne Rositch, PhD., states that the death toll from cervical cancer has not only increased substantially but is much greater than previously stated. In some cases, the difference is as high as 77% among black women (which may account for a discrepancy in health care in America), and 47% higher among white women, and as women age that risk only becomes greater (Rositch, 2014).

So, what has changed? In a nutshell, everything has changed.

Most of the foods Americans consume are genetically altered, green picked, chemically laced, and the soil, in which we grow our food, is depleted of most of its natural nutrients.

The water Americans drink needs to be filtered before it is safe for consumption. Several recent studies have found not only foreign chemicals and toxins in our water, but trace elements of a host of various pharmaceutical drugs.

The air we breathe contains less oxygen and is filled with foreign toxins and chemicals.

Our oceans are so polluted that eating too much tuna or sword fish can be fatal because of the high levels of mercury.

Even the way we live has changed, going from a lifestyle that was predominantly mobile to a lifestyle that is primarily sedentary, evidenced by the major increase in childhood obesity over the past several decades (Riely, 2011).

Maintaining a predominantly peaceful lifestyle has been replaced with one that includes chronic stress, dubbed "urban stress," or the "silent killer."

To make matters worse we have exchanged the ground we walk on (soil and grass), and the natural environment our ancestors lived under, to one made primarily of concrete and one inundated with electrical impulses, such as electric towers, power lines, airports, iPhones, microwaves, cable boxes, and a host of other electrical gadgets, all of which create a biological imbalance on our internal pulsating electro-magnetic field.

After conducting exhaustive research, for more than a decade, I am convinced that cancer needs to be approached from three different points of reference.

One point of reference has to do with eradicating cancer, the other point of reference has to do with cancer prevention, and the third and most important point of reference has to do with understanding cancer from a scientific point of view.

These points of reference will often overlap in the treatment of cancer, but they are as distinct as night and day.

This would explain why some countries, or cultures experience very low rates of cancer, while others show very high rates of cancer. This would also include why certain types of cancer are higher in certain regions of the world.

The good news is, while cancer is on the rise, estimated to overcome heart disease, as the number one killer in America, science has also advanced.

The cumulative effect of scientific information and research has been exponential. So much so that going back even 50 years, seems like going back to the Stone Age. The cumulative compounding of scientific information and research on cancer has created a paradigm shift in the scientific perceptions of how cancer develops, progresses, its biological effects, and how the human system naturally combats cancer and other diseases.

Equipped with this arsenal of recent scientific information, researchers have been able to develop multiple procedures and strategies on the war against cancer that often exclude outdated conventional therapies and their horrific side-effects.

Because there is no one direct cause for the onset and propagation of cancer, the avenues of scientific research cover a wide spectrum and piecing the cancer puzzle altogether has been an elusive task.

This book is an attempt to summarize the compilation of peer-reviewed literature and scientific research, from some of the greatest minds of the 20th and 21st centuries, in a format that diagrams how these various pieces of scientific information are forever linked biologically, genetically, physiologically, psychologically, and environmentally.

Disclosing their interdependence intricately weaved within the framework of life as we know it, the influences, both internal and external, and the repercussions that occur, in the form of cancer, disease and other illnesses, when interruptions within these interdependent life systems occur.

To fully understand cancer, it is important to first look to its past and gain a historical perspective.

Knowing that cancer has a historical linage that dates back indefinitely helps to dispel any 21st century anomalies. Being equipped with this knowledge provides a precedent for cancer within the mainstream of human existence, and a protocol for the onset of cancer that until recently was not fully understood. It is my hope that you will begin to understand that cancer is nothing new, but rather an ancient adversary that the human body has been successfully eradicating for centuries.

I have divided my research into two sections: i) The cancer paradigm – the ontology of a cancer cell and its biological repercussions; and ii) the secondary causes of cancer.

I begin from a historical perspective in order to create a baseline for its existence and to establish a historical pattern of notoriety.

This is followed by the scientific research and discovery of the primary cause of all cancers. It is here that we begin to understand the fundamental aspects of cellular respiration, and how cancer develops when a disruption occurs within this process. This is where and how all cancer begins.

Once we understand the fundamental origins of a cancer cell, based on 21st century science, we can design a cancer paradigm that is in line with the current scientific research. This is also where a revised definition of cancer is predicated.

Then this is followed by a series of common characteristics that all cancer cells maintain. Alterations in the genetic and immunological systems are the repercussions that follow when there are circumventing variables that interfere with the natural flow of biological events.

These genetic and immunological discoveries are part of the 21st century research, which details the breakdown in the biological mechanisms that allow for the uncontrolled growth of cancer.

The secondary causes of cancer often refer to environmental variables. For example, water, diet, stress, toxins and chemicals, all play an

INTRODUCTION 17

intricate secondary role in the ontology and propagation of cancer. It is their direct and indirect influence on the biological processes that are of major concern.

I'll briefly introduce you to one of our oldest adversaries – commercialism – and its ability to mitigate the ongoing discoveries that have filled the pages of scientific journals for decades.

I also introduce pH, which is an important indicator of oxygenation, a precursor to health and wellness.

This is followed by a brief discussion on conventional methods of treatment and their often-debilitating side effects.

Finally, I summarize and attempt to categorize the phenomenal 21st century discoveries and methods of cancer treatment in a format that attempts to explain their advantages, especially when used with specific types of cancer.

I would be remiss if I did not end my research with a brief acknowledgement of the scientifically proven power of spiritual endowment. As a Christian, I firmly believe that this spiritual power is endowed within those who believe in the God of all creation, and of His Son, Jesus of Nazareth.

In conclusion, the understanding of cancer has occupied the thoughts and minds of doctors, scientists, and psychologists for centuries. It wasn't until the advent of the computer, that the exponential computation of scientific research began to take massive strides, as the mathematical calculations and empirical formulations began to evidence themselves throughout the Internet.

Over the last 100 years there have been numerous doctors and Nobel Prize recipients that have advanced the knowledge and understanding of cancer, which we now can rediscover with a simple Google search.

In the aftermath of such a massive amount of information on cancer, one thing rings clear: there is no smoking gun. Cancer or the onset of cancer, is rarely the result of any one act or instrument, but of a combination of conditions that have evolved over an undetermined amount of time, often over the course of 10, 20, or 30 years.

Just as a cup of water is filled to the brim, and by adding even one more drop will result in an overflow, so too, untold variable conditions can act together creating a cup filled to the brim, then the one drop [the stressor] of water causes the cup to overflow, causing the onset of cancer. The stressor can be psychological, biological, or environmental, but more than likely, a combination thereof.

To make sense of the endless stream of information, three aspects of the human condition are evaluated, the psychological, the biological, and the environmental.

In order to begin to understand how these three components play a key role, it is first important to understand cancer from a biological perspective.

It is important to understand its characteristics, its likes and dislikes, how it functions, and what causes its demise.

Once this is understood, then piecing together these three major components, and how they play a critical role in the physiological condition, will be easier to understand.

Hopefully, this understanding will act as a precursor to the prevention of cancer and pave a road to wellness for everyone who reads this book.

The purpose of this book is to educate and inform, you, the reader, of the phenomenal scientific and medical breakthroughs in cancer.

Knowledge is power.

Getting equipped with this knowledge allows you to make informed decisions, decisions that will make the difference between life and death.

The intent of this book is not to debate issues or take sides over controversial therapies, but to inform and offer hope to families who have been stricken with cancer.

INTRODUCTION

The purpose of this book is four-fold:
i. to be a light of information to those in need.
ii. to save lives.
iii. to introduce you, the reader, to these scientific discoveries; and
iv. to disclose a paradigm shift that will revolutionize your perception of cancer forever.

I would be well satisfied if just one person, one child, whose parents read this book, was able to avoid the horrific side effects, and humiliating consequences that befall millions of cancer victims.

My heart grieves every time I see a child in a mall or supermarket whose head is absent any semblance of hair.

I am appalled at the insensitivity and ignorance of any doctor or medical establishment that fails to embrace, or even consider the vast amount of current research and scientific discoveries that have reshaped the very definition of cancer and the processes from which cancer should be viewed.

It is my hope that this book, at the very least, offers a ray of hope.

CHAPTER 4

UNDERSTANDING CANCER

THE HISTORY OF CANCER

"Those who do not remember the past are condemned to repeat it."
— George Santayana

"Ask the former generations and find out what their fathers learned, for we were born only yesterday and know nothing, and our days on earth are but a shadow. Will they not instruct you and tell you? Will they not bring forth words from their understanding?"
Job 8:8-10

Given the fact that over 30% of all Americans will be diagnosed with some form of cancer in the 21st century, a far cry from only 4% at the turn of the 19th century, there are countless questions that demand an answer.

For example, where does cancer come from? What causes it to exist? Has it always existed? If not, when did it first show up?

According to the latest research, it can be said with certainty that cancer has existed throughout recorded history.

The oldest evidence of cancer can be found among the remains of fossilized bone tumors and the ancient manuscripts of Egypt dating back to 3000 B.C.

One such manuscript is referred to as the, Edwin Smith Papyrus. Inside is an intricate part of an Egyptian medical textbook on trauma surgery, with a description of eight specific cases of breast cancer, as evidenced by ulcers and tumors.

Between 54 AD and 68 AD, there lived in Rome, during the time of Nero, a Greek physician, pharmacologist and botanist, Pedanius Diosscordes. In his writings, De Materia Medica (On Medical Matters), there is a description of a plant referred to as Red Clover, which was used to treat patients who had various forms of cancer. There is also a description of a drug, which was developed from the *autumn crocus,* an herb distinguished by its white, purple, lavender, and white flowers.

One of the most famous physicians and writers of Ancient Greece was Galen, who lived around 130 AD. He became the physician to Marcus Aurelius, the Emperor of Rome.

He writes extensively about malignant tumors and referred to the word, *karkinos*, which is a word related to carcinoma. According to the American Cancer Society (ACS), carcinomas are the most common of all cancers.

Carcinoma is the Greek word for crab, and the Latin word for crab is *cancer* (Moss, 1989; Murphy, n.d.). The Roman physician, Celsus (28-50 BC), later translated the Greek term into cancer.

Galen (130-200 AD), another Roman physician, used the word "oncos" (Greek for swelling) to describe tumors. Although the crab analogy of Hippocrates and Celsus is still used to describe malignant tumors, Galen's term is used as a part of the name for cancer specialists — oncologists.

Centuries later, in 1938 scientists found that the autumn crocus contains a substance known as *cholchicine,* an anti-tumor agent.

In 300 BC we find that the substance Galangal, a root in the ginger family of plants, was imported, and introduced by Arabian physicians and used by the Romans and the Greeks to treat skin cancer (The Romans in Britain, n.d.).

In 1861 Robert Bentley of King's College noted the anti-tumor properties found in the May apple, also known as Mayapple, Devil's

Apple, Hog-apple, Indian Apple, American Mandrake, American May Apple, Racoonberry and Wild Lemon.

The May apple is a perennial native herb found growing in moist soils in rich woods, thickets, and pastures. May apple roots are dark brown, fibrous and jointed, and are known to be very toxic (Murphy, n.d.).

It was not until 1946 that scientists discovered that a combination of substances found in the May apple (*picropodophyllum* and *picropodophyllic acid* called *podophyllotoxin*) acted against tumors by preventing cells from undergoing complete cell division.

In the 1700's Sir John Hill, of London England, observed that snuff, a form of tobacco, caused nasal tumors.

In 1775, Sir Percival Pott uncovered the first example of an "Occupational cancer" among chimneysweepers.

In 1801 a group of British and chemical investigators formed one of the first societies for the investigation of cancer. In their quest for answers, they established some basic questions:

- What are the diagnostic signs?
- Are there any characteristic changes in a tissue that proceeds the growth of cancer?
- Is cancer inherited?
- Is cancer associated with other diseases?
- Is it a localized condition?
- Is it produced by an unfavorable climate or environment?
- Is it ever susceptible to a natural cure?

Two hundred years later we are still asking some of the same questions.

Historically, cancer has been with us since recorded history, only the remedies have changed. Over the centuries, cancer has been a natural phenomenon but never a leading cause of death. Historically, its claim to fame did not occur until the late 1900's, with the advent of commercialism, the migration into urban dwellings, modern food processing, and the introduction of over 100,000 foreign toxins that have contaminated the soil, the water, and the air.

TYPES OF CANCER

According to the National Cancer Institute, all cancers are classified in two ways, according to the type of tissue (histology) from which the cancer originated, and the location of the initial cancer cells.

Histologically, there are hundreds of differing types of cancer, which are grouped into six categories:

1. **Carcinoma**: account for 80% – 90% of all cancers; in reference to malignant tumors of epithelial origin that consist of the outer or inner lining of the body.
2. **Sarcoma**: originate in the supportive and connective tissue (fat, tendons, muscle, and cartilage); occurring most often in young adults.
3. **Myeloma**: originating in the plasma cells located in the bone marrow.
4. **Leukemia**: often referred to as liquid cancer, or blood cancer; cancers of the bone marrow. There are various types of leukemia (Myelogenous, Lymphatic, and Polycythemia Vera).
5. **Lymphoma**: Cancers that develop within the nodes and glands of the lymphatic system. For example, within the spleen, the tonsils, or the thymus.
6. **Mixed Types**; In reference to a specific category or a combination of categories. Cancer types also take on the location from which it was originally diagnosed. For example, Leukemia is in reference to cancer of the blood. Pancreatic cancer refers to cancer of the pancreas, etc. The concern over labeling is that cancers often travel to other parts of the body (metastasis) and develop cancer colonies. Since some tissues

grow faster than others, certain locations are more dangerous than others (National Cancer Institute, n.d.).

FOUR KEY FACTORS FOR CANCER PROLIFERATION

There are four key factors or players in the creation and proliferation of all cancer cells.

The first key player in the creation of cancer cells is the lack of oxygen and the disruption of a process of transporting oxygen to the cell membrane.

Second, are the two-fold key players in the proliferation of cancer, which are: the lack of sufficient amounts of nutrients among foods that normally contain all the essential ingredients for healthy cellular metabolism, *and* the inhibition in the transportation of these essential nutrients.

Third, are the external and internal factors (x-factors) in the inhibitions of oxygen and the essential nutrients to the cell membrane, which takes into consideration psychological stress and excitotoxins.

Finally, the fourth key player, and one of the most important factors, is how the human system responds to the myriad of variables that take place incessantly. It may sound philosophical and possibly new age, but the truth is, the human system is highly integrated and dependent on its external environment and responds quite profoundly via its interdependent internal mechanisms.

For example, when a person contracts a cold virus, the effects can be extensive. The cold virus affects almost all systems beginning with physical discomfort and fatigue. Then there is inflammation of the bronchiole tubes, headaches, which is indicative of arterial pressures, and the list of repercussions continues. The point is multiple human systems and all their counterparts are altered in response to a simple cold virus.

Take into consideration, contaminated air, polluted and toxic water, processed foods, urban stress, and a human system, which is lacking sufficient supplies (nutrients) to deal with this ongoing and profuse invasion. The result is a human system that can easily become overwhelmed and eventually succumb to cancer, autoimmune disease, and a host of other illnesses.

It should be no surprise that one and a half million Americans will be diagnosed with some form of cancer for the first time, and 566,000 Americans will die of cancer every year.

It should also be no surprise that as a result of these unnatural conditions, the human body reaches its tolerance level quite quickly.

Once the tolerance level is reached the human body has passed the point of recovery and will succumb eventually to illness or disease, even with various forms of interventions.

All humans produce cancer cells. The difference is how each individual body responds to those cancer cells. If cancer cells can proliferate in excess of two billion cells, then that individual is diagnosed as a cancer patient.

It is important to remember that three million cancer cells can live on the point of a needle and be undetectable for decades. Very much like the tip of an iceberg, once the cancer has been detected there are always millions more under the surface.

There is no smoking gun. Becoming a cancer victim is never the result of any one factor, but rather a series of concerted factors and conditions.

For example, 20 years of prolonged exposure to an array of toxins and foreign chemicals, a poor diet that consists of processed foods, urban stress, no natural supplements to refortify the human body, and a lack of sufficient sleep, is a recipe for the propagation of cancer.

If this is true then the opposite must also be true: that a lifestyle fairly stress free, a diet that consists of organic foods, high in nutrients, minimum exposure to foreign toxins and chemicals, and for urban dwellers, food-based organic supplements, a sufficient amount of REM sleep, and adequate amounts of pristine water, could be a recipe for avoiding cancer.

It is believed, by many, that the body was designed to live approximately 120 years. How many people living in modern America even come close to that mark? Very few. And when some succeed, we applaud, as if they have accomplished some great feat, and we automatically assume it was because of good genes.

It is unfortunate that commercialism has polluted our planet to such an extent that we now require special precautions to maintain optimal health.

We now need to ionize and purify our water, filter our air, take care in choosing organic foods, and add supplements, such as vitamins, glyconutrients, minerals, and other natural nutrients to fortify our bodies.

SPONTANEOUS CANCERS

Our bodies consist of 75 trillion cells. Our bodies also re-produce about three billion new cells every day, and one out of every million or two of these newly-formed cells is mutant, many of which, eventually, become cancerous, often referred to as "Spontaneous cancers, " which occur due to errors in DNA replication, repair, or a combination of DNA sequences.

These "Spontaneous cancers," may also be inherited, which provides an avenue for the predisposition to cancer from one generation to another – although inheritability only accounts for approximately 5% of all cancers. It is estimated that *"Spontaneous cancers account for approximately 20% of all cancers. So, in effect: Every human being is pre-disposed to cancer"*. (Venitt, 1996).

Dr. Warburg, a Nobel Prize recipient, in his exhaustive experiments emphatically discovered that if one could reduce the oxygen content of a cell by 35%, one would invariably convert a normal cell into a cancerous cell (Warburg, 1956). Dr. Warburg further stated that 20% of all cancers were attributable to low levels of cellular oxygen. Recent scientific research has confirmed, "Spontaneous cancers," account for approximately 20% of all cancers and are primarily due to low levels of oxygen. This may be due, in part to "Free radicals," and low levels of antioxidants (Venitt, 1996).

CHARACTERISTICS OF A CANCER CELL

The face of evil, often, possesses the ability to adapt to its environment to evade detection, and covertly pursue its evil intent. - Estrada

Cancer cells maintain unique characteristics that distinguish them from normal cells. The following list is not complete because every day scientific research uncovers new information in the understanding of cancer, but it does identify key distinguishing features that can assist in the understanding of cancer and in our design of specific strategies against the propagation of cancer.

A shroud of protection.

A protective shield that allows the cancer cells to live undetected from the immune system. Under normal conditions the immune system patrols the human body looking for foreign elements that need to be eradicated. Cancer cells develop a shroud or protective shield that allows them to function and grow undetected by the immune system.

Apoptosis.

Apoptosis is defined as *programmed cell death*, which is a normal cellular function. It defines the life and death cycle of all living tissue. Without apoptosis cells would live indefinitely and continue to multiply (oncogenesis). Apoptosis regulates cell size and cell population creating a balanced cellular environment. For the human system to maintain homeostasis, apoptosis must occur naturally.

Apoptosis is the most common process the body uses to eliminate damaged and unneeded cells. If cell death occurs too often or not often enough an imbalance occurs that leads to dysfunctions and the onset of cancer. One hallmark of a cancer cell is its ability to avoid apoptosis, which allows the cells to continue to live indefinitely despite their damaged DNA and proliferate uncontrollably.

Oncogenesis

When a cell avoids apoptosis and continues to live and uncontrollably multiply, the formation and development of tumors occurs, referred to as oncogenesis.

Tumors are also known as neoplasms that are the result of uncontrolled growth of cellular tissue with no physiological purpose.

Fermentation

Under normal conditions a cell creates energy by combining oxygen with a glucose molecule and in a combustible reaction converts these elements into energy (ATP).

All cancer cells avoid this process and revert to a primitive process of producing energy without the use of oxygen, referred to as fermentation.

The difference on how a cell produces energy is the key distinguishing factor that differentiates a normal cell from a cancer cell. Dr. Warburg refers to this process as the primary cause of cancer, the inability to produce energy using oxygen.

Two Adenosine Triphosphate (ATP)

Normal cells produce 32 ATP per energy cycle. This energy is produced in the mitochondria of the cell membrane, and the amount of energy produced is enough to maintain the cell's specialized functions.

Cancer cells differentiate by producing energy in the protoplasm of the cell without combining oxygen resulting in the net production of only two ATP, which is far less than needed to maintain all the normal functions of a cell. This results in a breakdown in cellular function. To survive, all normal cellular functions cease, and the mutant cell reverts to only two cellular functions – to grow and multiply.

Angiogenesis

Because cancer cells are inefficient at producing energy (2 ATP) necessary for survival, they release growth factors that cause blood vessels to branch out and form new blood vessels that grow into the tumor, referred to as angiogenesis.

Under normal conditions, a healthy cell will use 50% of ATP production for cellular maintenance.

Because a cancer cell only produces 2 ATP, which is far less than required for survival, it needs to reduce its internal need for energy, shutting down most cellular functions. In order to survive a cancer cell needs to create other avenues to extract energy from the body.

This is where it develops its own vein system whereby it can extract vital nutrients directly from the blood supply, before the body is able to distribute those nutrients to healthy cells.

Nutrient Deficient

Because cancer cells are inefficient at producing energy (2 ATP), they are energy deficient. Angiogenesis occurs to provide an ample supply of blood from which the tumor cells extract vitally needed glucose (sugar) and other nutrients. By robbing healthy tissue of vitally needed nutrients, cancer patients become nutrient deficient, which further complicates their health status, compounding their health issues. In other words, the cancer patient is deprived of food on a cellular level, becoming malnourished.

Increased Metabolism

Because cancer cells are inefficient at producing energy (2 ATP) necessary for survival, they have a higher metabolism. Because they run hotter, they are easily detected by Thermo-Scans, which doctors use to detect heat signatures. Thermo-Scans are non-intrusive and even more efficient that an x-ray, except without the radiation of an x-ray.

Microscopic

Cancer cells are also microscopic, living most of their existence undetected. It is estimated that three million cancer cells can live on the head of a needle. It is not until they reach around two billion in number that they are detected, and one is diagnosed with cancer.

Lactic Acid

Because cancer cells produce energy without the use of oxygen, a byproduct or waste material is lactic acid. Lactic acid is highly acidic, which means it is low in oxygen (low pH) polluting the lymphatic fluid surrounding the cell.

This creates a toxic environment and inhibits the flow of oxygen, nutrients, and other enzymes from entering surrounding cells, creating an environment that starves healthy cells.

Lactic acid also provides a haven for cancer cells to grow and thrive. Lactic acid is also ideal for viruses, fungi, and other diseases. It is estimated that cancer patients can be a thousand times more acidic than a non-cancerous individual.

An acidic environment equates to a low oxygen environment. Without sufficient amounts of oxygen, cells become damaged and die.

Mucus

Mucus Is a slimy mixture secreted by the glands that line the nasal cavity, esophageal, and other cavities in the body, whose primary purpose is to lubricate and protect surfaces.

What scientists find intriguing is that various cancer cells produce up to 50 times more mucus than normal cells. Scientists have discovered that protein receptors on the surface of cancer cells go into overdrive to stimulate the production of mucus.

Mucus and lactic acid are the preferred environments for all cancer cells. Recent research has discovered that the overproduction of mucus is an important variable in the formation of tumors, which also assists in making them resistant to radiation, drugs, and the immune system by covering them completely.

This is one of the key reasons Killer cells have a difficult time recognizing and tagging cancer cells (Cromie, 2004; Williams, 2013).

Low Oxygen

Because of the production of mucus and lactic acid, cancer cells live in an oxygen-deprived environment.

Dr. Warburg, a Nobel-Prize recipient for his work on cancer, discovered that all cancer cells would die if the oxygen level was increased by 35%.

Lack Anchorage Dependence

Every tissue was created for a specific function and place in the human body.

Tissues do *not* migrate, they remain fixed, and this is called *anchorage dependence*. This is a phenomenon that requires cells to attach to a particular surface to reproduce.

Individual cells interact with one another within the confines of a matrix. This is an essential process required for homeostasis, and the regulation of cell growth and differentiation.

Cancer cells lack anchorage dependence and will often travel to other parts of the body creating new cancer colonies.

Metastasis

When cancer cells detach from their original place of origin and migrate to other tissue, traveling through the blood vessels and the lymphatic system within the body and establish new colonies, this is referred to as metastasis.

Cancer cells maintain the ability to break through natural tissue barriers and invade surrounding tissue and other organs.

Lack of Contact Inhibition

The naked mole rat, which lives in Africa, has the longest longevity of all rodents, living up to 28 years, as compared to a typical house mouse that lives approximately four years. They are also resistant to cancer, since cancer or tumor growth has never been observed in these mammals.

Scientists believe that this is because of their two-tiered contact inhibition.

Contact inhibition is a natural occurrence that displays itself by arresting cell division when the number of cells within a specific region or area reaches a specific threshold. This prevents overpopulation and acts to maintain homeostasis.

However, cancer cells lack contact inhibition and uncontrollably multiply, resulting in oncogenesis (Seluanov, et al., 2009).

Non- Specialized

Normal cells are created with a specific purpose and are therefore referred to as *specialized* (e.g., a red blood cell, a liver cell, a brain cell, etc.).

Because cancer cells are poor producers of energy and are the result of damaged DNA, they lose all specialized function, becoming non-specialized, and revert to a primitive mode of existence.

It is as if someone turned off the lights in the factory and shut down most of the operating equipment except for one small light. A cancer cell maintains only one purpose: to survive, viewing their host as their enemy with a mantra that states – survival at any cost.

Dormant

Not all cancer cells are readily self-revealing. Some cancer cells can lie dormant for years and even decades until stimulated by promoting agents, which makes it even more difficult to determine the exact cause of the initial cancer.

Promoting agents can consist of numerous catalysts such as toxins, and chemicals.

Growth rate varies

Not all cancer cells are created equal, which is why some cancers develop rapidly and others take years to propagate. The exact reasons for such discrepancies are not always clear, which makes it difficult to determine the exact causes for the onset of cancer.

There are countless variables that can either promote the growth of cancer, or inhibit its growth, all of which are active in our daily lives.

Some cancers can take years and even decades before they are detected, while others can take five years or less before they are detected.

Low Calcium Levels

Cancer cells maintain low amounts of calcium. Cancer cells contain only 2% of the calcium of a normal cell, which means that they maintain a very low oxygen level.

A REVISED DEFINITION OF CANCER

$E=mc^2$ ~Albert Einstein

"Nothing in the world is more dangerous than sincere ignorance...."
–Martin Luther King Jr.

When Albert Einstein introduced the Theory of Relativity to the world, he re-defined the order of a phenomenal and complex creation.

Understanding cancer is very much like Einstein's Theory of Relativity. From a purely scientific point of view Einstein's Theory of Relativity can be expressed as a simple equation: $E=mc^2$.

At face value it looks relativity simply, but in reality, it is an extremely complex equation. If you were to open this theory, <u>slightly</u>, it might look like this:

$$E = mc^2 = \frac{g_{00}m_0}{\sqrt{g_{00} - \frac{v^2}{c^2}}} = m_0\left(1+\frac{2\phi}{c^2}\right)\left(1+\frac{2\phi}{c^2}-\frac{v^2}{c^2}\right)^{-1/2} c^2$$

$$\approx m_0 c^2 \left(1+\frac{2\phi}{c^2}\right)\left(1-\frac{\phi}{c^2}+\frac{1}{2}\frac{v^2}{c^2}\right)$$

$$\approx m_0 c^2 \left[\left(1-\frac{\phi}{c^2}+\frac{1}{2}\frac{v^2}{c^2}+\frac{2\phi}{c^2}-\frac{2\phi^2}{c^4}+\frac{2\phi v^2}{c^4}\right)\right]$$

And if you were to get into greater detail, the formula becomes even more mind boggling.

Yet it is precise and exact in its calculation. This is because the science of math is a precise science.

Re-defining cancer can be viewed in a similar way.

As a formula it could be defined as:

$$C = TV^2$$

If you were to open this formula, slightly, it might look like this:

$$C = TV^2 = \frac{S_{oo}A_oRV^2}{T^2P^2} \left[1 + \frac{SD^2H}{W^2A^2} \right] \left[1 + \frac{v+^2}{H^2 C_2} \right]$$

From any perspective, the cancer formula becomes even more complex when considering the countless variables responsible for its proliferation within the human body.

For example, there is a multitude of key variables such as: time, age, sex, race, place, state of mind, diet, exercise, health, water, oxygen, soil, etc.

Then consider the multitude of sub variables such as: the magnitude of exposure, length of exposure to, air, water, foods, radiation, environment, and 100,000 different toxins and chemicals.

The variable formula for cancer becomes incalculable.

This is one of the reasons why most of us survive cancer and many of us succumb.

For example, you can have two patients of the same age, sex and same type of cancer, which has progressed to the same degree. Each patient is given the exact treatment, yet one lives, and one dies.

The difference could be any one of countless variables that play a determining role. The deciding variable could have been one's state of mind, the will to survive, a diet lacking adequate nutrients, or a combination of countless variables acting in concert.

The exact reason for success or failure is undeterminable.

For millions of people who are diagnosed with cancer each year, an accurate definition of cancer determines their perception, bias, actions, and direction.

In battling cancer, there is nothing more important that an accurate definition.

Martin Luther King Jr. said, *"Nothing in the world is more dangerous than sincere ignorance."*

In a battle with cancer, adequate knowledge or the lack of knowledge could mean the difference between life and death, **and** also death *with* dignity or *without* dignity.

Based on 21st century research and scientific discoveries of our understanding of cancer, a 21st century definition could read as follows:

> *"Cancer is not a disease but a symptom or a condition of an efficient biological system whose daily production of three billion new cells also produces defective cells, from which "Spontaneous cancers" originate. This efficient biological system can be compromised due to a lack of adequate nutrition (vitamins, minerals glyconutrients, trace elements, etc.), oxygen, overwhelming exposure to foreign toxins (100,000), excessive amounts of prolonged stress, lack of adequate sleep, electro-magnetic imbalance, or a combination of any of the above. The guardians of this biological system are genetically and immunologically linked. Once this biological system has been compromised and the genetic and immunological links have been disrupted, or substantially inhibited, cancer is allowed to grow unchecked or inadequately checked. The result is, uncontrolled growth, and the spread of abnormal cells with no physiological function other than to cause bodily harm, destroy healthy tissue, and multiply, causing death or serious disablement unless effectively treated."*

The secondary causes of cancer are varied and undeterminable, as to exact cause. There can be a multitude of factors working in concert, that set the groundwork for the onset of cancer.

The proliferation of cancer does not stem from one isolated factor, but rather from a multitude of factors acting in concert with one another, usually over an extended period.

If one were to consider the environmental factors, such as increased levels of carbon dioxide, smog, chemicals – such as those to build and preserve one's house, pesticides, ionizing radiation, asbestos, food additives, high fat, and high sugar foods, refined, processed foods, the use of constraining under garments, and synthetic clothing.

Then consider tobacco smoke, secondhand smoke, alcohol, drugs, prescription drugs, junk food, fast foods, and processed sugars.

Add to this emotional factors, such as stress, anxiety, depression, toxic thoughts and emotions, and other psychological ailments.

Finally adding, the lack of exercise, green picking, poor soil, nutrient-deficient foods, synthetic vitamins or no vitamins, fluoride, chlorinated water, free-radicals, the introduction to electronic devices, power lines, concrete floors, it is easy to see how the human system succumbs to a tolerance level that is easily overwhelmed, and an immune system that is compromised.

All these factors conveniently fit into the cancer paradigm – the genetic connection, the immune system, cellular metabolism, X-factors, stress and the disruption of the body's natural electro-magnetic field.

It is no wonder that in developed countries like America and Europe, cancer has reached epidemic proportions, killing one in four (Calbom & Mahaffey, 2006).

The human body is made up of multiple systems, all of which are interdependent to both internal and external forces. A deficiency in one area affects the entire system, creating an imbalance, from which it desperately attempts to compensate.

While the human body is resilient and compensatory, any long-term insufficiencies will result in the proliferation of disease and illness.

In addition, the absence of essential nutrients and the presence of foreign elements can create havoc to any immune response. These lead to a host of problems that affect the systems already in place, which assist in detoxification, especially of the liver, and the cellular gatekeepers (glycans) that regulate immune response and direct all cellular communication (glycans).

The absence of these essential nutrients and the presence of foreign toxins and chemicals is one of the key factors in the proliferation of cancer throughout the body. Without these natural defenses, cancer cells grow unabated.

Certain cancer cells spread faster than others and the logic behind the rate of growth is a combination of factors: first, the body's ability to defend itself, and the second factor being the type of cancer cells involved.

For example, blood cells are duplicated much faster than bones cells.

It is estimated that there are more than 200 different types of cancer. The type of cancer one contracts depends on its origin, which is where it receives its name. For example, to be diagnosed with leukemia, the cancer must have originated in the bloodstream. The same can be said about lung cancer or pancreatic cancer. The cancer must have originated in the lungs or the pancreas. While there may be 200 different types of cancer it is important to note that all cancer cells maintain specific fundamental characteristics.

For example, all cancer cells produce energy without the use of oxygen, produce lactic acid, are non-specialized, and maintain a higher metabolism. [For a complete list, refer to the chapter: Characteristics of a Cancer Cell.]

There are also some fundamental differences. For example, some cancers can remain dormant for years; some cancers take years to grow, while other types of cancer grow quite rapidly.

Finally, it is important to note that there are also genetic predispositions that can be carried on from one generation to another.

Contrary to what most of us believe, genetic links only account for approximately 5% of all cancers.

CHAPTER 5

THE PRIMARY CAUSE OF CANCER

"If you know the enemy and know yourself you need not fear the results of a hundred battles." –Sun Tzu

The Persian Gulf War began in January 1991 with six weeks of air bombardments against key strategic points, disrupting communications, troop movements, and supplies.

In the background, waiting for orders, were 700,000 coalition troops, including 540,000 Americans. The air campaign was immediately followed by 100 hours of ground offensive that resulted in the expulsion of Iraqi troops from Kuwait, and the annihilation of an entire army.

What few people realize is that well before the first plane struck an enemy target, General Schwarzkopf had taken into consideration the strength of his enemy, the capability of their air force, their troop placements, and their communication network. With this information in hand he could prepare a detailed plan of attack.

In Sun Tzu's book, "The Art of War," the author makes a famous statement, "Know thy enemy."

Before sending one solder into battle during the Kuwait war, General Norman Schwarzkopf had spent years preparing his battle plan, making sure he had a complete profile on the Kuwaitis' methods and strategies, and how they had responded in past battles with Iran.

This inside intelligence provided the edge that General Schwarzkopf required in preparing a successful plan of attack, one that Schwarzkopf could be confident in, well before committing a single troop or firing the first missile (Tzu, 2010).

Make no mistake, preparing a battle plan against cancer is no less serious, and preparing a successful strategy requires a complete understanding of cancer, including all the latest scientific and medical breakthroughs, which can be compared to the latest military intelligence.

Today, our understanding of cancer is much more defined.

To begin with, we now know that somewhere along the line we got off track.

So how do we get back on track and uncomplicate our understanding of cancer, its origins, characteristics, and, most importantly, how to effectively eradicate it?

The answer is, we start at the beginning by examining cancer from a cellular perspective.

In preparing for battle, it is important to first understand how cancer cells form, what environment they thrive in, what adversely affects their livelihood, and some of the practical applications that can prevent, or mitigate their advances.

Our quest begins with a basic understanding of normal cellular respiration, as it relates to the production of energy, and the various mechanisms that can inhibit normal energy production.

If we can develop a detailed profile, we can establish a baseline from which to compare, and we can begin to formulate a winning strategy against cancer.

In the early 1920s Dr. Otto Warburg, a Nobel Prize recipient, discovered and defined the primary cause of all cancers. Dr. Otto Warburg discovered emphatically that the primary cause of cancer is because of a cells *damaged respiration*. Based on his exhaustive research and discoveries, he stated:

> *"Nobody today can say that one does not know what the prime cause of cancer is. On the contrary, there is no disease whose prime cause is better known, so that today ignorance is no longer an excuse for avoiding measures for prevention" (Warburg, 1966).*

As Dr. Otto Warburg discovered, all cancers begin when the human cell metabolizes energy without the use of oxygen (anaerobically), in the same way plants metabolize energy.

In other words, when a normal cell suffers from a damaged respiration and begins to metabolize energy by way of fermentation (without the use of oxygen) that normal cell transforms into a cancer cell, a process that is irreversible. This would also take into consideration all "Spontaneous Cancers."

Since Dr. Warburg's initial discovery, science has been able to substantiate his findings, concluding that the primary cause of cancer is because of a cell's *damaged respiration*. In a recent study from the University of Georgia, researcher found that *"low oxygen levels in cells, is proven to be a key driver of certain types of cancer"* (Yang, 2012).

In August 2017, a team of Belgian scientists confirmed that cancers grow by rapidly breaking down glucose, referred to as the "Warburg Effect" (Peters, et al., 2017).

Given this discovery, Dr. Warburg could demonstrate empirically that oxygen was a key variable in the war against cancer. Dr. Warburg demonstrated that if one were to increase the oxygen content by 35% all cancer cells invariably die. Dr. Warburg's discoveries mark the beginning of our scientific journey of understanding the etiology and propagation of all cancer cells (Warburg, 1956; Nobelprize.org, (2015).

Dr. Warburg's discoveries were so phenomenal that his discovery was referred to as the "Warburg Effect."

In 2008, Whitehead Institute for Biomedical Research and Massachusetts Institute of Technology Department of Biology re-examined the "Warburg Effect," reemphasizing the key variable of low oxygen as the pre-cursor to cancer growth (Hsu & Sabatini, 2008).

After Dr. Otto Warburg made this amazing discovery, he became frustrated with the direction of the medical community with regard to cancer, and on June 30,1966, when addressing Nobel Laureates at Lindau Germany, he stated:

> *"How long prevention will be avoided depends on how long the prophets of agnosticism will succeed in inhibiting the application of scientific knowledge in the cancer field."*
>
> *"In the meantime, millions of men and women must die of cancer unnecessarily."*

THE BASICS – UNDERSTANDING NORMAL CELLULAR FUNCTION

Every human body consists of approximately 75 trillion individual cells, and all 75 trillion cells have a specific function and a predetermined lifespan.

For example, red blood cells have a life expectancy of approximately 127 days, which means that every 127 days the entire human red blood supply has been replaced with new red blood cells.

Bone cells, which are very dense, have the longest lifespan lasting between 25-30 years.

Then there are granulocyte and eosinophil cells that have a lifespan of only hours.

All 75 trillion cells in the human body are designed for a specific purpose (VitaNet, 2006).

It is estimated that the human body produces approximately three billion new cells every day. In the daily production of new cells, several thousand are produced with defects. Many of these defective cells either become cancerous or have the potential to become cancerous. They are referred to as "spontaneous cancers."

It is estimated that the body produces about 200 spontaneous cancer cells each day, which the body, by way of the immune system, normally eradicates (Conley, 2004).

It is important to note that this process of developing "spontaneous cancers" and the natural eradication process is a cancer paradigm that has remained consistent since the beginning of human existence.

In fact, this cancer paradigm is so precise that the immunological method of eradication has been remarkably effective throughout the centuries. This immunological process is so effective that cancer deaths were considered rare, until the 20th century. It is only during this recent period in history that cancer deaths have been elevated to epidemic proportions.

In normal cellular respiration – the production of energy – every cell in the human body requires oxygen, nutrients, and glucose to function properly. Fats and proteins are also used in exceptional cases.

Most human cells produce energy-rich chemicals, referred to as Adenosine Triphosphate (ATP). This energy is required to provide for daily and specialized functions, such as thoughts, the blinking of an eye, the movement of a hand, etc.

All of life's functions require the use of energy. For example, nerve impulses are electrically charged pulses of energy.

It is also important to note that every essential chemical that the cells produce, including estrogen, testosterone, thyroid hormones, neurotransmitters, white blood cells, cortisol, adrenaline, antibodies, etc., require, as pre-requisites, vitamins, minerals, essential fatty acids, glyconutrients, amino acids, trace minerals, etc. Without these essential nutrients, cellular respiration and the production of energy could not be achieved effectively.

To transport these raw materials and essential nutrients into the cell membrane, and to remove all the waste material out of the cell membrane, the human body contains two transport systems: blood and the lymphatic system.

Blood, by way of veins and arteries, supplies our cells with oxygen, nutrients, enzymes, hormones, white blood cells, antibodies, etc. A healthy blood environment maintains a pH balance of 7.40.

The lymphatic system serves to remove toxins and waste material from the individual cells, and provide a fluid called lymph that contains infection-fighting white blood cells.

The lymphatic system is also the railway of the immune system, where lymph nodes are junction points, which is why removing any lymph node severely hinders the body's ability to cleanse and remove waste products, toxins, and other foreign elements from the cell.

The lymphatic system is an elaborate and intricate system from which lymph fluid flows to and from every cell. Its purpose is to remove toxins, waste, and debris from the cell membrane, and to replace lymph fluid with fresh fluids, maintaining a hygienically clean environment from which oxygen and other vital nutrients can easily be transported. A healthy fluid environment maintains a pH balance of 7.0.

NORMAL CELLULAR RESPIRATION (AEROBIC RESPIRATION)

Just as a car uses oxygen and combines it with gasoline to produce energy, during normal cellular respiration, glucose is burned using oxygen to produce energy (ATP). Thirty-two units of ATP are produced for every glucose molecule.

The significance of ATP is seen every time one moves a muscle, blink an eye, and think a thought. Every time a heart beats, or a breath is taken.

What is so phenomenal is that every human cell is a manufacturing facility that produces energy (ATP), except for bone and muscle cells, and as a result, requires daily maintenance.

This entire process of maintenance and production of energy requires a constant importing of raw materials – oxygen, nutrients and fluids, *and* the export of waste and debris (IUPUI Biology, 2004).

ABNORMAL-CELLULAR FUNCTION (ANAEROBIC RESPIRATION)

According to Dr. Otto Warburg, a Nobel Prize recipient, the genesis of a cancer cell begins when a normal cell loses its ability to produce ATP through the use of oxygen and begins to produce energy without the use of oxygen (fermentation), a process referred to as anaerobic respiration.

Once a normal cell reverts to producing energy anaerobically the process is irreversible. Not all cells that produce energy anaerobically are cancer cells, but all cancer cells produce energy anaerobically.

Normal cellular production is far more efficient (32 ATP) as opposed to a cancer cell's production of energy (2 ATP) (Warburg, 1956; IUPUI Biology, 2004).

This is significant because normal cells are highly specialized (intelligence) and require more energy to function efficiently. A normal cells DNA structure is designed to perform specific functions, whether it involves muscle function or brain function.

Cancer cells lose all specialized function and revert to basic, rote activity, primarily involved in survival: eating and reproducing.

The possible reason for the loss of specialization is because the source of ATP production is outside the mitochondria, whereas normal production of ATP is inside the mitochondria.

Another reason for the loss of specialized function is because a cancer cell produces an insufficient amount of energy (2 ATP) to maintain normal cellular function. Cancer cells are incapable of producing sufficient amounts of energy because they have a damaged respiration (Warburg, 1956).

This creates a major problem for the cancer cell: where to attain the necessary energy to survive.

THE CAUSE OF CANCER ON A CELLULAR LEVEL

Dr. Otto Warburg defined the root cellular cause of cancer in the late 1920s; all other causes of cancer are considered secondary. He discovered that all cancer cells originate on a cellular level.

According to Dr. Warburg's exhaustive research, on a cellular level, oxygen is transported into the cellular membrane with the help of oxidative enzymes. These oxidative enzymes include iron, vitamin A, B2, B3, B5, B12, zinc, selenium, and water.

Whenever these nutrients are inhibited, oxygen transport is inhibited and if this inhibition of vital nutrients continues, irrevocable cellular damage occurs.

If the inhibition of vital nutrients is left unchecked, the short- and long-term effect is that a normal functioning cell (*aerobic*) reverts to an abnormal functioning cell (*anaerobic*) – the etiology of a cancer cell.

In a nutshell, Dr. Warburg was able to describe the origin of a cancer cell and the process from which it originates. (Warburg, 1956).

What Dr. Warburg discovered in the 1920s has been substantiated by 21st century biology. Today's scientists understand that all living beings require energy to sustain life, energy is created by cellular respiration, and that essential enzymes, which Dr. Warburg referred to as, "The Active Group," are catalytic in this process, (Campbell, et al., 2008; Hsu & Sabatini, 2008; Yang, 2012;).

It is the blocking of oxygen to the cell by the inhibition of essential enzymes and nutrients that causes cancer cells to form (Warburg, 1956).

We all understand that human life is totally dependent on oxygen, and without it human life would cease. For example, how long can a person hold their breath? Oxygen is transported to *every* cell in our body, and those cells use it to create energy.

Oxygen is a critical ingredient in the normal conversion of glucose into energy. This entire process of transporting oxygen is dependent upon nutrients being imported into the cell membrane. The inhibition of oxygen and the lack of sufficient nutrients to complete this process is a focal point of scientific investigation and are of grave concern, as scientists have come to realize the importance of essential nutrients in the transportation of oxygen, pre-requisites to cellular respiration.

A PARADIGM SHIFT ON CANCER

The ultimate question is why would a normal cell lose its ability to produce energy using oxygen? What caused a normal cell to become incapable of producing ATP using oxygen? What hindered the oxygen process?

These are the questions that Dr. Otto Warburg asked himself back in the 1920s.

In addressing these issues, Dr. Warburg came to believe that there are two possible causes.

First, the supply of oxygen was inhibited or reduced significantly, to prevent normal cellular respiration.

Second is the possibility that the process of producing ATP was interfered with (Warburg, 1956).

Recent scientific research has validated these assumptions, but has also expanded on Dr. Warburg's discoveries, noting countless reasons for the interruption of ATP.

All cellular function and reproduction are necessitated by a daily supply of vitamins, minerals, enzymes, fatty acids, glyconutrients, etc. Any deficiency in supply will inhibit the transport of oxygen into the cell membrane.

Here's one reason for the interruption of ATP.

In the 20th and 21st centuries a major shift has taken place in the way foods are produced and prepared for market. Because of pasteurization, the introduction of genetically modified organisms (GMO), green-picking, toxins in our soil, depleted soil, contaminated water, and the introduction of chemicals to preserve and prevent maturation, our foods are far less superior then those produced a century earlier. Some of our foods may not even be biologically recognized because they have been altered on a genetic level (GMO).

Keep in mind that the human system was designed to recognize foods from its environment, not from a laboratory. As a result, they contain fewer nutrients, or synthetic nutrients, which require a laboratory to process. As an example, it is estimated that it takes 50 peaches to equal the same nutritional value of a peach produced in 1950.

The results are devastating. When people buy produce, they assume they are receiving the maximum nutrient value from that produce. In reality they are only receiving a fraction of the nutrient value compared to previous generations. As a result, the body is deficient important vitamins, minerals, enzymes, fatty acids, trace elements, and glyconutrients, prerequisites for the transportation of oxygen into the cellular membrane.

Another way to destroy the process of respiration of body cells is to remove the oxygen or to inhibit its availability. For example, if an embryo within its mother's womb has the umbilical tied around its neck preventing oxygen from flowing brain damage would follow. In the same way, if oxygen is somehow hindered from flowing freely cellular damage ensues.

Inhibiting the flow of oxygen can easily be accomplished using toxins, and foreign chemicals.

At present, there are numerous known poisons that inhibit the flow of oxygen such as arsenic (found in pesticides, wood preservatives, alloying additive, glass and nonferrous alloys), certain hydrogen sulfide derivatives (such as those used in fruit preservatives), and Ethylene Thiourea (a hydrogen sulfide derivative found in rubber).

Radiation is also a prime example of inhibiting the respiratory process, resulting in damaged cellular function, which results in cancerous cells and the potential for cancerous cells to mutate several generations later (McNally Institute, 2000).

In the 21st century more than 100,000 foreign chemicals have been introduced into our environment and many have found their way into the human system, most of which are stored in our fatty tissue. It is estimated that the average American is contaminated with more than 700 toxins that may account for an extra 15-23 pounds.

In a recent study, scientists examined the umbilical cord blood of 10 babies and found over 200 foreign chemicals. This would correlate with the rise in infant defects, auto-immune disease, and the growing number of cancers among small children (Goodman, 2009).

It is important to understand that the body consists of approximately 75 trillion cells, many of which produce energy as a pre-requisite for normal cellular function. While oxygen and glucose are used in the combustion of energy, the transportation of oxygen and glucose into the cellular membrane is dependent upon vital nutrients, which was first introduced by Dr. Otto Warburg and expanded upon with the advances of science.

Piecing the cancer puzzle together begins on a cellular level and has everything to do with cellular combustion.

Dr. Warburg referred to the malfunction in this process as the primary cause of cancer.

The inhibition of this process is referred to as the secondary causes of cancer. The number of variables involved in the inhibition process and their arrangement are limitless, which is why there is never a smoking gun, or exact cause of cancer.

> **THE PRIMARY CAUSE, AS OUTLINED AND DEFINED BY DR. OTTO WARBURG, IS THE PRODUCTION OF ENERGY ANAEROBICALLY (WITHOUT THE USE OF OXYGEN), A PROCESS REFERRED TO AS FERMENTATION. THE SECONDARY CAUSES OF CANCER HAVE EVERYTHING TO DO WITH THE INHIBITION PROCESS, WHOSE VARIABLES RANGE FROM DIET RELATED NUTRIENT DEFICIENCIES, CONTAMINATED WATER, TOXINS, STRESS, AND ENVIRONMENTAL ANOMALIES.**

The primary cause, as outlined and defined by Dr. Otto Warburg, is the production of energy anaerobically (without the use of oxygen), a process referred to as fermentation. The secondary causes of cancer have everything to do with the inhibition process, whose variables range from diet related nutrient deficiencies, contaminated water, toxins, stress, and environmental anomalies.

The evolutionary process of a cancer cell continues as a once-specialized normal cell becomes a non-specialized mutant cell maintaining a unique set of characteristics.

One such characteristic is the inability to produce enough energy to maintain normal function, thus they revert to a survival modality. A cancer cell's survival modality consists of robbing the body of vital nutrients, growing and multiplying indefinitely, and invading surrounding tissue.

THE PRIMARY CAUSE OF CANCER

When a cancer cell produces energy through a process called fermentation, it produces as a byproduct, lactic acid. Lactic acid not only inhibits the flow of oxygen into the cell membrane, it exacerbates the problem by polluting the water (lymph fluids) surrounding adjacent cells.

Lactic acid also lowers the body's pH balance by inhibiting the flow of lymphatic fluids rich in oxygen, while at the same time providing a haven for cancer cells to grow and thrive.

Understanding the fundamental principles of cellular respiration and the primary and secondary causes of cancer can be compared to General Schwarzkopf's pre-emptive and exhaustive preparations in designing a successful battle plan against a seasoned enemy.

In preparing for that battle, every small detail was scrutinized, and every minute factor was dissected before a directive was issued.

CHAPTER 6

THE SECONDARY CAUSES OF CANCER

"In the beginning God created the heavens and the earth... Then God said, "Let there be light"; and there was light.... [and He gave it life - called - an Electro-magnetic field] .... Then God said, "Let Us make man....God created man.... [and He breathed into him life, called - Electric-magnetic field..."] – Estrada's version of Genesis 1:1,3,26

In the 17th century a scientist by the name of John Canton discovered that electricity was present in the air. Benjamin Franklin, who also lived in the 17th century, was credited for his belief that lightening was electrical charges.

In 1862, for the first time in history, a scientist by the name of Lord Kelvin (1824-1907) was able to measure the atmospheric electric field, which was referred to as the "Potential Gradient." Using air balloons scientists were able to measure atmospheric electricity up to five and a half miles (9km) above the surface of the earth. But when measured at 13.5 miles (22km) above the earth, no atmospheric electricity was present. Thus, they concluded that atmospheric electric field existed between the earth's surface and the earth's upper atmosphere.

The earth's electro-magnetic field (EMF) consists of electrons, which travel around the earth in the form of currents, creating an electro-magnetic current. Without these electromagnetic charges, life could not exist (Aplin, Harrison, Rycroft, 2008).

In a similar way the human body functions on an atomic level via electrical charges, which consists of the interaction of protons (positive), electrons (negative), and neurons (neutral). The body generates electricity via chemical reactions that occur between atoms and molecules within the body, and without these electric charges, human life could not exist.

What is important is that these chemical reactions are dependent on the foods we consume. The foods we eat contain specific elements such as oxygen, potassium, sodium, calcium, magnesium, phosphorous, chloride, and electrolytes, which maintain specific number of electrons and protons. The interaction between these electrons and protons in the foods we eat with other electrons and protons within our bodies, allows for the creation of energy (Bowers, 2015; Interdisziplina re Gesellschaftfur Umweltmedizine. 2002; Weil, 2012).

Electrolytes producing electrical discharges are a simple example of the incalculable ways the human body transform the foods we eat to produce energy and enables us to function.

Every nerve impulse, thought, muscular action, brain function, emotion, and cell function begin with an electrical impulse.

In the same way, electro-magnetic charges are required in order to reverse disease and maintain optimal health.

In an age of processed foods, depleted soil, foreign toxins, etc., most of these essential elements have been destroyed or have been minimized, creating a deficit in electrolyte interaction.

The repercussion of this deficit could be part of the reason for the massive increase in autoimmune disease, cancers, and other illnesses and diseases (Bowers, 2015; Interdisziplina re Gesellschaftfur Umweltmedizine. 2002; Weil, 2012).

Dr. Warburg was also able to demonstrate that there are secondary causes of cancer. He was able to discover that the absence of certain nutrients, which he referred to as the "Active group" was the secondary cause of cancer. The "Active group" consisted of enzymes that promotes the transporting of oxygen into the cellular membrane, which included iron, vitamin A, B2, B3, B5, B12, zinc, selenium, and water (Warburg, 1966).

It is because of his efforts that we can understand the pre-cursors to cancer and the metabolic etiology of a cancer cell.

In the years that followed there would be numerous other pioneering doctors and scientists who would validate the work of Dr. Warburg and expand on his discoveries. For example, based on current 21st century science, we know that the environment and the human biological system in concert, play a pivotal role in the creation of cancer cells, and in the deterring, or abetting the onset and progression of cancer cells (Warburg, 1956; Warburg, Nobelprize.org, 2015).

It is estimated that the human body produces approximately 200 spontaneous cancers every day. Thus, every human being has cancer cells. So, then how does a doctor distinguish between "not having cancer" and being "diagnosed with cancer."

To understand this distinction, you need to know that three million cancer cells can live on the tip of a needle. In other words, cancer cells can be very tiny and even undetectable to conventional detection devices.

When cancer growth continues unabated, those growths eventually become visible and detectible, which is when a person is officially diagnosed as having cancer.

The human body has always had some cancer cells, but up until that point, the body's immune system was efficient enough to eradicate them. It is when the body's immune response becomes compromised or is overwhelmed by a combination of inhibiting factors that cancer cells can propagate unabated.

CHAPTER 7
THE BIOLOGY OF LIFE - FOODS

"One quarter of what you eat keeps you alive, the other three quarters keeps your doctor alive" –Ancient Egyptian Proverb

"The cancer trail often begins with nutrition."
–Dr. Campbell, Dr. Esselstyn, & Dr. McDougall

"Every ailment, every sickness, and every disease can be traced back to an organic mineral deficiency." –Dr. Linus Pauling, two-time Nobel Prize winner, addressing the 74th U.S. Congress

Thomas Jefferson once wrote, *"Was the government to prescribe to us our medicine and diet, our bodies would be in such keeping as our souls are now."* Almost 200 years later, according to the American Medical Association, each year over 100,000 people die as a result of taking FDA approved drugs. That's 300 people per day, one death every five minutes.

In 1978 Dr. Coldwell Esselstyn, an Oncologist, was on the breast cancer task force at the Cleveland Clinic. As a surgeon, he soon realized that he had not been able to make a difference on the prevention of breast cancer. He began researching the global statistics on breast cancer, which called into question the traditional methods of treatment he had been administering.

He discovered that in Kenya in 1978, a woman's chances of developing breast cancer were 82 times lower than in America. He also discovered that in Japan in 1958, the number of prostate cancer deaths totaled 18, while in America, during the same period, the number of prostate cancer deaths was 14,000. While the population of America was almost twice that of Japan, the number of prostate related cancer deaths was far greater per capita (Jefferson, 1781; Stone, Campbell, & Esselstyn, 2011).

In the early 1970s the risk for heart disease was 14 times lower in China than in America and almost non-existent in the highlands of Papua New Guinea. A common denominator between these countries was their diet, which was primarily vegetable-based, no dairy (Stone, Campbell, & Esselstyn, 2011).

Another study that has long been overlooked was just prior to and following WW II, when the Germans occupied Norway, and confiscated all the livestock and farm animals to provide for their own army. This meant that the Norwegian people were left to eat mainly a vegetable-based diet. Prior to their occupation the Norwegians reached a peak in deaths due to heart disease and stroke. During the occupation, when they were forced to eat a vegetable-based diet their death rates plummet (Stone, Campbell, & Esselstyn, 2011).

There has never been a situation in which cardiovascular disease dropped so dramatically, in all of medicine, even with the latest drugs and therapies. When an entire population is forced to abstain from particular foods, their health improves, and cardiovascular disease and strokes fell to an all-time low. Once the hostilities were over and the population returned to a diet consisting of dairy, their rate of heart disease and stroke regained its prior status (Stone, Campbell, & Esselstyn, 2011).

Dr. John McDougall began practicing medicine on a sugar plantation in Hawaii during the mid-1970s. What he discovered was that the health of the local population differed depending on how long they had lived in Hawaii. Those raised in Japan, the Philippines, Korea, and China were always trim and never experienced heart disease, prostate cancer, breast cancer, or colon cancer. They never had rheumatoid arthritis or multiple sclerosis. They were fully coherent and functional even into their 80s and 90s (McDougall, n.d.).

Their offspring, however, began to experience many of the ailments that their parents seemed to have avoided, and their children's children were just as sick as those in American society.

The major difference was diet.

The first generation had been raised on a diet that consisted mainly of rice and vegetables. The following generations began to replace the traditional diet for an American diet. They began to eat at McDonald's and adapted to a fast food diet, which consisted of dairy products.

In America, by the 1950s the introduction of convenience foods began to take a foothold and the American diet was forever altered (McDougall, n.d.).

Dr. Campbell, compelled by recent research, decided to replicate a recent research study that indicts an animal protein called "casein" as a major contributor for the onset of liver cancer. Over a 12-week period Dr. Campbell fed one group of rats a diet consisting of 20% casein and the second group of rats was fed a diet consisting of only 5% casein. Casein is a major protein found in dairy products, including milk, sour cream, ice cream, yogurt, butter, and cheese. Casein also comes as a protein dietary supplement.

At the end of 12 weeks the rats that were administered the 20% casein developed liver cancer, while the rats that were administered only 5% casein did not develop liver cancer (Stone, Campbell, & Esselstyn, 2011).

According to the Mayo Clinic, for an average individual who maintains a 2,000 (daily) calorie diet the consumption of casein (protein) should be no more than 175 grams per day, or 35% of your calorie intake. A typical nine-ounce steak has between 70 and 78 grams of protein.

While casein may be an excellent source of low-fat slow burning protein used for weight loss and muscle gain, in this case "too much" is not better. In fact, "too much" could put you at risk for liver disease, osteoporosis, diverticulitis, and kidney problems (Schuna, 2017).

Dr. Campbell took this experiment one step further. He took the group of rats that were administered 20% casein and altered the amounts fluctuating from 20% to 5%, and back to 20%, to 5%. He did so for 12 weeks. What he discovered was that the tumor clusters fluctuated with the differing amounts of casein. At 20% casein the tumors grew, when the amount was dropped to 5% the cancer tumors reduced in size. When the 5% was, again, increased to 20% the tumors began to grow, but when Dr. Campbell reduced the amount to 5% the tumors, again, began to shrink in size (Stone, Campbell, & Esselstyn, 2011).

What is so phenomenal about this study is that Dr. Campbell could manipulate the cancer growth simply by altering the dosage of this one protein, casein. Time and time again the tumor growth or reduction in size was determined by the administration of specific amounts of casein.

To determine if this is indicative of just animal proteins or if it is also true of vegetable-based protein, he conducted the same studies using proteins found in soybean and wheat, but there was no evidence of cancer growth. Dr. Campbell argued that vegetables have enough amounts of protein to sustain excellent health (Stone, Campbell, & Esselstyn, 2011).

Dr. Campbell estimates that the human body requires about 8% - 9% protein to maintain optimal health and an animal-based diet that exceeds 20% adversely affect the liver.

According to Dr. Campbell, Americans are often misinformed, believing that they need to eat meat for the purpose of obtaining calcium and that vegetables do not contain calcium (Stone, Campbell, & Esselstyn, 2011).

Nothing could be farther from the truth. The truth is a person does not need to eat meat to obtain calcium or to sustain life. There are over 34 vegetables that are high in protein. For example, sun dried tomatoes are 14% protein, and soybean sprouts are 13% protein.

To further substantiate his hypothesis that the consumption of too much animal protein is toxic and leads to cancer, Dr. Campbell turned to China. In 1974 the premier of China, Zhou Enlai, was hospitalized with bladder cancer. Realizing that his cancer was terminal, the premier of China decided to broaden the understanding for the onset of cancer.

So, China began one of the largest and most exhaustive scientific studies on cancer ever undertaken.

650,000 researchers painstakingly cataloged mortality patterns caused by several types of cancer between the years 1973-1975. The study included every region in China and 880 million people.

This study was so comprehensive that it would take 10 years to complete.

The results of this study are described and mapped out in the 200-page atlas entitled: "Atlas of Cancer Mortality in the People's Republic of China" (Zhonghua Renmin Gongheguo e xing zhong liu di tu ji bian ji wei yuan hui, 1981).

At the time of the study, fat intake was less than half of that found in the U.S. Animal protein consumption was only 10% of that found in the U.S. In rural China cholesterol was 127 mg/dL compared to 203 mg/dL for the U.S. (adults age 27-74). Coronary artery disease was 16.7 times greater for men in the United States and 5.6 times greater for women in the United States (Zhonghua Renmin Gongheguo e xing zhong liu di tu ji bian ji wei yuan hui, 1981).

What is unique about this exhaustive study is that certain cancers were more apparent in certain regions of China than in others. There seemed to be hot spots, where certain cancers flourished, while in other areas these cancers were almost non-existent.

For example, cancer of the esophagus showed a 400% difference between different regions (in the U.S. cancer of the esophagus revealed a 2% difference between differing counties). Why such a disparity among a common people (Zhonghua Renmin Gongheguo e xing zhong liu di tu ji bian ji wei yuan hui, 1981)?

In collaboration with the Chinese government Dr. Campbell and his Chinese associates embarked on one of the most comprehensive studies ever conducted. They decided to examine why such disparities existed.

The study took into consideration 367 diet and health related variables. Researchers collected and analyzed mortality information for more than 50 diseases, including 14 types of cancer (stomach, esophagus, liver, cervix, lung, colon and rectum, breast, nasopharynx, leukemia, brain tumors, malignant lymphoma, cancer of the bladder, prostate, and choriocarcinoma), from 65 regions and 130 villages, in rural and mainland China. Blood, urine, food samples, and complete dietary information were gathered from a sample of 50 adults from each location. The information was analyzed for nutritional, viral, hormonal, and toxin contributions.

The study would be conducted in 65 different rural and semi-rural counties scattered across China. They chose rural areas because the people living there rarely move and maintain a specific lifestyle that spans 20 to 30 years, which adds stability to the study. In preparation for this study more than 350 workers were trained to study and document the lifestyle and dietary habits of 6500 people within the 65 counties (Chen, Campbell, Li, & Peto, 1990).

In 1983 Dr. Campbell and his colleagues began to analyze the enormous amount of information that had been collected. In 1990 they published their findings. The study referenced no less than 90,000 correlations between diet and disease. The study included hundreds of detailed tables and charts (Chen, Campbell, Li, & Peto, 1990).

The central message from this study is that a diet that is primarily food based, consisting of cereal grains, vegetables, and fruits is always associated with low mortality of certain cancers, strokes, and coronary heart disease (Chen, Campbell, Li, & Peto, 1990). The New York Times published an article stating that this was one of the *"most comprehensive large study ever undertaken of the relationship between diet and the risk of developing disease"* (Brody, 1990).

Dr. Campbell's exhaustive and comprehensive studies were all consistent and for the first time he could demonstrate, empirically, that a diet that is food-based promotes a healthy lifestyle, while a diet that is animal based promotes disease (Campbell, Parpia, & Chen, 1998; Chen, Campbell, Li, & Peto, 1990; Stone, Campbell, & Esselstyn, 2011).

In the end Dr. Campbell could identify different pieces of the cancer puzzle, the interaction between genes, chemicals, and nutrition. Dr. Campbell concluded, after exhaustive research that an animal-based protein, casein, when consumed in excess of 20% of a normal diet, promotes cancer growth, and that casein, exceeding 20%, is toxic to the liver (Stone, Campbell, & Esselstyn, 2011).

At the time of his research, Dr. Campbell was unaware of the research being conducted by Dr. Burzynski, and his work on antineoplastons (a peptide produced by the liver) and gene therapy, which would, forever, link casein as an indirect inhibitor in the liver production of antineoplastons (Stone, Campbell, & Esselstyn, 2011; Burzynski, n.d.).

Dr. Campbell believes there is no single variable responsible for the onset of cancer. What is clear is that a diet that consists of 20% or more of dairy is toxic to the liver (Stone, Campbell, & Esselstyn, 2011). Overall health and well-being is accomplished by an orchestration of events that include the consumption of certain foods and how they interact biologically to provide the proper amount of vitamins, minerals, enzymes, antioxidants, sugars (glyconutrients), trace elements, etc., which provides the necessary mechanisms for healthy biological function and the eradication of cancer and other diseases. There are also external variables such as toxins, foreign chemicals, and green picking of fruits and vegetables that adversely influence cellular health (Stone, Campbell, & Esselstyn, 2011).

Meat consumption rose substantially after WW II. What is also of interest is beef consumption doubled after the first McDonald's restaurant opened. While the consumption of dairy, and in particular meat, has risen substantially and a diet that exceeds 20% is clearly toxic to the liver, there are countless other toxins (as of 2016, over 100,000 foreign toxins and foreign chemicals) that have been introduced, many of which are carcinogenic and toxic to the liver, inhibiting its natural functions. For example, in 1830 annual sugar consumption was 15 pounds per person. Today it is 150 pounds per person. According to the FDA there is "no conclusive evidence" that sugar is responsible for chronic disease. Today (2011), in excess of 25% of the American caloric intake consists of sugar, and nothing else (Stone, Campbell, & Esselstyn, 2011).

Between 1880 and 1910, 33% of the U.S. population lived on a farm and consumed the produce from the farm, which consisted primarily of vegetables, fruits, grain, and raw, unpasteurized milk. Today only one percent of the U.S. population lives on a farm. In 1910 the risk of Type II diabetes was one in 30. Today (2013), according to the Center for Disease Control (CDC), Atlanta, it is one in three.

In 1910 Americans consumed 18 pounds of butter annually, and the mortality from heart disease was below 10%. In 2000 that total consumption of butter dropped to four pounds annually, having been replaced with synthetic substitutes referred to as margarines, which is a major source of trans fats (estimated to be in excess of nine pounds per year), and the mortality from heart disease rose 40% to 45% (2000).

In 1910 lard that came from pigs raised outdoors was consumed by 70% of Americans. It contained vitamin D and palmitoleic acid, a monounsaturated antimicrobial fatty acid that eradicates bacteria and viruses. Today lard has been replaced with processed soybean oil that contains no vitamin D.

In 1911 Proctor and Gamble (P&G) introduced Crisco to the American people as an alternative to lard, a shortening made from hydrogenated vegetable fat, which was originally designed to make candles but with the advent of electricity the candle industry almost disappeared. Crisco claimed it had a longer shelf life and over the decades to follow would contribute hundreds of millions of pounds of trans fatty acids. Margarine, vegetable shortening, corn oil, and other vegetable oils, contain excess amounts of Omega six. Excess amounts of Omega six inhibit the flow of oxygen and nutrients by injuring and inflaming bodily tissue.

In 1934 the first blood test for cholesterol was introduced and cholesterol was blamed for several chronic diseases. However, in 1937 two biochemists, David Rittenberg and Rudolph Schoenheimer from Columbia University provided scientific evidence that dietary cholesterol had minimal effect on blood cholesterol.

While this has never been refuted the national guidelines restrict dietary cholesterol to less than 300 mg. per day. By 1948 vegetable fat, which contains trans fatty acids, consumption reached 28 pounds per person, and by 1956 it was a high as 55 pounds per person. During the same period obesity and diabetes became public health concerns. In 1949 arterioslcerosis, for the first time, is added to the International Classification of Diseases.

During WW II inexperienced creamery workers and recent replacements produced a batch of tainted milk, which resulted in several deaths. At the time, the government blamed the deaths on the raw milk and not on the inexperienced workers, and in 1949 mandated pasteurization. Pasteurization not only kills essential nutrients, including Vitamin B-12, it also kills the enzymes necessary for the absorption of the milk proteins. The government solution thus far is to add synthetic Vitamin D.

In 1955, at the age of 64, President Eisenhower suffers from a heart attack. The doctors recommended a low fat, low cholesterol diet. His cholesterol, at the time of his attack was 165 ml/dl. Despite his low cholesterol diet, his cholesterol continued to rise until it reached 259 on his last day in office. Eisenhower would suffer from several more heart attacks and eventually would die of heart disease.

In 1955 John Gofman (1918 – 2007), at the time, Professor Emeritus of Molecular and Cell Biology at the University of Berkley, stated that carbohydrates elevate very-low-density lipoprotein (VLDL). VLDL is the lipoprotein that transports blood fats (triglycerides) produced in the liver from surplus carbohydrates. He stated, "Restricting carbohydrates would lower VLDL" (a surplus of carbohydrates → elevated triglycerides → the manufacturing of more VLDL → increased risk of heart disease). John Peters, from Yale School of Medicine, using the latest technology of the day, confirmed the work of John Gofman.

Despite these findings the American Heart Association conducts a national fundraiser promoting a low fat, low cholesterol, low saturated fat diet recommending margarine, corn oil, breakfast cereals, and skin milk. Ironically this was the same diet that Eisenhower was placed on. It was in 1956 that John Gofman stated that people with heart disease had elevated triglycerides and depressed high-density lipoproteins (HDL), which was due to a high intake of carbohydrates, which consisted primarily of high consumptions of white breads and processed sugars.

In 1957 Hilde Bruch, an American psychoanalyst, recognized for her work on eating disorders and obesity wrote: *"The great progress in dietary control of obesity was the recognition that meat was not fat producing; but that it was bread and sweets which lead to obesity."* Obesity, because of its overall contributions to bodily dysfunctions, is a precursor to the onset of cancer.

In 1999, Walter Willett, in a Harvard Nurses Study, where 3000 nurses had contracted cancer, concluded that a low-fat diet increases the risk of cancer. *"Saturated fat seems to be protective…"* The real culprits are excess amounts of sugar and carbohydrates.

In conclusion, current research clearly indicates that a diet that consists primarily of fruits and vegetables is consistent with a very low risk of cancer. While a diet that consists primarily of processed sugar, carbohydrates, and 20% or more in dairy equates to a high risk of cancer, heart disease, and other illnesses. There are a multitude of factors that have changed in what people eat and in how foods are prepared for market in the past 110 years.

Essentially with the advent of pasteurization and modern food processing, foods naturally abundant in nutrients are stripped of these vital nutrients or are harvested green and lacking in these essential nutrients. It is also important to note that dairy, in and of itself, does not cause cancer, however, when a diet consists of 20% or more in dairy over an extended period the liver is affected adversely. When the liver becomes toxic it fails to produce an important peptide (antineoplastons) necessary for the modulation of our two cancer genes, which is often referred to as our second immune system.

Finally, in piecing the cancer puzzle together, the work of Dr. Campbell, Dr. Esselstyn, and countless others, clearly demonstrates that the type of diet a person consumes directly and indirectly dictates their state of health. It is also clear that the bodily functions are dependent on a diet that provides the required nutrients. Any absence in this daily requirement will result in a malfunction of bodily functions that ultimately leads to cancer and other illnesses and diseases.

CHAPTER 8

BIOLOGICAL REPERCUSSIONS

Hippocrates, the father of medicine (431 B.C) said, *"Let food be thy medicine and medicine be thy food."*

People rarely consider why we need food, or why the body requires food, and for what purpose. People almost never take into consideration why the digestive track is 30 feet long and not one-foot-long, or why foods come is such an array of colors, and how these colors contribute to health and well-being.

How does the body respond to a dinner consisting of one hamburger, a coke, and fries as compared to a leafy green vegetable salad, fresh fruit and unprocessed milk or fresh water? Have you ever thought about the differences between fresh foods verses a TV dinner, or organic verses non-organic, pasteurized verses non-pasteurized, margarine verses butter? These are questions we rarely ask ourselves or even think about.

Up until the 1900s the world was not familiar with pasteurization, or non-organic foods, or processed foods. The world had never seen a TV dinner, pre-packaged vegetables ready to pop into the oven, let alone McDonald's fast foods, where all you have to do is drive up to the window.

It all has to do with one of the most amazing mechanisms ever created – the human body. The human body is made up of 75 Trillion cells. If you consider all the moving parts both within the cell and outside of the cell, the actual number of moving parts is closer to infinity. What is of prime importance is that the human body and all its systems (immune system, nervous system, etc.) are interdependent and all these moving parts require continued maintenance. To maintain optimum performance there is a constant need for raw materials in the form of nutrients.

When foods are consumed, they begin a digestive process, via the intestinal tract, that extends 30 feet from mouth to rectum. This elongated tube is where all nutrients are extracted from the foods we consume. The nutrients required for normal cellular function include: Oxygen, Carbon, Hydrogen, Nitrogen, Calcium, Phosphorous, Potassium, Sulfur, Sodium, Chloride, Magnesium, Iodine, Iron, Chromium, Cobalt, Copper, Manganese, Molybdenum, Selenium, Vanadium, and Zinc. The Body's massive manufacturing facilities also requires: Vitamin A, B1, B2, B6, B12, C, D, E, H, K, folic acid, and a host of trace minerals.

The body also requires eight essential monosaccharides referred to as, glyconutrients (Glucose, Galactose, Mannose, Fucose, Xylose, N-Acetyl-Glucosamine, N-Acetyl-Galactosamine, and, N-Acetyl-Neuramanic Acid). A deficiency in any of these necessary nutrients will result in an imbalance that can result in biological dysfunction, including the inhibition of oxygen and vital nutrients to the cell. We acquire all of these for optimal health and we acquire them, primarily, from unprocessed fruits, vegetables, nuts, and grains. All are required for maximum biological function (New Health Guide, 2015).

This biological process has not changed since human creation. What has changed that would jeopardize this process? In brief, what has changed is how a society processes its food. Humans are the only species that processes its foods before consumption. All other created animals, birds, and sea creatures eat their foods as produced by nature. In other words, they consume their foods naturally.

What has changed is the introduction of foreign chemicals at such a massive scale (100,000) that it has polluted the air we breathe, the water we drink, and the soil in which we grow our crops. The amount of chemicals is so overwhelming that it has created an ecological imbalance that has not existed since the beginning of time. What has changed is the comingling and dwelling of millions of people within a small confined space.

Finally, what has changed is the overwhelming introduction of electro-magnetic waves (from microwaves to cell phones) that create havoc to the body's natural pulsating electro-magnetic field.

This inter-dependent relationship between human systems and nutrients extends universally. It is becoming even more apparent how extensively the human species is dependent on its environment for existence and well-being. Just as plants depend on the sun for its energy, people depend on plant life for nutrients used to convert simple sugars (glucose) into energy – ATP. This interdependency has been well established, but not until recently has it become of critical concern or fully understood.

For centuries human beings have taken for granted the intertwining relationship between human biology and the external relationship from which people obtain their sustenance. Since this interdependent relationship is in jeopardy and the effects overwhelming as well as devastating, people are beginning to re-examine the natural co-relationship people have with their environment.

Normally, the body extracts essential nutrients from the foods consumed daily. Today, with the advances in scientific research scientists know so much more about nutrients and why they have become deficient in the American diet. US Senate Document #264, Published in 1936, states: *"The alarming fact is that foods (fruits, vegetables, and grains) now being raised on millions of acres of land that no longer contain enough of certain minerals and are starving us. No matter how much of them we eat, no man can eat enough fruits and vegetables to supply his system with the minerals he requires for perfect health because his stomach isn't big enough to hold them...The truth is that our goods vary enormously in value, and some of them aren't worth eating as foods..."*

Paul Bergner compiled data from the USDA and other sources, which shows the decline in mineral and vitamin content of several fruits and vegetables in 1914, 1963, and 1992. He analyzed oranges, apples bananas, carrots potatoes, corn, tomatoes, celery, romaine lettuce, broccoli, iceberg lettuce, collard greens, and chard. According to the USDA: average changes in mineral content of some fruits and vegetables, 1963-1992

Minerals	Average % Change
Calcium	-29.82
Iron	-32.00
Magnesium	-21.08
Phosphorus	-11.09
Potassium	-6.48

(Bergner, 1997).

The Immunological Connection & its Link with the Modern Diet

The human body can be compared to a car. To run, it requires fuel, adequate oil, water or coolant, and a periodic tune-up. For example, within the human body, when a muscle loses only 3% of its water it results in a 10% drop in strength and an 8% drop in speed. Drinking five glasses of water a day decreases the risk of colon cancer by 45% plus it can slash the risk of breast cancer by 79%, and one is 50% less likely to develop bladder cancer (Holisticresearch.org, n.d.).

Two hundred and fifty years ago, it was discovered that the reason sailors contracted scurvy was because they were not getting sufficient amounts of vitamin C. What do you think would happen if commercial manufacturers removed all the vitamin D in milk, and most of the vitamins and minerals in the foods you consume at your local restaurant, fast food facility, and grocery store? How would your body acquire all these vital nutrients it requires in order to function effectively and efficiently? What do you think would happen if this scenario continued for years, or decades? Do you think there might be a breakdown in one or more systems, and how would that reveal itself?

When the human body is deprived of vital nutrients, pristine water, clean air, and is subjected to prolonged periods of stress, there are major biological repercussions. Dr. Warburg would have referred to these countless variables as secondary causes for the onset and propagation of cancer. But because every human being is unique, maintaining their own exclusive risk tolerance, the absence of these essential biological requirements plays out distinctively, which is why doctors and scientists can never pinpoint the exact cause of cancer.

This is also why the repercussions of nutrient deficiencies reveal themselves in varying forms, distinct from one individual to another. In some cases, cancer will ensue ten years later, while others may react more quickly. Still others will be affected with various forms of autoimmune disease, heart disease, or some other illnesses and disease. In the end, prolonged deficiencies of vital nutrients, or the prolonged consumption of fast foods with result in illness and disease, it's only a matter of time.

The Genetic Connection & its Link with the Modern Diet

In the early 1970s, Dr. Burzynski was the first scientists to discover the disruptive link between the environment and cancer suppressor genes and oncogenes. The variables were peptides called, antineoplastons. Antineoplastons regulate the body's cancer suppressor genes by turning them on and by turning off the oncogenes. Dr. Burzynski discovered that cancer patients are highly deficient these antineoplastons, which are produced in the liver.

Dr. Campbell was also one of the first researchers to discover a link between casein, an enzyme found in dairy products, and liver toxicity. He first came upon this truth by noticing that the poor people of the Philippines did not suffer from cancer of the liver, while it was more common among the wealthier inhabitants of the island. This truth was also validated in the "China Study," which was one of the largest studies on cancer ever conducted.

Dr. Otto Warburg was the first to discover that the secondary cause of cancer was diet related. Any deficiency is specific nutrients that he referred to as the "Active group" resulted in the inhibition of oxygen to the cell. More recent research reveals that nutrients are necessary for every human function, including immune response, which is our first line of defense against illness and disease.

In piecing this part of the cancer puzzle together, which has much to do with diet, it turns out that large consumptions of dairy are toxic (in excess of 20%) to the liver, inhibiting its normal function. Without the normal production of antineoplastons, the body's genetic mechanisms are adversely affected. Without adequate amounts of antineoplastons the body is unable to adequately regulate its cancer genes, resulting in the proliferation of cancer cells. Finally, without sufficient amounts of nutrients all of the body's systems are jeopardized.

Processed Sugar (Glucose)

In July 1988 Gregory Grosbard of Miami, Florida, received a United States patent on a process to improve the strength of plastic by using sugar. The problem was every time plastic went through a dishwasher heat cycle, it lost strength because oxygen in the atmosphere would penetrate the material and create what was referred to as oxygen "holes." Mr. Grosbard found that by mixing a small amount of processed sugar into the plastic material during its development it strengthened the plastic, and when it was subjected to a dishwasher's heat cycle, the sugar grabbed onto the oxygen first, preventing the oxygen holes and making the plastic stronger.

Research has shown that:

- Processed sugar **blocks** the absorption of calcium.
- Processed sugar produces a low oxygen environment.
- Processed sugar is extremely acidic (a haven for cancer).
- Too much processed sugar suppresses the immune system. It interrupts the Krebs's energy cycle, which in turn suppresses the immune system's ability to manufacture killer cells and antibodies (killer cells are a major part of the anti-cancer arsenal).

- Processed sugar depletes B vitamins which are key players in the transference of oxygen molecules to the cell, and without cellular oxygen, cancer cells are created. The liver is the most important organ in healing the body.

Cancer has become the number one "killer disease in children" in the past few years. A major contributor is sugar consumption, which is robbing the oxygen out of their bodies and making their cells extremely acidic while severely suppressing their immune systems. Sugar averages for children are around 36 teaspoons a day (96 teaspoons = one pound; 36 x 365 = 13,140 teaspoons of sugar annually. 13,140/96 = 137 pounds per year). That's 137 pounds of processed sugar a year.

The negative side effect of such an enormous amount of processed sugar is not only a depressed immune system but also Attention Hyperactivity Disorder (ADHD) and attention Deficit Disorder (ADD). A diet high in processed sugars and bleached white flour provides an ideal environment for cancer to grow.

Recently there was a story of a young boy who had just undergone chemotherapy. His face and eyes showed the horrors he had experienced. He appeared to be lifeless and unwilling to live due to the ill effects of his treatment. He was subjected to chemo, in the form of mustard gas (a highly toxic poison) that had destroyed his immune system.

To ease his suffering his doctor offered him a vanilla milk shake. What they were oblivious to was that the high sugar content of the milkshake is highly acidic, which feeds his cancer cells. The sugar also lowers his body's pH, causing it to become more acidic, an environment that cancer cells thrive in. The reality is ignorance can kill.

Sugar Substitutes

To make matters worse, to circumvent the effects of sugar, sugar substitutes were created such as NutraSweet, which is made from aspartame. Aspartame is 10% wood alcohol, which the body metabolizes into various carcinogens (one of them is DKP, which has been linked to brain tumors). According to the Ramazzini Foundation of Oncology and Environmental Sciences, aspartame, when consumed, breaks down into formaldehyde and formic acid. The formaldehyde attaches to the DNA causing multiple breaks (double-strand breaks) in the DNA, which are associated with the onset of cancer.

Aspartame is accumulated within the body and is responsible for the increase is leukemia, lymphoma, breast cancer, and brain tumors. Aspartame is also responsible for neurological diseases such as Alzheimer's and Parkinson's. Finally, aspartame is highly addictive. Other side effects, as reported by the FDA, include headaches, dizziness, mood changes, numbness, vomiting, nausea, muscle cramps, and spasms, abdominal pain, vision problems, skin lesions, memory loss, and seizures (Somers, 2008).

Another sugar substitute that has been introduced into our food supply, Sucralose, which is a synthetic organochloride that is a common ingredient in most of the world's food supply. It is being marketed under the name, Splenda, which is being promoted as healthy, but is proving to be extremely detrimental. Common ads refer to it as being made from sugar, and referred to as, "natural," when, it is more closely linked to a chlorinated pesticide.

Splenda is creating a host of health problems including, promoting the onset of cancer, autoimmune disease, and skin problems., to name a few (Mercola, 2013; Carpenter, 2012; Schiffman, 2013).

It all begins in the gut, where there are several trillion healthy bacteria, or microorganisms that are essential for optimal health. In fact, these microorganisms outnumber our cells 10 to 1. Scientists are just beginning to understand the link between these microorganisms and a variety of bodily functions, including their ability to facilitate proper digestion, synthesize nutrients from the foods we eat, maintain proper immune function, prevent autoimmune disorders, and prevent the onset of cancer (Mercola, 2013; Carpenter, 2012).

These microscopic bacteria (several trillion) communicate directly with nerve endings in the digestive track and the nervous system, which then communicate with the brain. According to the American Psychological Association (APA), these microscopic bacteria produce neurochemicals that are utilized by the brain for psychological and other mental functions, including the regulation of mood, memory and learning. According to the APA most of our serotonin is produced by these microscopic bacteria located in our gut (Perlmutter, 2015; Carpenter, 2012; Schiffman, 2013).

According to some of the latest research, we now know that all our bodily systems are interrelated and the functions of one system, or the dysfunctions of one system affects other systems. This is important because, if the proper balance of microbiomes in our gut is disrupted, this could cause a leaky gut, and or inflammation. If so, this would create a host of problems, and Splenda can destroy up to 50% of your gut bacteria, destroying primarily the good bacteria, and disrupt the pH balance in the gut.

Remember, inflammation is the precursor to disease, including the onset of cancer, Alzheimer's disease, Parkinson's, Multiple Sclerosis, type 2 diabetes, and insulin resistance. Also, pH is directly related to oxygen. If you lower the oxygen levels, the result is acidity, a precursor to cancer (Perlmutter, 2015; Carpenter, 2012; Mercola, 2013; Schiffman 2013).

Splenda (sucralose) promotes toxicity, damage to our DNA, and is carcinogenic when used in cooking. When used in cooking or when heated sucralose releases a chemical known as chloropropanols, which is related to dioxin, an element found in Agent Orange.

A list of consumer complains can be found at the website: www.truthaboutsplenda.com. Finally, The Canadian Journal of Gastroenterology (2011), strongly suggests that Splenda may be responsible for their high rate of Inflammatory Bowel Disease (IBD) (Xiaofa, 2011; Mercola, 2013; Perlmutter, 2015; Schiffman, 2013).

It is important to note that there is a major difference in how the body reacts to processed sugars as compared to the eight natural sugars required for optimal health, which are found in nature and in fruits and vegetables.

An excellent natural sugar substitute is, organic, Stevia. I have eliminated all sugars from my pantry, and when I need a sweetener, I reach for Stevia. It is an excellent sugar substitute for diabetics and is many times sweeter tasting than sugar.

Processed Foods

There are approximately 320 million Americans, most of which live in urban settings. If you can imagine, for a minute, that all 320 million Americans, from Alaska to Main, want to eat a salad for dinner, one that consists of ripe red tomatoes. How can tomatoes producers provide 320 Million Americans, from Alaska to Main, ripe red tomatoes every day? Under normal circumstances it would be impossible, unless you could circumvent Mother Nature. Today we call it "food processing."

Food distributors use chemicals to delay maturation, extend the life cycle of foods, and to enhance flavor. Most of these chemicals are also carcinogenic and excitotoxic. Because foods are picked well before they mature, "Greened picked," they lack much of their original flavor, and as food manufacturers prepare different food varieties for sale they are greatly concerned about flavor.

Once fruits and vegetables are picked a set of chemicals is applied to delay maturation, which extends the life of the foods, and allows for transport. Just before these foods are put on display a set of chemicals is applied to promote maturation. To enhance flavor MSG (monosodium glutamate) was added to foods, post WWII. Because MSG was so toxic and considered a neurotoxin, the public began to complain of its ill effects, so it was substituted for other less known flavor enhancers, which are also excitotoxins (Somers, 2008).

Excitotoxins are amino acids that are the building blocks of specific proteins called glutamate, aspartate, and cysteine, which are found in food enhancers. These excitotoxins are commonly added to foods, including baby foods to enhance flavor. Excitotoxins stimulate neurons causing them to rapidly fire off their impulses until they become exhausted and die, as if these cells were excited to death, thus the name, excitotoxins.

MSG has been replaced with several food enhancers, all of which contain, either, glutamate, aspartate, cysteine, or combinations of all three. For example, MSG was replaced with hydrolyzed vegetable protein, which also contains three known excitotoxins. Other food enhancing excitotoxins include caseinate, autolyzed yeast extract, beef or chicken broth, and natural flavorings. Ironically, the FDA allows food manufacturers to add these toxic additives if the glutamate content is less than 99% (Somers, 2008).

Glutamate, as a natural amino acid, is one of the most common neurotransmitters, which stimulates neurons. Because glutamates are so common the body goes to great lengths to regulate their number, too many can cause brain damage. Recent scientific discoveries have revealed that every human tissue maintains glutamate receptors, and overstimulation of these receptors can lead to a host of problems, including the acceleration of cancer growth and metastasis as well as other diseases such as diabetes, atherosclerosis, heart failure, and damage to the lungs (Somers, 2008).

Glutamates play an extensive role in a variety of areas, including brain function, the endocrine system, regulating of hormones, and in food addictions. If glutamate levels become too elevated during critical periods of development it can have major effects on menstrual periods, premature puberty, and infertility. When consuming foods laced with glutamate additives or drinking large amounts of diet sodas, you increase your addictive behavior (Somers, 2008).

It is almost impossible to find processed foods not treated with food additives that increase the flavor of foods. Commercialism demands it, competition encourages it, and people expect it. What they do not realize is how detrimental and addictive these additives are. How they have been linked to the onset of cancer as well as the increased growth of some cancers, along with the onset of other diseases and illnesses.

It is important to note that the list of foreign chemicals and toxins is quite exhaustive, and this chapter attempts to shed light on a few of the most influential players, and the impact they have on our environment and on our biological system.

Table Salt

Over the past 20 or so years salt has been given a bad rap, which led to the low salt craze. But the reality is, salt is not only necessary for healthy bodily function, it is an essential ingredient, without which we would all die.

Here is a list of some of the benefits of salt:

- It regulates blood pressure
- It is required for electrolyte function
- It regulates the balance of fluid and water retention.
- It supports nerve function.
- It helps to prevent muscle cramps
- It aids in digestion.
- It affects positive kidney function
- It helps the body retain nutrients that are extracted from the foods we eat.

What is bad for you is processed salts that have been altered. Most Americans are not aware that table salt, or commonly referred to as, iodized salt, may have some or all of the following added ingredients, glass, sand, sodium chloride, iodine (used to prevent goiters), MSG, white sugar (used to stabilize the iodine), aluminum derivatives, (such as sodium solo-co-aluminate), ferrocyanide, and talc (Barendse, 2013; Zeratsky, n.d.).

According to Katherine Zeratsky, R.D., L.D., in an article for the Mayo Clinic, sea salt is produced by evaporating ocean water or from saltwater lakes, which when completed leaves trace minerals and other natural ingredients. Table salt, on the other hand, is taken from underground sources and is "more heavily processed" to eliminate minerals. Various elements are added to prevent clumping. However, there is no mention of what is added to prevent the clumping. Some have suggested that sand and glass are added to prevent clumping (Barendse, 2013; Zeratsky, n.d.).

In the manufacturing process of table salt, the natural minerals are removed, and the salt is heated to 1200-degrees Fahrenheit. During this extreme heating process, the chemical composition of the salt is completely altered, killing any nutritional benefits. Once the salt is stripped of any nutritional value, additives are added as supplements, such as, ferrocyanide, silica aluminate (a by-product of aluminum), and talc, to prevent clumping and to promote a free-flowing effect.

Aluminum is known to lead to neurological disorders. Also, the body does not eliminate aluminum from the body, storing it in fatty tissue, which causes further bodily degeneration over time. Talc is a known carcinogen that was once added to baby powder, since removed from most products because of its health risks. However, the FDA still allows up to 2% to be added to table salt, despite its toxic effects (Barendse, 2013).

Any added glass and sand, used to prevent clumping, cuts your veins and causing your veins to bleed, bruise, and tear. In response, your body's cholesterol acts as a band-aid and promotes healing. In the end, too much table salt leads to high blood pressure, heart disease and high cholesterol. While the body requires salt for optimal health, it does not need processed salt (Barendse, 2013).

According to Sarah Barendse, in her article, "The Truth about Salts," sea salt was once the best alternative. But because of the environmental changes that have occurred in recent times, such as oil spills, nuclear radiation leaks (Fukushima nuclear power plant), and contaminated ocean waters, Himalayan salt, or pink Himalayan salt is probably your best choice. It is currently sold at most Costco stores.

Himalayan salt is found well below the earth's surface. It was created when the primal sea was dried up by the sun and then compressed over thousands of years. Extracted from the Himalayan mountains and sun dried is a natural process that allows the salt to maintain its natural ingredients, which contain 94 different minerals and trace minerals that our bodies require and are made up of, calcium, magnesium, potassium, copper and iron, to name a few.

Below is a list of some of the benefits of Himalayan pink salt:

- Create an electrolyte balance
- Increases hydration
- Regulate water content both inside and outside of cells
- Balance pH (alkaline/acidity) and help to reduce acid reflux
- Prevent muscle cramping
- Aid in proper metabolism functioning
- Strengthen bones
- Lower blood pressure
- Help the intestines absorb nutrients
- Prevent goiters
- Improve circulation
- Dissolve and eliminate sediment to remove toxins

Because of its extensive nutrient value, some doctors recommend taking ½ or a ¼ (I prefer one quarter) teaspoon and adding it to one gallon of purified water (Barendse, 2013).

CHAPTER 9

WATER

"Not All Water is created Equal." –Estrada

"How wet is your water?" –Estrada

"Drinking five glasses of water a day decreases the risk of colon cancer by 45% plus it can slash the risk of breast cancer by 79%, and one is 50% less likely to develop bladder cancer." (Holistic-research.org, n.d.)

All of life is dependent on water. When scientists explore other planets the first thing they look for is water. Because they know that without water, life, as we know it, could not exist. The earth is 70% water, and life is abundant. Nobel Prize recipient, Albert Szent-Gyorgyi, who discovered vitamin C, referred to water as the mother and matrix of all life (Edsall 1986). The 20th century was the dawn of new viruses and diseases, including the exponential growth of cancer, worldwide. It is now believed that the quality water is an intrical part of the cancer dilemna.

Scientists have recently discovered that water is the most influential nutrient to health and well-being, and a key ingredient to a cancer free lifestyle. What has also been discovered is that the very structure of the water people drink effects health and longevity. Up until the 21st century water was the key ingredient for optimal health, that was taken for granted.

Scientists have recently discovered that not all water is created equal.

Scientists now know that there is a connection between longevity and the source of water, which is why many scientists believe some cultures live longer than others.

Another connection between water and cancer has to do with contamination. Because of the rising concerns over contaminated water, many American water manufacturers have introduced a variety of different filtering systems, along with the addition of electrolytes, minerals, and oxygen; but those introductions have proven not to be completely effective, especially as it relates to how the body assimilates water.

There are three major concerns regarding the consumption of water, **absorption**, **quality**, and **contamination**, which scientists believe play a vital role in the cycle of life and death, health and disease, cancer and the mitigation of cancer. In America, the concerns over water absorption, quality, and contamination, is so grave that Americans spend billions of dollars annually hoping to duplicate that natural spring water that their ancestors drank.

According to the Environmental Working Group (EWG), whenever an American drinks a glass of water they are ingesting industrial, and or agricultural contaminants linked to cancer and other diseases, including infertility developmental defects, neurological disorders, and hormonal issues. What is even more alarming is that the EPA has not updated their list of water contaminants in over 20 years. Based on outdated regulations, drinking water falls under the contaminant limits set by the EPA, but are well above safety levels based on current research (EWG, n.d.).

Between 2010 and 2015 EWG collected data for all 50 states, from the EPA and state agencies, consisting of 48,712 water utilities and found 267 contaminants out of the 500 contaminants tested. Over 40,000 utility systems were linked to carcinogens that exceeded Federal and State safety guidelines. Sixty-three systems were said to be harmful to small children and fetuses. Thirty-eight system were linked to infertility problems. Seventy-eight were linked to nervous system damage. And forty-five were linked to hormonal problems (EWG, n.d.).

EWG found 19,000 Utilities that had high levels of lead. High enough to harm formula fed infants. In Flint Michigan (2015) a mother concerned about water safety, after her children became ill, contacted the EPA, only to discover that her drinking water was contaminated with high levels of lead (EWG, n.d.).

Another concern is pharmaceutical drugs found in the drinking water. It seems that when our water is filtered, before being dispensed to the general public, our current filtering systems are unable to filter out certain pharmaceutical drugs, so, in effect, when an individual drinks a glass of water, they are ingesting small particles of a variety of pharmaceutical drugs.

Keys to drinking water:

A human body consists of 77% water. Ironically, the earth is made up of 75% water. Drink half your body weight in ounces of water. For example, if you weigh 180 pounds, you should drink 90 ounces of water. By dividing 90 ounces by eight to 10-ounce servings you know how many glasses of water you should consume daily. In this case dividing 90 by 10 would mean that you would drink nine glasses of water per day.

Electrolyte Balance

Electrolytes facilitate the process of re-hydration. Too much pure water dissolves vital nutrients such as salts, which can impede cellular function. Too much pure water without enough salt can lead to water poisoning. This can occur when athletes train, using up vital nutrients such as salt. Waters that contain electrolytes allow the body to replenish without any ill effects (Kellum, 2000; Lyobebe, 2012).

Intracellular function also depends on electrolytes, which facilitate cellular metabolism. Without electrolytes the cell fails to function properly and if left unchecked may contribute to a process known as cellular fermentation. Electrolytes consist of Sodium (Na), Potassium (K), Calcium (Ca, Magnesium (Mg), Chloride CI), Phosphate (HPO4), Sulphate (SO4) and Bicarbonate (HCO3). The major Intracellular electrolytes, which are part of the "Active group" that Dr. Otto Warburg identified, consist of Potassium and Phosphate (Kellum, 2000; Lyobebe, 2012; Warburg, 1956).

Bottled Water

In America water can take on a myriad of types. There is exotic water from the Fiji Islands and Iceland. There is sparkling water, artesian water, spring water, water with added proteins, water with added calcium, waters sweetened with Splenda, and there are waters with caffeine.

In 2005 Americans spent more than 10 billion dollars and consumed more than eight billion gallons of water, which is 26 gallons per person. Ironically nearly 40% of all bottled water is nothing more than repackaged tap water. What is even more disconcerting is that currently there is no federal testing of bottled water for bacteria, or other hazardous chemicals (Donn, Mendoza, & Pritchard, 2008; Mendoza, 2008).

A recent report by the Associated Press revealed that our water supplies are also contaminated with pharmaceutical drugs, many of which are resistant to water treatment processes. Do not be surprised if your bottled water contains trace amounts of various pharmaceutical drugs, along with other known and unknown toxins (Donn, Mendoza, & Pritchard, 2008; Mendoza, 2008).

If that is not enough, toxic chemicals get leached into the bottled water when placed directly in sunlight. Do you taste plastic in your bottled water? It is not plastic that you taste but rather carcinogenic toxins that have been leaching into your water from the plastic container.

Scientists have also discovered the link between the lack of absorption of vital nutrients, such as vitamin supplements and water absorption.

Many Americans are taking enough amounts of vitamins and other supplements with little or no effect. In several studies scientists have erroneously concluded that vitamins supplements are not an effective means of absorbing nutrients. What scientists have recently discovered is that the assimilation of vital nutrients and vitamin supplements has everything to do with the structure of the water one is consuming (the wetness of water), age, and the source of vitamins (synthetic compared to organic).

In dealing with these issues and concerns let's begin by understanding the relationship between water and overall health. One of the greatest contributors to the understanding of water comes from the "Father of fluid dynamics," Dr. Henri Coanda. Consider the following facts:

- Our blood is made up of 92% water.
- Our brain is made up of 80% water.
- Our muscles are made up of 75% water.
- Our bodies are made up of 70% water.
- Our bones are made up of 60% water.
- 99% of all chemical reactions, which sustains life, require water.
- Water is responsible for all bodily processes, including digestion, absorption, circulation, and excretion.
- Water is responsible for the transportation of all nutrients to the cellular membrane.
- Water is the vehicle used for the extraction and elimination of all toxins and waste products from within the cell.
- The kidneys require water for the removal of all waste products.
- Water regulates bodily temperatures.
- Water is used to lubricate joints.
- Water is required to breathe.
- The body uses 1.5 liters of water daily to eliminate toxins, through the kidneys, lungs, and skin.
- The body cannot survive longer than 7 days without water.

- Fruits and vegetables consist of 90% water, which makes it easy for the body to assimilate all the vitamins and minerals and natural sugars.
- The body loses approximately 8 cups of water daily, which needs to be replenished.
- The daily allowance of water required for metabolism is about 1/3 liter.
- For optimal health the minimum daily intake of water required is 2 liter a day, which can be consumed, in part from fruits and vegetables.
- Four servings of vegetables and four pieces of fruit, consisting of 1.1 kilograms, provides 1 liter of water, leaving a daily deficit of one liter that can easily be taken in the form of liquid water or herb and fruit teas.
- Alcohol, tea, and coffee are diuretics, causing the body to lose water.
- If a muscle loses only 3% of its water, it can cause a 10% drop in strength and an 8% loss in speed.
- Approximately 90% of the world's population is dehydrated.
- Dehydration causes the blood to become thicker, which causes the heart to work harder.
- As people age the body becomes less capable to recognizing dehydration. The trigger mechanisms are not sent to the brain, making it even more important to monitor how much water one consumes.

(Williams, 2005; Greviskes, A. 2014).

Absorption

It is clear from the above list of facts that water is not only essential; it has a multitude of purposes, all of which are indispensable for the maintenance of life. Yet as we age, we absorb less of the water we drink, which results in dehydration. One of the major health concerns lies in the individual's ability to absorb vitamins and minerals from the foods and supplements consumed, which requires the absorption of water. Water is the vehicle that transports the vitamins and minerals into the cellular membrane, yet the average absorption of water by the body is only between 2% to 30% (Flanagan, 1995).

Scientists have only recently discovered that the body's ability to absorb water has everything to do with the surface tension of the water, thus the phase, "How wet is your water?"

Wetter water equates to lower surface tension and easier absorption. At one time scientists used a "dyne" as a unit to measure surface tension. For example, distilled water has a surface tension of 72 dyne compared to the surface tension of body fluids, which is 45 dynes.

An excellent example of surface tension is in observing the "water strider," which lives on the surface of ponds, marshes, and slow streams. The Water strider can walk on water because its weight is not heavy enough to pierce the surface tension of the water.

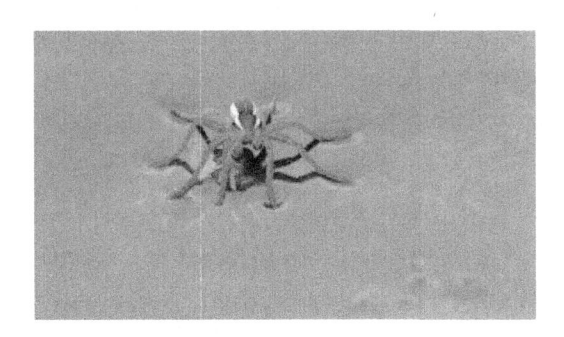

For optimal absorption of water, by the human body, to occur water tension must equal a bodily fluid tension of 45 dynes. In other words, in order to properly hydrate a human cell, allowing for the extraction of toxins and debris and the absorption of nutrients, minerals, sugars, and oxygen, the surface tension of the water needs to be reduced (Nave, 2014).

One of the investigative questions for scientists was why some waters have lower surface tension, while other waters have a naturally high surface tension? What was even more astounding was that the correlation seemed to align itself with longevity. Those societies whose water surface tension is naturally lower live longer than those societies whose water surface tension is higher (Flanagan, 1995).

Another concern for scientists is the fact that as humans' age they absorb less water and nutrients, becoming more and more dehydrated. Some would argue that dehydration is equivalent to aging, in other words, we don't get old we simply dry up. No matter what amount of water one consumes the ability to absorb water and vital nutrients are a common concern, associated with aging. When the body becomes deficient of vital nutrients disease occurs (Flanagan, 1995).

Establishing a Baseline

The average life span of an American male is 76 and the average life span of an American female is 81. The average life span in Russia is 69.85 years, in China the average life span is 74.99 years, in South Africa the average life span is 49.48 years. Yet the people of Valcabambia in Ecuador and the people of Hunza land in the Karakoram Mountains of Northern Pakistan live to be 100 plus years of age, with no signs of cancer or autoimmune disease. (National Geographic, n.d., infoplease, 2013).

In creating a baseline for why some waters have a lower surface tension than others; one of the best places to begin is with the Hunza people of Northern Pakistan. A unique characteristic of these amazing people is the water they drink.

Dr. Henri Coanda, a Romanian Physicist and the "Father of Fluid Dynamics" (Imats, 1966), spent 60 years examining the glacier water of the Hunza Valley and determined that the water was high in oxygen (high alkaline pH), active hydrogen, mineral content, and has a naturally lower surface tension.

According to Dr. Coanda, water has a life of its own, maintaining its own unique characteristics, which is why every snowflake is different.

This uniqueness can also determine why some cultures live longer than others. Doctor Coanda was able to determine the lifespan of a people based on the unique qualities of their water (Flanagan, 0995; Imats, 1996).

Dr. Coanda examined the differing waters from all over the world and discovered that the water of the Hunza valley and the water of Valcabambia had unique qualities, which he referred to as, "anomalous water." Dr. Coanda originated the phrase, "you are what you drink" (Flanagan, 1995).

In examining the water from the Hunza valley scientists discovered several unique qualities:

- The water does not contain the mineral salts typically found in mountain springs or in well water.
- The trace minerals found in the water are in a special clusterized form.
- The water contained large amounts of negatively charged ionized hydrogen atoms. "The negatively charged hydrogen protons that are contained in the Hunza water are the most powerful electron donors known in chemistry" (Flanagan 1995).
- The negatively charged electron donors are the ultimate antioxidant.
- The Hunza water resembles, in many respects, the same properties of the fluids that surround our cells.
- The water was high in oxygen (high alkaline pH) and active hydrogen, and mineral content

The trace minerals found in the Hunza water are in a unique clusterized form. They are silicate colloidal minerals, which are microscopic minerals that are insoluble in water. They maintain their stability within the water by a negative electrical charge, also referred to as electro kinetic potential, which attracts and organizes the water molecules in this unique clusterized form, (Flanagan, 1995).

These microscopic silicate trace minerals are responsible for reducing surface tension and increasing the water's negative charge, creating naturally "wetter water." These two natural processes reduce the surface tension of the water allowing the water to be absorbed within the cell, thus, allowing for the flow of nutrients and the extraction of toxins from within the cell.

Another unique quality found in the Hunza water are the large amounts of negatively charged ionized hydrogen atoms, which are not found in such abundance in ordinary water. *"The negatively charged hydrogen protons that are contained in the Hunza water are the most powerful electron donors known in chemistry"* (Flanagan 1995).

These negatively charged electron donors are the ultimate antioxidant, which are the most effective free-radical scavengers. Remember, free-radicals damage healthy cells and are the precursors to, aging, disease and cancer. Free radicals are spawned by such factors as pollution, radiation, cigarette smoke, herbicides, stress, and other known contaminants (Flanagan 1995).

What is unique is the large amounts of negative charges coincides with the mineral content, and together they form a unique colloidal structure that cannot be duplicated by merely adding minerals or by adding electro-charges to the water. What is so phenomenal is that this very structure of the Hunza water resembles, in many respects, the same properties of the fluids that surround our cells. This similarity allows for the ease of assimilation, which sets this water apart from all other waters (Flanagan 1995).

Scientists believe that the primary variable that sets the Hunza people apart and contributes to their longevity is the very structure of their water, which begins on a microscopic level. The combination of the high number of negatively charged ions together with the large mineral content creates "wetter water," which strongly contributes to a cancer free environment.

Keep in mind that glacier water is old water, centuries old, which contains no mineral salts found in well water or spring water. It is this very structural affect that sets Hunza water apart and contributes to the absorption of water, oxygen, and vital nutrients into the cellular membrane, and allowing for the removal of toxins, and debris. The abundance of negatively charged ions is the ultimate antioxidant.

Together these qualities provide for longevity and the absence of disease, such as cancer. This could also be why the people of Iceland, whose water comes from glaciers, have a history of longevity.

Quality & Contamination

As the United States (U.S.) became populated it was common for people to settle near a river where the source of water was abundant. For example, Los Angeles was settled near the Los Angeles River. In the middle of the U.S. people often settled along the banks of the great Mississippi River. Unfortunately, as the U.S. moved into the industrial age, most manufacturers also based their operations near a large river or lake. At the time it was expedient to dump all their waste into the water. But as the rivers and lakes became contaminated concerns heightened and laws were passed preventing the ostentatious pouring of contaminants into the lakes and rivers.

As pharmaceutical drugs became more common, as an antidote for every form of illness, concerns over pharmaceutical contamination of the drinking water became an issue. A recent report by the Associated Press revealed that our water supplies are also contaminated with pharmaceutical drugs, many of which are resistant to water treatment processes (Donn, Mendoza, & Pritchard, 2008; Mendoza, 2008).

Another concern is over the use of plastic containers. When plastic containers are exposed to sunlight toxic chemicals get leached into the bottled water, which is why people often taste plastic when drinking their bottled water. It is not the plastic that they are tasting but rather carcinogenic toxins that have been leaching into the water from the plastic container.

What is even more alarming is fluoridated water, which I talk in length about under the chapter on toxins. Fluoride is listed with the FDA as a toxin, and according to the National Science Foundation, fluoride is listed as a hazardous contaminant at 4.0 mg/L (Blaylock, 2011; Odiyo & Makungo, 2012; Durrant-Peatfield, 2004, National Science Foundation, n.d.).

If you want to know what is in your drinking water, just type into your favorite search engine, "Home water testing kit" and see for yourself. There are over 100,000 known toxins in the environment and 2,100 known carcinogens in our drinking water. In America women now have a one in three chance of contracting cancer and men have a one in two chance. In America (2014) there are over 19 major cities whose water is not suitable for consumption, including San Francisco, San Diego, New Orleans, Atlanta, Detroit, Denver, and Phoenix. You can obtain more information about bottled water at: http://www.nrdc.org/water/drinking/bw/appa.asp (NRDC, n.d.).

There was a time, not long ago, that even the thought of bottled water was unheard of. As water pollution reaches epidemic levels Americans have become concerned over the quality of their drinking water. To compensate for these discrepancies in water quality, for commercial purposes, manufacturers began to add various elements to water.

In America, water can take on a myriad of types. There is exotic water from the Fiji Islands and Iceland. There is sparkling water, artesian water, spring water, water with added proteins, water with added calcium, waters sweetened with Splenda, and there are waters with caffeine, and waters with added oxygen.

As we discussed earlier, in 2005 Americans spent more than 10 billion dollars and consumed more than eight billion gallons of water, which is equivalent to 26 gallons per person. Ironically nearly 40% of all bottled water is nothing more than repackaged tap water. What is even more disconcerting being that currently there is no federal testing of bottled water for bacteria, or other hazardous chemicals (Donn, Mendoza, & Pritchard, 2008; Mendoza, 2008).

In piecing together, the cancer paradigm, water is "the" essential nutrient, and having access to pristine water is paramount. In the last

100 years scientists have discovered numerous differences in the water people consume. These differences are influential to health and well-being, longevity, and illness and disease, including the onset and avoidance of cancer. Scientists have discovered that it's not just about what is in the water that is influential but the very structure of the water that affects the individual drinking it. Adding oxygen and various minerals supplements may help in one respect or another, but it is not enough. Water quality has everything to do with an orchestrated event between negatively charged ions and the corresponding minerals within the water, which creates a unique water structure.

Coke or Water

When I go grocery shopping, I am always appalled to see parents buying large quantities of bottled sodas. Most of them have no clue to the tremendous dangers they have introduced into the lives of their children. Americans often believe that drinking a Coke is comparable to a glass of water. Let's examine what happens when there are discrepancies or deficiencies, which can contribute to cancer.

The active ingredient in Coke is phosphoric acid, which has a pH of 2.8. Keep in mind that the human body has a pH of 7.35. Phosphoric acid, when consumed, leaches calcium from the bones, contributing to osteoporosis. The calcium being leached is used to neutralize the acid from the Coke. This is because the human body strives to maintain a pH of 7.35 and when anything acidic is consumed calcium is the body's first line of defense. The same can be said about chemotherapy. It is so toxic that the body uses calcium to neutralize its toxicity.

CHAPTER 10
AGING

Another concern is the natural occurrence of aging, which hinders the absorption of water, resulting in dehydration, preventing the intake of vital nutrients, and the elimination of toxins and cellular debris. This results in illness and disease, including cancer. To compensate, there are several solutions, all of which are not cure all. Filtered water would be the first step, but far from adequate. Drinking water that has been treated with reverse osmosis is of upmost importance, since reverse osmosis is the only way to remove fluoride.

Many larger health food stores offer water that has been treated with reverse osmosis. For example, in Seattle, Washington, the Puget Sound Cooperatives (health food stores) offer water that has been treated with reverse osmosis. The same can be said of the health food stores in Minneapolis, Minnesota.

Drinking glacier water would be ideal, since glacier water is high in pH and has more negatively charged ions allowing for a lower water tension, which allows it to be accessibly absorbed into the cell membrane, allowing for the intake of vital nutrients and the extraction of waste and debris, including toxins. Also, glacier water does not contain any fluoride or chlorine.

As a source of bottled water, one that I prefer is water from Iceland. Iceland water can be found in many large grocery stores, but make sure that it is imported from Iceland. Another brand is called Essentia, which goes through a reverse osmosis, has added electrolytes, and maintains a pH of 9.5. Finally, well water, contains no fluoride, chlorine, and has natural minerals and it higher in pH. But the quality of water depends on the source of the well water. In some countries, such as Africa, the well water is not as "wet" as glacier water, and in America well water could be contaminated by pesticides that are applied to plants and vegetation, which ultimately ends up in the soil and eventually finds its way to our water supply. Given the abundance of environmental toxins it would be wise to periodically test the water you drink for contaminants.

CHAPTER 11

ELECTRO-MAGNETIC POLLUTION

Since the beginning of time the earth and human beings have maintained a harmonious and stable electro-magnetic relationship. This relationship is derived from the earth and the sun, as it emits extremely low frequency and ultra-low frequency rays and high energy gamma rays that give life to the human body. With the advent of technology, it has been estimated that the electro-magnetic density of many of our major cities is now 50 million times greater than it was 100 years ago, under natural conditions.

A group of Danish ninth grade girls took 400 seeds, which consisted of rapidly growing herbs, and evenly divided them and placed them in two different rooms. They cared for them in similar fashion except for one difference, in one room the seeds were placed near two Wi-Fi routers. After 12 days of care the seeds that had been exposed to the Wi-Fi routers showed no signs of growth, while the other seeds showed normal growth (Weil, 2012).

Richard Box, from Bath, England took 1301 fluorescent bulbs and placed them underneath power lines. The electro-magnetic energy was so great that the energy caused the fluorescent tubes to light up. The display, referred to as, "Field" attracted hundreds of people passing by. The image can be seen at: http://www.richardbox.com/ (Allan, 2004).

Since 1977 the explosion of electronics has been unfathomable, ranging from electronic wiring, appliances, Wi-Fi, computers, air conditioners, electronic appliances, televisions, cell phones, cell phone towers, power lines, transformer, power stations, radio frequencies, microwaves, etc. According to many experts EMF pollution is a primary environmental concern affecting physical, emotional and mental health, and a major contributor to illness and disease. Electro-magnetic fields in our environment affect our system by interfering with our own natural electrical impulses (Bowers, 2015; Interdisziplina re Gesellschaftfur Umweltmedizine. 2002; Weil, 2012).

Electro-magnetic pollution has been attributed to insomnia, headaches, fatigue, poor concentration, irregular heartbeat, dizziness, leukemia, chronic disease (including genome/DNA damage), and various other cancers. Researchers have strong evidence to suggest that there are adverse biological effects from the continued use of cell phones, including leakage of the blood-brain barrier and broken DNA within blood cells. It has become clear the extended use of cell phone, 10 years or more, doubles the risk of a brain tumor on the side of the head that the cell phone leans against (Bowers, 2015; Khurana, et al., 2009; The Interphone Group, 2010; Lehrer, 2011).

The World Health Organization has categorized ionizing radio frequency radiation (emitted from cell phones) as a 2B (possible) carcinogen, which is the same category classification they give to DDT, lead, and engine exhaust. According to Dr. Gandhi from the University of Utah, children are much more vulnerable than adults, because their cranium is thinker than that of an adult, which allows for the absorption of 10 times more microwave radiation than an adult (WHO, 2014; Gandhi et al., 2011).

It seems clear that the introduction of an electronic environment has played havoc with the body's electro-magnetic impulses facilitating a host of problems and concerns, including illness and disease, and cancer. There may be a partial solution, the introduction of Pulsating Electro-Magnetic Field (PEMF) devices. They are one of the newest innovations that could reverse the effects of electro-magnetic pollution (Bowers, 2015; Khurana, et al., 2009; The Interphone Group, 2010; Lehrer, 2011).

CHAPTER 12

STRESS

"Most of the diseases of abnormal immune function are remarkably linked to psychological stress" –Robert Scaer, MD. The Trauma Spectrum

Sam Johnson was only 20 years old when he answered the call to serve his country. He would sign up and became an Airforce fighter pilot. He would fly 62 missions during the Korean War and 25 missions during the Vietnam War. It was on that fateful 25th mission that his F-4 Phantom II was shot down. His right engine was hit by enemy gunfire and as his plane descended, he parachuted out. As he hit the ground his right arm and back were broken, and left arm was severely injured. It was on that fateful night that he would find his way to the infamous Hoa Lo Prison, otherwise known as the "Hanoi Hilton."

The Hanoi Hilton became famous for its inhumane torture of American prisoners of war. At the time Sam Johnson was 35 years old, a husband and father of three small children. A family that he would not see for almost seven years. At the time, what he wasn't aware of was that he had entered HELL. Sam Johnson would have to endure constant torture, deprivation, and solitude for almost seven years.

One of the images that he would remember for the rest of his life was the meat hook that stood suspended above his cell. The Vietcong would bind both the hands and feet of their prisoners and then tie their hands to their feet, extending the hands forward or from behind, aching the body to its full extent. Then they would hang them on the meat hook for hours, even for days. Often coming in to tighten the ropes. The prisoners were left hanging there until their limbs turned purple and swelled to twice their normal size.

When the prisoners were not being tortured, they were left in leg irons and leg stocks that confined their movement. As part of their imprisonment they were unable to talk to any other prisoners. They were left in solitude. Sam Johnson would learn the prison code, allowing him to communicate, via, taps on the wall, with other prisoners. Over the course of seven years he was able to say that he got through HELL through the Grace and mercy of God. As Sam Johnson walked through a hellish situation, he was able to meditate and acknowledge the Grace and mercy of God, that helped him take one day at a time (Johnson, 2015).

Dr. Rudolph Willis, MD, and Vice Chief of Staff for Clinical Affairs at Cancer Treatment Centers of America (CTCA) at Eastern Regional Medical Center states: *"For some time oncologists have known that two different patients with the same cancer, with the same stage of progression, and treated with the same therapy, might have completely different outcomes. One dies and the other doesn't. There are innumerable frays in the battle for life, but the true war is fought by the most important warriors of all – one's spirit and one's faith"* (Barry, 2011).

Robert Ader, past director of the Center for Psychoneuroimmunology Research in the Department of Psychiatry at the University of Rochester Medical Center, coined the term *"psychoneuroimmunology"* to describe a relationship that links one's behavior disposition, neurological function, and endocrine factors, to its respective counterpart, the immune system (Barry, 2011).

As 500,000 men and women in America contract cancer this year, it is not uncommon to hear about those individuals who lived well, ate well, slept well, exercised regularly, yet could not understand how they contracted cancer, or why their treatment was not effective when so many others had experienced success. What they may not have taken into consideration is one of the most influential, yet most underrated elements of human health, their current mental state (Barry, 2011; Baum, Revenson, & Singer, 2007).

Most of us have not seriously taken into consideration the link between psychological impulses, such as anxiety, depression, hypertension or distress, and their biological/physiological imprint. Yet, recent terms such as, "urban stress" and "the silent killer" are acronyms that have been coined to describe one of the most underrated urban killers in modern times.

What is even more alarming is that this genetic linkage can pass from mother to infant and is directly responsible for cancer, reproductive failure, diabetes, heart disease, and other biological dysfunctions, including neurological diseases that may play a pivotal role for the onset of autoimmune disease.

Over the past 50 years there has been extensive research on stress and its implications yet there is still no absolute definition for stress that everyone can agrees on. Part of the problem is that stress can be categorized into several different elements, **physical stress, emotional stress, oxidative stress, cellular stress,** and **psychological stress**.

For the sake of argument let us focus specifically on psychological stress and how it relates to the onset of cancer. It is important to understand where stress originates and how it expresses itself to understand its implications.

Ultimately, stress is a neurological impulse that expresses itself as a biological chemical reaction, in response to a psychological or physiological stimulus. As a biological chemical reaction, it affects most of the major systems and can sometimes be observed through physical measures, such a sweating, increased heart rate, indigestion, agitation, etc. This chemical reaction can have devastating repercussions, inhibiting normal cellular, and other biological functions (Baum, Revenson, & Singer, 2007).

Even if one were to exercise regularly, eat properly, avoid commercial foods, drink natural contaminant free water, and live in a toxic-free environment, if there is evidence of a high stress lifestyle, this could easily circumvent all of the above, and one could eventually succumb to cancer, autoimmune disease, or other illnesses and disease. Stress influences multiple functions, including psychological, physiological, and biological behavior, covering every aspect of health and well-being, and often overrides other healthful measures.

For example, psychologists, in investigating the impacts that stress plays on biological function, designed a series of experiments that centered on a term referred to as, "fight or flight response." This is a physiological response that occurs when one experiences a perceived threat or harm to one's survival. On the surface, such a reaction lends itself to a prepared reaction, but underneath, biologically, a cascade of adrenal stimuli produces a cascade of hormones, adrenaline, and cortisol that prepare the human body for extreme circumstances.

Adrenaline is released to help us act quickly in the event of an emergency, and cortisol provides the fuel. The human body was designed for survival and a "fight or flight response" is an intricate part of that design. However, the human body was never designed to maintain a high state of stress for an extended period, let alone months and years, which, often, exemplifies itself in urban living.

For example, during a state of chronic stress the body releases cortisol, continuously however, during psychological stress the body does not deplete the extra cortisol. Maintaining too much cortisol creates a host of problems. For one, cortisol breaks down bone density, which leads to osteoporosis. Chronic stress also leads to diabetes, heart disease, and neurological diseases. This biological crisis has been blamed on an urban environment plagued with countless inhibiting catalytic variables (Baum, Revenson, & Singer, 2007).

These stress factors are exacerbated by abnormal demands at work, loss of employment, mortgage payments, divorce, in-laws, taxes, conflicts, abuse, domestic, and community violence, financial issues, etc. All of these variables are associated with acute or chronic anxiety, depression, psychological disposition, and various coping mechanisms that directly influence the biological and psychological mechanisms that act in concert to maintain a balanced and well-tuned system and can adversely affect the role each system plays in maintaining health and well-being (Brydon, Walker, Wawrzyniak, Chart, & Steptoe, 2009; Kemeny & Schedlowski, 2007).

The science of psychoneuroimmunology has established a definitive link between the psychological and physiological features for the onset and progression of cancer. In a chronic stressful event immune response is impaired, which contributes to the onset and progression of certain types of cancer. Studies have shown that in chronic stress cellular and molecular immunological elements are compromised, which is further evidenced by decreased T-cell and Killer cell activity. This decrease in T-cell and Killer cell activity reduces immune surveillance of tumors, allowing them to grow unchecked (Reiche, Nunes, & Morimoto, 2004).

When stressful life situations exceed a person's ability to cope, a psychological stress response is initiated, which is composed of negative cognitive and emotional elements that directly alter immune function, increasing the risk of acute infectious respiratory illness. Creating an environment vulnerable to even a common cold (Cohen, Tyrrell, & Smith, 1991).

Researchers from Harvard Medical School and Brigham and Women's Hospital enlisted 557 families consisting of pregnant women who lived in urban areas. When the infants were born, researchers investigated the differences in immune function of those born to mothers in a high stress environment as compared to those mothers who lived in a low stress environment. This was accomplished by collecting blood samples, isolating immune cells and stimulating these immune cells with several allergens such as dust, viral, and bacterial stimulants, and cockroaches.

The blood was analyzed for indications of how the child's immune system was prepared for its environment. Researchers found a significant difference in those infants whose mothers lived in a high stress environment as compared to those infants whose mothers lived in a low stress environment. Their research concluded that infants whose mothers lived in a high stress environment were less protected against environmental allergens, evidenced by altered innate and adaptive immune response in core blood samples. They further concluded that urban stress may impact the expression of allergen disease with mothers who live in a high stress environment (Abbott, Blazek, & Foster, 2010; Wright, 2010).

Psychological stress has also been linked to reproductive failures, acting on three plausible mechanisms of the reproductive system, the endocrine, immune, and nervous system. Neurologically, in response to acute or chronic stress, inhibiting stimuli affect the reproductive system. Specific hormones are released inhibiting the release of estrogen, progesterone, and luteinizing hormones (LH). LH, among other things, promotes ovulation, and at the same time producing an inflammatory environment and inhibiting any anti-inflammatory response. Together, these adversely affecting the reproductive cycle. In 28 separate studies, two-thirds found a direct correlation between stress and subsequent pregnancy rates (Gourounti, Kapetanios, Paparisteidis, Vaslamatzis, et al., 2009; Parker &Douglas, 2010).

A wealth of recent research shows that psychological stress impairs innate and adaptive immune function and plays a pivotal role in the progression or suppression of disease. Psychological stress suppresses an array of immune functions, which result in impaired resistance to disease, reduced response to vaccinations, wound healing, and increases the propagation of cancer.

Understanding that stress has an adverse effect on immune response, several researchers have concluded after extensive experimentation that relaxation therapies have a positive effect on immune response and can reverse stress induced immunological dysfunction (Barry, 2011; Baum, Revenson, & Singer, 2007; Conner, 2008).

Here are four ways to reduce your stress and improve your mental health:

1. Take the time to meditate. Keep in mind that you can only have one thought at a time.
2. Take the time several times a day and focus on your breathing. If you are like most, you will note that you are have shallow breaths. Take in deep breaths and hold those breaths for several seconds and then let out. Try this several times a day and you will notice a reduction in stress.
3. Slow down. Take the time to examine your activities, especially driving. If you are like most, you should have been to your appointment 10 minutes ago. Stop and slow down. Realize that nothing is going to change, if your late your late. Realize that life will continue, and, in the end, what will be will be. Learn to flow with life rather than constantly trying to manipulate life.
4. Take the time to self-examine your present metal condition and make a positive difference by learning to walk through life rather than constantly running through life.

It has become quite evident in the 21st century that almost every aspect of one's existence is directly or indirectly influenced by foreign toxins and chemicals that threaten our very existence. As stated earlier, there are more than 100,000 foreign chemicals and toxins that have been introduced into our environment, most of which are carcinogenic and excitotoxic.

Although it is impossible to detail each of these foreign intruders, it is important to take note of their existence and their power to create illness and death. It is also important to examine a few of these carcinogenic and excitotoxic intruders to gain a better understanding of how influential they are in inhibiting health and well-being.

In designing the cancer paradigm, x-factors is listed to describe a few of those variables in our environment that play an active role in the onset and propagation of cancer, which are outside the realm of diet and stress.

CHAPTER 13
TOXINS

Toxins act as inhibitors of normal cellular metabolism, which has far reaching consequences, including the etiology of cancer cells, autoimmune disease, and other biological disorders. It is estimated that in the past 70 years more than 100,000 foreign toxins have entered the atmosphere, many of which are carcinogens, and fat soluble, which means they are stored in the body, especially breast tissue. These foreign toxins and carcinogenic chemicals are present in the air we breathe, the water we drink, and the foods we eat. Two excellent examples of a highly toxic chemical that affects Americans are mercury and fluoride.

Mercury

Two thousand years ago the Spanish discovered that the slaves who worked the mercury mines eventually got sick and died. Today, most Americans are probably unaware that since the 1930s, Thimerosal, which is a version of mercury, is used, as a preservative, in several biological and pharmaceutical products, including vaccinations. It is also used in local antiseptics for abrasions and minor cuts. Concerns over toxicity have resulted in the FDA recommending lower dosages, but they continue to be used, despite their inherent toxicity. What is even more alarming is that the human body stores mercury, usually in fatty tissue, so the negative effects are a result of the cumulative amounts, which can span from birth, because child vaccines often contain Thimerosal (FDA, 2012).

In the 1960s and 1970s there was widespread mercury poisoning in

Minamata, Japan from contaminated fish and the long-term effects were devastating. Mercury is a developmental neurotoxin that affects neurological functions and is especially dangerous to pregnant woman, evidenced by brain lesions and birth defects (Harada, 1995). Recent studies conducted in the Faroe Islands reveal that even low doses of mercury in mother's who are pregnant can lead to negative brain development in developing fetuses (Folk, 2007).

Today's American power plants account for approximately 41% of all harmful mercury emissions. When examining blood levels, the Centers for Disease and prevention found that between 316,588 and 637,233 children, annually, have levels of mercury greater than 5.8 ug/L. At these levels the neurological affects can be measured by lower IQs (Trasande, Landrigan, & Schechter, 2005).

American power plants release mercury in aerosol form because of its low boiling point. Once airborne these mercury particles can travel long distances and eventually dropping onto farmland, rivers, lakes, and oceans. This is where microorganisms convert mercury into methylmercury, which biomagnifies in marine foods, reaching high and dangerous concentrations in tuna, swordfish, king mackerel, and shark (Trasande, Landrigan, & Schechter, 2005).

The current scientific research shows that even low doses of mercury negatively affect the central nervous system, especially in developing babies, still in the womb. Mercury is also linked to harmful effects on the cardiovascular, immune, and reproductive systems. Mercury also affects the kidneys, liver, immune response, vision, and hearing. Mercury is also involved in paralysis, insomnia, and psychological instability. During pregnancy, mercury crosses the placental barrier and interferes with neurological development and can cause attention deficit disorder (FDA, 1995; Folk, 2007; Trasande, Landrigan, & Schechter, 2005).

The recent scientific studies and universal recognition of the destructive impact of mercury, even in low dosages has raised urgent questions about the current pharmaceutical call for increased vaccines to infants, children, and adults, all of which, use mercury as a preservative.

In April of 2017 John F. Kennedy Jr. met with President Trump and agreed to form an investigative commission on vaccines. John F. Kennedy Jr. created the "World Mercury Project," which will pay $100,000 to anyone who can prove, scientifically, that thimerosal is safe, in their current dosage, when administered to children and pregnant women. He has also gained the support of leading actor Robert Deniro, whose son has autism.

Kennedy's aim is to remove highly toxic mercury, a neurotoxin that is 100 times more toxic than lead, from all vaccines. If you need more convincing, I encourage you to go to their website (https://worldmercuryproject.org/), it is filled with current information (Kennedy, 2017).

One of the major concerns is the number of vaccines given to children. In 1960 the total number of vaccines given was estimated at eight. By 2014 that number has escalated to 26. It is estimated that by the age of 18 an individual has been administered up to 66 vaccines (Vaccines.gov, n.d.).

Fluoride

Fluorine (Fluoride)
Atomic Number: 9
Symbol: F
Atomic Weight: 18.998403

When fluoride was first added to America's drinking water (Grand Rapids, Michigan), back in 1945, the world of science was quite limited in its knowledge of human biology. It was during this era that Chemotherapy (Alfred G. Gilman and Louis S. Goodman) was first introduced as a form of treatment against cancer and the microscope that could peer into the human cell had not yet been invented. Today, 72% of the American public that is served by the public water system drinks fluorinated water. Scientific discoveries and knowledge have increased exponentially since 1945. Today scientists are aware of the detrimental effects of fluoride.

On October 4, 2011 Pinellas County, Florida, voted to discontinue the addition of fluoride to their drinking water. The discontinuance was implemented December 31, 2011. Approximately one million people who have been subjected to fluoride will no longer be subject to its ill effects (Pinellas County Florida Utilities, n.d.). Ever since the introduction of fluoride into the American drinking water (1945), it has not been without controversy.

For decades dentists hailed it as an anti-cavity fighting agent with no adverse side effects. Today we know, emphatically, that most of the stories about fluoride and its origins are true. Recent research indicates that fluoride has far reaching detrimental effects on human health (Blaylock, 2011; Odiyo & Makungo, 2012; Durrant-Peatfield, 2004).

The United Kingdom's (England) Poisons Act 1972, a provisionary act for the regulation of non-medical poisons included a "poisons list," which spells out specific known poisons, including Sodium Silicofluoride (used in drinking water). In the United States the Environment Protection Agency (EPA) lists fluoride as a contaminant, setting the maximum contaminant level at 4.0 milligrams per liter (4 parts per million – 4 ppm). The EPA also lists "some" of the detrimental effects of excess levels of exposure, including bone disease. Ironically, according to the EPA, children age eight and younger who are exposed to excess amounts of fluoride have an increased risk of developing pits in their tooth enamel (Poisons Act 1972, n.d.; EPA, n.d.).

Chemical weapons, also referred to as nerve agents because they affect the transmission of nerve impulses in the nervous system, have been of interest beginning with WW I. Nerve agents are considered highly toxic and have a rapid affect when absorbed through the skin or when inhaled. In 1938 a highly toxic chemical weapon (CW) agent was introduced called *sarin*, which was followed by the introduction, in 1944, of a third

CW agent call *soman*. Both *sarin* (CH3-P(=O)(-F)(-OCH(CH3)2) and *soman* (CH3-P(=O)(-F)(-CH(CH3)C(CH3)3) compounds consist, in part, of fluoride components (Ivarsson, Nilsson, & Santesson, (eds). (1992).

Today, whether fluoride is a toxin or not is not a question for debate, even the EPA lists fluoride as a toxin. What is in question is how much exposure proves to be detrimental? In 1945 when fluoride was introduced into the drinking water it was estimated that the maximum exposure would be set at 4 mg/L. Today, 70 years, and 10 thousand experiments later, there are grave concerns over the amount of fluoride exposure, especially considering recent research that indicates that even 1 mg/L is detrimental to human health. Another important element to consider is that the amount of exposure has increased substantially with the addition of fluoride in underarm deodorants, toothpaste, and other products (Blaylock, 2011; Odiyo & Makungo, 2012; Durrant-Peatfield, 2004).

According to Dr. Blaylock's recent research, a board-certified neurosurgeon, fluoride has devastating effects not only on the nervous system but also on every organ in the human body. Dr. Blaylock conducted an exhaustive investigation on the effects of fluoride to the human body and his research reveals an epidemic of neurological disorders tied to toxins, including fluoride, in our environment.

Even though it has been scientifically proven that fluoride is not only toxic and does not prevent tooth decay, currently 60% of England's water is forced fluoridated, while the countries in mainland Europe, realizing that fluoridation has detrimental effects on health, refuse to fluoridate their water. Ireland is forced fluoridated, and many counties in America have been pressured into fluoridating their water (Blaylock, 2011). According to the National Science Foundation, fluoride is listed as a hazardous contaminant at 4.0 mg/L. The detrimental effects of ingesting fluoridated water include skeletal and dental fluorosis. The recommendation for decontamination is distillation and reverse osmosis (National Science Foundation, n.d.).

According to Coplan, Patch, Masters, & Bachman (2007), various derivatives of fluoride, such as silicofluorides (SiFs), fluorosilicic acid (FSA) and sodium fluorosilicate (NaFSA), hexafluorosilicic acid (H2SiF6), and sodium hexafluorosilicate (Na2SiF6) are used to fluoridate US municipal water supplies. They studied the blood level in more than 400,000 children in three different samples and concluded that fluoride derivatives are associated with neurotoxins.

This is primarily evidenced by twice the uptake of lead in children drinking fluorinated water versus those who drink unfluorinated water. According to the Center for Disease Control (CDC, 1992), sodium fluoride was introduced into the American drinking water in 1945 but has since been replaced with SiFs and other cheaper derivatives of fluoride, which have never been tested for their effects on humans or animals. They concluded, *"We should stop using silicofluorides in our public water supply until we know what they do"* (Coplan, Patch, Masters, & Bachman, 2007, p. 1).

21st century science has concluded that fluorides are also detrimental to the immune system. Fluorides cause the immune system to malfunction. Fluorides act as toxins and cause the immune system to fail to distinguish between healthy proteins and abnormal proteins, which can lead to autoimmune disease, such as asthma and Graves' disease. Because fluoride is toxic, it also damages cell tissue. For example, fluorides damage the collagens, along with other cell tissue that make up bones, tooth enamel, ligaments, tendons, and muscle (Blaylock, 2011; Odiyo & Makungo, 2012; Mundy, 1963).

Fluorides also have a toxic effect on the body's chromosomes, causing genetic alterations in structure, which has been linked to defects in genitalia and birth defects, such as Down Syndrome. Fluoride also acts as a mutagen, altering the genetic DNA information, creating cellular mutations. Once a cell is damaged two mutations can transform a damaged cell into a cancerous cell, a process that is irreversible (Blaylock, 2011; Odiyo & Makungo, 2012).

In the mid-1930s a group of European scientists used fluoride to treat an over-active thyroid. In their experiments their patients drank fluorinated water, consumed fluoride pills or were bathed in fluorinated water. As a result of these treatments the once over-active thyroid was greatly depressed, and in many patients the thyroid ceased to function (Benagiano, 1965; Litzka &Mundy, 1937).

In 1945, the New England Journal of Medicine reported a 400% increase in cancer of the thyroid, which was linked to the addition of fluoride to the water (Durrant-Peatfield, 2006). Today's scientists have discovered that fluoride not only damages the thyroid but also is linked to thyroid cancer (Blaylock, 2011; Benagiano, 1965; Durrant-Peatfield, 2006; Galleti & Joyet, 1958; Hillman, 1979; Odiyo & Makungo, 2012; Stole & Podoba, 1960).

According to recent research, fluoride is detrimental because of its ability to inhibit enzymes. Enzymatic reactions are pre-requisites to life. Enzymes are complex protein compounds that accelerate the biological reactions necessary to produce energy and sustain life. For example, SiFs inhibit cholinesterase, an enzyme that plays an important role in regulating neurotransmitters.

Fluorides affect the nervous system very much like chemical agents and could be responsible for a host of puzzling conditions that affect millions of Americans. Because enzymes are required for all bodily functions the use of fluorides places the entire human system at risk. Enzyme inhibitors are also found in pesticides and herbicides because of their immediate effect on the nervous system (Coplan, Patch, Masters, & Bachman, 2007).

Other Toxins

Recently, tamoxifen, an antiestrogen medication, has been used to treat women who have already undergone chemo and radiation therapy for breast cancer. The purpose is to reduce the possibility of reoccurrence. However, new research has concluded that tamoxifen is NOT effective for 95.5% of those who take it. One must consider the risks if there were no side effects. Unfortunately, that is not the case, the side effects include, uterine cancer, an increased risk in stroke, blood clots, problems with the liver, high calcium levels in the blood, and early onset menopause (Brownstein, 2017).

CHAPTER 14
DR. BURZYNSKI – GENETICS AND DNA THERAPY

"All of cellular life begins with a code. This physiological code of life is dependent on the equilibrium of biological systems that are dependent on the inflow of nutrients, which in turn is dependent on the environment."
— Estrada

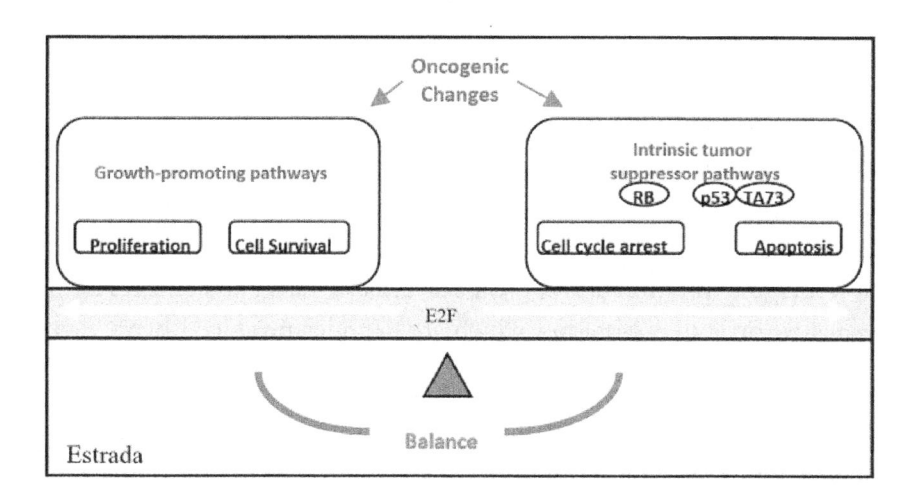

Our DNA is said to be the human body's second immune system. Recent research has substantiated the genetic link that leads to either the suppression of cancer cells or the propagation of cancer cells. The propagation of cancer is a multi-step process, steps that involve the dysregulation of oncogenes, tumor suppressor genes, and specific changes or disruptions in genetic expression. This entire process occurs on a molecular level that ultimately leads to changes in cell growth, cell differentiation, and the natural pathways that lead to cell death (pro-apoptotic signals).

These irreversible abnormal alterations from normal cellular processes culminate in the proliferation of cancer. Recent studies of those who have contracted colon cancer serve as a paradigm for this multi-step process of molecular deviations from the normal processes that culminate in the propagation of cancer cells (Raulet & Guerra, 2009).

Since the beginning of time a natural immune response has been the elimination or eradication of "Spontaneous cancers." Under normal conditions components of the immune system detect cellular abnormalities through a process called cellular stress, which results in an immune response (Raulet & Guerra, 2009).

First, natural killer cells and other lymphocytes are called into action, whose sole purpose is to identify, tag, and eliminate initial cancer cell formations, which prevents the growth of tumors.

Second, our tumor suppressor genes (our second immune system) are called into action, which genetically, suppress the multiplication of these damaged cells, preventing the propagation of cancer cells and tumor growth. Simultaneously oncogenes are suppressed, which also prevents the proliferation of cancer cells. This genetic response is regulated by antineoplastons, which are peptides produced by the liver (Raulet & Guerra, 2009).

The disruptions in genetic expression, which results in the mutation of oncogenes and tumor suppressor genes, are responsible for the abnormal changes in cell growth, cell differentiation programs, and the natural pathways that leads to cell death. This disruption inhibits the body's second line of defense against cancer growth leaving the individual vulnerable to the proliferation of cancer (Raulet & Guerra, 2009).

In 1967 Dr. Burzynski discovered naturally occurring peptides (amino acid derivatives), called antineoplastons, in the urine and blood, produced by the liver, which is lacking in sufficient numbers in advanced cancer patients. He hypothesized that if he could extract this peptide from healthy donors and synthesize them and reintroduce them into the body of cancer patients, this possibly could reverse their cancer. (Burzynski, 2008; NCI, 2012a, NCI, 2013).

"In every cancer there is a network of mutated genes (50 to 650) usually developing during patient's lifetime." These genes develop an information processing network, much like an advanced computer program, which can NOT be eradicated by chemo or radiation therapy. Currently, the only way to eradicate this network of mutated genes is through Antineoplaston therapy, which is confirmed by a genomic blood test, which is an extremely sensitive test that measures the concentration of mutated genes in nanograms/cc (one billionth of a gram). antineoplastons effect over 100 of the most crucial genes (Burzynski, n.d.).

Thus, from 1970 to 1977, partially funded by the National Cancer Institute, Dr. Burzynski conducted exhaustive research as an assistant professor at Baylor University College of Medicine. Dr. Burzynski worked in collaboration with researchers from the National Cancer Institute, the Medical College of Georgia, the Imperial College of Science and Technology of London, the University of Kurume Medical School of Japan, the University of Turin Medical School of Italy, et al. As a result of his research, he authored and co-authored 16 publications, which also included his research on peptides (antineoplastons) and their effect on human cancer (Burzynski Clinic, n.d.).

Over the course of four decades Dr. Burzynski, by way of hundreds of government studies, developed a gene targeted therapy (a cyber war) using his newly discovered peptides as catalysts. Antineoplastons act as molecular switches, turning off the activity of the mutated genes. Genetically there are two types of cancer genes: Oncogenes, influential in the initiation of cancer growth, and tumor suppressor genes, which inhibit cancer growth. The tumor suppressor gene, TP53, which is the most important gene, primarily because it controls 1,700 other genes, plays a critical role in regulating cell death by suppressing tumor growth, disrupting the cell cycle, and preventing cellular division. The tumor suppressor genes can have numerous mutations. The ONLY medications available, which turns off the TP53 mutated gene and other mutated tumor suppressor genes and activate the normal suppressor genes are antineoplastons (Burzynski, n.d., Elbendary, Cirisano, Davis, Iglehart, Jet, et al., 1996).

It is important to note, that mutated tumor suppressor genes promote cancer growth rather than protecting against cancer. Oncogenes are also directly influenced by tumor suppressor genes. Antineoplastons provide two benefits, that cannot be overstated, the removal of mutated genes from the body and increasing the expression (to 70 times) of normal tumor suppressor genes in a healthy body.

These peptides called, antineoplastons control neoplastic (cancer) cell growth by using the patient's biochemical defense system in collaboration with the body's immune system. Recent scientific research indicates that cancer genes are directly linked to immunological function. During uncontrolled cancer growth this link is severed, by the mutation of these cancer genes (Burzynski, et al., 2008; National Cancer Institute, 2012a).

Antineoplastons modulate DNA by turning off oncogenes and turning on tumor suppressor genes when required, a normal function of the body's natural defense against the proliferation of all cancer cells. These antineoplastons were first discovered by Dr. Burzynski in the 1970s. He discovered that these molecular peptides were abundant in non-cancer patients but scarce in cancer patients.

In phase II trials antineoplastons were found to be effective in low grade Glioma (brain tumors consisting of neuroglia), brain stem glioma, high grade Glioma, and hepatocellular carcinoma. In recent studies with children who had low-grade glioma's 74% of these patients obtained objective response, and adults with adenocarcinoma of the colon, which had metastasized into the liver, had a median survival rate of 67 months versus only 39 months survival rate using conventional chemotherapy (Ogata, et al., 2015).

What is also important to note is that the administration of antineoplastons resulted in "no serious toxicity, including bone marrow suppression, liver or renal dysfunction" (Ogata et al., 2015).

Dr. Burzynski also began to treat stage four inoperable brain tumors of those who had undergone chemo and radiation therapy with no success, and to the amazement of all concerned, he had a success rate just under 30%. With conventional treatment the success rate had been 0%, 100% fatal, yet Dr. Burzynski was able to save almost three out of 10 patients.

It is important to keep in mind that these patients had undergone extensive radiation and chemotherapy, and as a result their immune response was highly compromised, which could account for only a 30% success rate (Burzynski, et al., 2008).

In a recent study Antineoplaston therapy was conducted on Glioblastoma (a very aggressive and rapidly growing brain tumor), ONLY after surgery, radiation and chemotherapy had been applied with no success. The success rate was 85% (An MRI scan indicated that the active tumor was either gone or reduced by no less than 50%, and after four weeks most patients showed no signs of tumor growth). Again, keep in mind that after a patient undergoes chemo and radiation therapy, their immune response has been compromised. Currently, Glioblastomas do not respond to conventional forms of treatment (surgery, chemo, and radiation), until the advent of Antineoplaston therapy, these types of tumors were a death sentence.

The world was beginning to take notice of his phenomenal discoveries and accomplishments and Dr. Burzynski soon found himself on the Larry King Show and on May 17, 2011, Dr. Oz interviews Dr. Burzynski on Oprah radio for the first time. Dr. Oz, states that Dr. Burzynski discovered a scientifically based alternative approach to the treatment of cancer.

Dr. Burzynski could demonstrate that genes play an intricate role in the suppression or expression of neoplastic (cancer) growth, and that antineoplastons (peptides) act as cancer gene modulators, and that these peptides are produced by the liver (Burzynski, 2004).

The link between Dr. Burzynski and Dr. Campbell centers on the liver and has everything to do with diet and toxicity. Dr. Campbell could demonstrate, emphatically, that a diet high in dairy (20%) is highly toxic to the liver, by way of an animal protein called casein (Stone, Campbell, & Esselstyn, 2011). Liver toxicity also can be attributable to external factors, such as toxins and chemicals (x-factor).

Since the early 1900s there have been more than 100,000 toxic chemicals that have been introduced into the environment, of which many are considered carcinogenic. As a result, these toxins are also present in our food, our water, and in the air we breathe. One element of toxicity that directly affects the liver, which has been underrated, is pharmaceutical drugs. Every time a person swallows a pill it passes through the liver. Too many pills result in a toxic liver, and it is not uncommon for one individual to have several drug prescriptions.

What is even more disheartening is that recent research into the American water supply has found that antibiotics, mood stabilizers, sex hormones, and dozens of other prescriptions drugs, including heart medication, cannot be filtered out of our drinking water, using conventional methods, and, as a result, they find their way into our tap water (Jessup, 2008).

Whatever the source of toxicity, if the liver is affected, it is inhibited from functioning normally. This can inhibit the production of antineoplastons, which are critical to the regulation of our cancer genes (Burzynski, et al., 2008; Stone, Campbell, & Esselstyn, 2011).

Dr. Burzynski's discovery of antineoplastons is one of the most phenomenal discoveries in the 20 century. Critics are quick to point out that this genetic therapy results in the deaths of seven out of 10. What they fail to remember is that these particular cases are in stage four and have already undergone extensive bounds of chemotherapy and radiation therapy, which, by default, impairs their immune response, leaving the patient vulnerable to a common cold virus, of which many die of pneumonia.

What Dr. Burzynski's critics also fail to mention is that those who, initially, underwent his treatments had already been given a death sentence by conventional medicine. An excellent example is dealing with inoperable brain tumors, which are 100% fatal using chemotherapy and radiation therapy. In this scenario, a 100% death sentence is reduced to just under 70%. In other words, approximately 30% or 30 out of 100 lived, who would have otherwise died. Keep in mind that when a person reaches stage four, the cancer has metastasized, and the human body is nearing its maximum risk tolerance. Once a person's risk tolerance has been breached death is imminent.

What is important to remember is that Dr. Burzynski's discoveries have provided immeasurable scientific information on what regulates our cancer genes as well as shedding light on the processes that the human body goes through in fighting cancer and what occurs when dysregulation occurs. Dr. Burzynski's gene targeted therapy also gives hope to the hopeless, saving lives one at a time.

Science has come a long way in uncovering the secondary causes of cancer growth. Scientists once believed that the human system consisted of just one major immune system. Today's scientists have discovered that our DNA plays an active role in the propagation or suppression of cancer.

What science has learned is that there is a direct link from our DNA to the production of specific peptides, called antineoplastons, which are produced by the liver. As we have learned, these antineoplastons regulate our cancer genes. What is imperative at this point is that the production of antineoplastons requires a healthy and functioning liver.

What science has also recently discovered is that cancer patients suffer from a toxic liver, and a toxic liver inhibits the production of certain peptides. Without these specific peptides the role of our DNA in suppressing cancer is directly inhibited. Ironically, the condition of our liver is directly related to diet, and toxic and chemical exposure, including the use of pharmaceutical drugs.

It is important to note that antineoplaston therapy may be covered by insurance. Contact the Burzynski Clinic for more information (www.burzynskiclinic.com).

CHAPTER 15

DR. REG MCDANIEL AND THE SCIENCE OF GLYCOBIOLOGY

*"...their fruit will be **for food** and their **leaves for healing**."*
Ezekiel 47:12

Glycobiology is the study of sugars and how these sugars interact biologically. Scientists are just now discovering just how significant glyconutrients are to human health and well-being and the adverse effects that occur when these simple sugars are found lacking in the diet. Since the late 1970s extensive scientific research has taken place on glyconutrients, especially those from the University of California, San Diego, Department of Glycobiology (UCSD, n.d.) and other major scientific universities and institutions, worldwide.

Simple sugars are key players in the biological functions of life, including the initiation of life (egg to sperm) cellular communication (cell to cell communication), cell growth and differentiation, regulation (gatekeepers to the cell; modulating the immune system), metabolism, repair (DNA; Stem cells), healing (cancer, autoimmune disease, etc.), cognition, and memory.

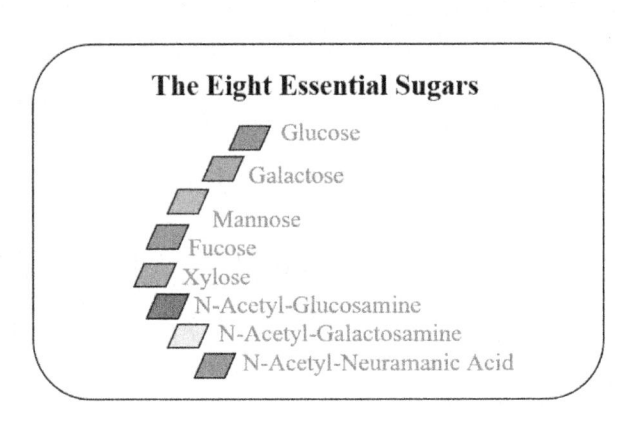

> **The Eight Essential Sugars**
> - Glucose
> - Galactose
> - Mannose
> - Fucose
> - Xylose
> - N-Acetyl-Glucosamine
> - N-Acetyl-Galactosamine
> - N-Acetyl-Neuramanic Acid

There was a time, not long ago when a specific bacterium would claim 50% of its victims, not discriminating between young or old, rich or poor, white or black. Each year 100,000 Americans would fall victim to a bacterium called, pneumococcal pneumonia. It is a rapidly moving disease that quickly moves from the lungs to the bloodstream. Within just three to four-days, crisis occurs as the fever intensifies and the struggle between the immune system and the bacteria wages on.

In September 1928 Dr. Alexander Fleming, returning from a summer vacation in Scotland, returns to Saint Mary's Hospital laboratory, located in London, England, only to discover that a penicillium mold would inhibit the growth of the bacteria, staphylococci. Unknowingly, he had discovered a substance that would, forever, change the course of medical research. It would take another 14 years, and the exhaustive work of Doctor Howard Florey, Dr. Ernst Chain, and a host of others, before the first vaccine would be administered. It was the world's first antibiotic, referred to as, "The wonder drug." Throughout history, during wartime more soldiers would die from infection than from actual war injuries.

In World War I the death rate from bacterial pneumonia was as high as 18%. In World War II, with the introduction of penicillin, the death rate from bacterial pneumonia was reduced to less than 1%. In 1945, Dr. Fleming, Dr. Florey, and Dr. Chain were awarded the Nobel Prize in Physiology or Medicine (Nobelprize.org, 2015).

CELL MEMBRANE

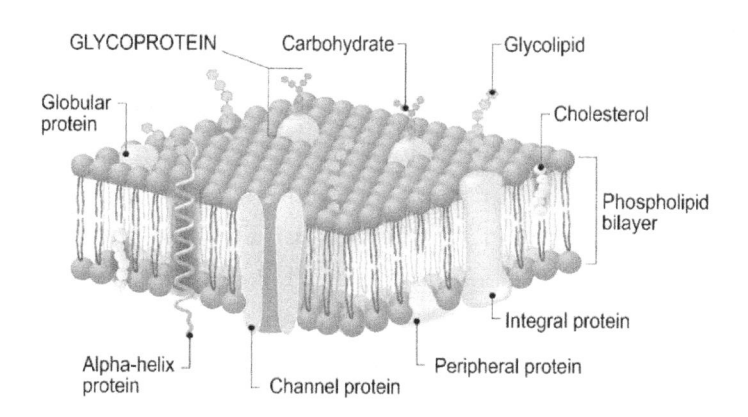

Diagram of cell membrane showing: Glycoprotein, Carbohydrate, Glycolipid, Globular protein, Cholesterol, Phospholipid bilayer, Integral protein, Peripheral protein, Channel protein, Alpha-helix protein.

The same can be said about the phenomenal story of the science of Glycobiology and its introduction into the world stage, which began back in the late 1970s when a pharmacology student asked the question: "Why has Aloe Vera gel been used for over 5,000 years by every civilization on every continent for health its restoring properties?" Hence, a study was initiated as a group of doctors (including Dr. Reg. McDaniel), scientists and researchers began a quest to discover the real healing power hidden within the leaves of the Aloe Vera plant.

Dr. Alexia Eberendu, PhD., an analytical chemist discovered that the bioactive ingredient in the Aloe Vera plant was a chain of mannose sugars (beta I-4 polymannose), otherwise known as, polymannose. These polymannose would later be referred to as glyconutrients.

Experimenting with glyconutrients began in August 1985 when a group of AIDS patients reported improved health and functionality after drinking an Aloe Vera drink. Another observation with these AIDS patients was the shrinkage of tumors. When these nutritional supplements were withdrawn, hemostasis was lost, and cancer and autoimmune diseases return.

Traditionally, doctors and patients, as well as the general public have been taught to believe that simple sugars (derived from complex carbohydrates) do not, cure cancer, or aid in major biological functions, but rather are used to burn energy in order to sustain human life. But recent scientific evidence now shows that these simple sugars support the body's immune defense and are key players in the biological functions of life, including the initiation of life (egg to sperm) cellular communication (cell to cell communication), cell growth and differentiation, regulation (gatekeepers to the cell; modulating the immune system), metabolism, repair (DNA; Stem cells), healing (cancer, autoimmune disease, etc.), cognition, and memory.

Because of the radical changes in our environment and how we go about food production, beginning with the depletion of the natural raw materials found in our soil, our foods are found to be grossly deficient in vitamins, minerals, enzymes, trace elements, and monosaccharides.

It is important to note, that these glyconutrients (monosaccharides) provide the necessary molecules for cellular synthesis (the building blocks) in establishing normal function and structure within the human biological system. They do not, in and of themselves, cure cancer or disease, but rather, act as a necessary ingredient in the biology of life and biological synthesis.

Ironically, 2000 years ago, Greek scientists referred to the Aloe Vera plant as the universal remedy for all diseases and illnesses. The Egyptians referred to the Aloe Vera plant, as the "plant of immortality." Alexander the Great and Christopher Columbus used the Aloe gel to treat wounded soldiers.

In piecing the cancer puzzle together, scientists have recently discovered a link between essential nutrients normally found in most vegetables and fruits, and the body's interdependent systems that regulate life, including immunological function. According to John Axford, BSc, MD, FRCP, president of the Section of Clinical Immunology and Allergy, Royal Society of Medicine, *"in the late 1970's, a recent discovery was made that the human cell is covered with a dense layer of certain simple carbohydrates or monosaccharides, known collectively as, glycocalyx, which are found in plants. Because of their microscopic size, they are impossible to detect with a normal light microscope and impossible to detect under routine visual inspection of cells or tissues"* (Macmillan & Daines, 2003).

According to 21st century science these saccharides were found to be responsible for the cellular communication for all cells in the human body. *"The study of these simple saccharides, which are now called the glycosylation (the addition of saccharides to proteins or lipids to form a glycoprotein or glycolipid) on the human cell, is called the science of glycobiology. Glycobiology is now taught in every medical school...."* (Macmillan & Daines, 2003; Oxford Journal of Glycobiology, 2009).

According to the Oxford Journal of Glycobiology, 2010 issue, *"Glycobiology provides a unique forum dedicated to research into the biological functions of glycans..."* The importance of monosaccharides (sugars or glycans) was first recognized in the late 1970s, when a simple monosaccharide was extracted from the Aloe Vera plant. What was discovered was the sugar, mannose, which is produced naturally in types of natural foods, including rice and wheat. While this simple sugar is found in the rice fields of China and India as well as in all other countries, it is absent, or deficient in most foods produced in America. (McDaniel, 20112).

The study of sugars (glycans) and how the body utilizes these sugars for numerous purposes, including their ability to heal the body of illness and disease has been so phenomenal that Science Magazine, March 23, 2001, devoted an entire issue, "Carbohydrates & Glycobiology," to educate doctors and other scientists on glyconutrients, Glycobiology, and Glycoscience (Science Magazine, 2001).

Dr. Reg McDaniel and other researchers and scientists have recently discovered that there are over 200 sugar compounds, technically known as saccharides that occur naturally in plants. And ten of them, known as glyconutrients, have been identified as essential to optimal human health." Unfortunately, researchers have also discovered that most of these essential sugars are absent or significantly absent from foods found in the American diet. According to Science Magazine (2004), scientists are beginning to understand that these sugars are biomarkers for various diseases. According to the National Cancer Institute (2007), the study of Glycobiology could help scientists to better understand cancer risk and cancer detection (Marano, 2004; Murray, Granner, Mayes & Rockwell, 1996).

Scientific American, in its July 2002 issue stated that: *"Scientists have long recognized that certain sugar structures, which are attached to protein and lipid molecules, may be important as markers for cancer development,"* said NCI Director John E. Niederhuber, M.D. *"While this area has compelling scientific interest, its biological and chemical complexities have often discouraged investigation. Today, with the advent of advanced technologies to conduct protein and carbohydrate chemistry, research into this intriguing area has experienced renewed interest"* (Scientific American, 2002).

In 2007 The National Cancer Institute, part of the National Institute of Health stated that it is, *"funding a new $15.5 million, five-year initiative to discover, develop, and clinically validate cancer biomarkers by targeting the carbohydrate (glycan) part of a molecule"* (NCI. 2007).

In the October 26, 2002 issue of New Scientific magazine (pp34), they state that *"This is going to be the future"*, declares biochemist Gerald Hart of Johns Hopkins University in Baltimore. *"We won't understand immunology, neurology, developmental biology or disease until we get a handle on glycobiology"* (New Scientist Magazine, 2002).

The University of Liverpool, Centre for Glycobiology is conducting exhaustive research on the interactions of glycans on biological function (University of Liverpool, 2017).

Currently, one of the foremost center for the research of glycobiology is conducted at the University of California San Diego, as demonstrated in the third edition of their textbook, "The Essentials of Glycobiology". According to Peter C. Doherty, Nobel Laureate in Medicine 1996, and a contributing editor in the textbook, glycans play a central role in the recognition of cancer and other diseases, and any glycan abnormalities or dysfunctions can hinder this recognition process (Varki, A., Cummings, R., Esko, J., 2017).

According to James E. Rothman, Nobel Laureate in Medicine, 2013, Bruce Beutler, Nobel Laureate in Medicine, 2011, and Kurt Wuethrich, Nobel Laureate in Chemistry, 2002, these essential sugars are key players in human biology. They not only direct intercellular movement, they also act as gatekeepers to cellular function and act as protectors and defenders in the recognition of pathogens. Their central and functional roles in human biology are numerous and undetermined (Varki, A., Cummings, R., Esko, J., 2017). If you were to search for images of "The Essentials of Glycobiology", you would begin to visually discover the complexity in the study of glycobiology, the study of simple sugars that have taken the scientific community by storm.

Dr. McDaniel was among one of the first scientists to conduct government studies on glyconutrients. He is a renowned pathologist, known internationally, who lectures on the significant biological role glyconutrients play in health and well-being. Dr. McDaniel tells of the incredible healing power of glyconutrients and how these monosaccharides, when administered as a supplement, have affected the lives of tens of thousands of people around the world. Based on his scientific discoveries and exhaustive research Dr. McDaniel remains a staunch advocate of an organic food-based diet consisting primarily of vegetables and fruits as well as a staunch advocate of glyconutrient supplements (McDaniel, n.d.).

In 1996 Harper medical textbook, Harper's Biochemistry, was revised to include eight essential monosaccharides as essential for cellular function. Those essential sugars include not only Glucose, Fructose, and Mannose, which we all recognize, but also, Galactose, N-acetyl-neuraminic Acid (sialic acid), N-acetyl-glucosamine, N-acetyl-galactosamine, and Xylose.

Keep in mind that this was 1996, today we know so much more, including the fact that these simple sugars are more important to a healthy system than we all realized, and the absence of these simple sugars from the American diet raises a host of questions. If the body must produce them rather than extract them from the foods that we eat, the body is exposed to tens of thousands of free radicals that only damage healthy cells. Today, science has now identified 10 monosaccharides.

In 2001, Science Magazine (March 23, 2001) devoted an entire issue of its magazine to the education of Glycobiology (Science, 2001). Carbohydrates and Glycobiology. Science, 2001. In 2001 Dr. Emil I. Mondoa published a book on Glyconutrients entitled, "Sugars That Heal." He states:

> *"Saccharides are essential in virtually all intelligent interactions between the cells of the body; they're a critical part of the cell intelligence and activity. Glyconutrients affect how our cells form the structure of the body and the daily repair of our tissues. They play an important role in helping our body distinguish what belongs in it from what does not belong, and so they are vital to how our cells react to bacteria and viruses. Virtually every change within our multi-cellular bodies, from conception until death, is to some degree mediated by this language of sugars"* (Mondoa, 2001).

As a follow up Psychology Today, in their June 2004 issue stated that "*Over 200 sugar compounds, technically known as saccharides, occur naturally in plants. And eight of them, known as glyconutrients, have been identified as essential to optimal human health.*"

Science has recently discovered that these complex sugars are not only a major component in the human system, they are essential for the well-being of human tissue, and the lack of these essential components leads to disease and death.

Glyconutrients are not a cure all, but they are, according to modern scientific research, essential agents in the healing process, and for the maintenance of cellular metabolism. To date, there are countless scientific documents that validate the important significance of glyconutrients.

What do glyconutrients do in your body? According to 21st century science, a normal healthy cell in your body would have its surface covered with glycans (sugars) that are attached to either a protein (glycoproteins) or a fat (glycolipids). These glyconutrients form a type of "language," or code that allows the cells to communicate with each other. The cells of your body trying to communicate without the presence of these glycans would be like trying to write the dictionary with some of the letters of the alphabet missing. It would be impossible!

Why do cells need to communicate? A major function of your immune system is to recognize disease-causing bacteria, viruses, cancer cells, and toxins. Once recognized, these foreign cells are "tagged" as dangerous to your body.

Your immune system must communicate the message to the appropriate cells of your immune system responsible for neutralizing or destroying these harmful foreign cells. This ongoing process of recognizing, tagging, and destroying foreign cells requires glyconutrients. Glyconutrients make it possible for the cells in your body to "talk" to one another. If the disease-causing foreign cells are not identified and destroyed, they will grow and multiply causing horrendous damage to the body (Science Magazine, 2001; McDaniel, 2012).

The cells of your body also must be able to distinguish the foreign cells from the normal healthy cells. If normal healthy cells are "tagged" by mistake and subsequently destroyed, your body can develop an "autoimmune disease." There are no less than 87 autoimmune diseases that have currently been identified.

Another phenomenal 21st century discovery is that glycans have been shown to be immune modulators, not immune stimulants. An immune modulator assists the immune system to achieve balance; in other words, glyconutrients regulate the immune system by either stimulating or depressing the immune system as the need is determined. This discovery alone has enormous implications in the war against cancer and autoimmune disease. The most significant player in successfully combating cancer and autoimmune disease is immune response. This single bit of information is as significant as vitamin C is to the sailors of the 1800s or the discovery of penicillin during the mid-1900s.

The role of glyconutrients as immune modulators is quite significant because autoimmune disease is the result of an overactive immune system, while cancer growth, in part, may be the result of an underactive immune system. This is especially true in the initial stages of cancer when the immune system, under normal circumstances would have detected the cancer growths and eradicated them.

The mere fact that they progress allows for the possibility that the immune system is compromised. Since, initially, it would not have been overtaxed, unless other foreign agents came into play, such as overwhelming amounts of radiation or foreign toxins, or if there were insufficient amounts of glyconutrients, which would normally be supplied by the foods we eat.

According to recent research adding supplements of glyconutrients reacts biologically by communicating to the immune system, causing the increase of natural killer cells, which is the front line of defense against cancer cells. Researchers can demonstrate that glyconutrients stimulate the production of killer cells by more than 300%. T-cell and B-cell production is also increased by more than 250% and 200% respectively (U.K., 2006; Cimoch, Chou, Chang, & Tilles, 1998).

These ten essential glyconutrients, at one time, were prominent in the American diet, but because of how America processes its food, these naturals sugars are now absent, or deficient in most foods. The long-term results are devastating. Without these essential nutrients the body's immune response becomes compromised and cancers and autoimmune diseases can grow unchecked, resulting in death and disability.

Glyconutrients are essential for:

- Normal cellular processes
- Cellular immunity
- Recognition and response
- Antibody function
- Signaling and recruitment
- Modulating immune function
- Assisting is combating free radicals
- Assisting the bodies healing properties
- Memory
- Cognition
- Combating infertility
- Cell-to-cell communication
- Activating immune response
- Biological synthesis

Fortunately, the body was created with a "back-up" plan and can manufacture the missing ten sugars found in the American diet, however, this occurs at a great cost. During the conversion process your cells are exposed to tens of thousands of free radical daily. This requires time, energy, and a host of other micronutrients to complete the conversion.

Viruses can also interfere with our body's ability to make these conversions. People who are ill or who have inborn errors of metabolism are especially vulnerable to a breakdown in the process. When the monosaccharides cannot be made, communication is slowed down or impaired and as a result, disease, and premature aging are likely.

In the human body there are four blood types, "A," "B," "O," and "AB." What most people are not aware of is that the only difference between each blood type is a sugar molecule. While there are four different blood types (A, B, O, and AB). Most people also know that transfusing the wrong blood type to someone can result in illness or death.

What most people do not know is that the difference between the different blood types is a saccharide (glyconutrient). Type "A" and B have an additional sugar molecule that Type O does not have, while Type "A" has the terminal sugar molecule N-acetylgalactosamine (GalNAc) and Type B has the terminal sugar molecule Galactose (Gal).

Another function of glyconutrients has to do with reproduction. A woman's egg recognizes suitable healthy sperm of its own species from the complex of sugars at the tip of the sperm that "talk" to corresponding sugars and proteins on the surface of the egg cell.

Cells communicate their needs for all nutrients via sugars (glyconutrients). It is important to note that absent of these critical sugars could be one of the reasons for infertility, and the addition of glyconutrient supplements could, possibly, reverse infertility (Murray, Granner, Mayes, & Rockwell, 1996; Diekman, 2003).

There are countless textbooks, conferences, doctors, and journals, and medical schools around the world involved in the study of glycobiology. On April 19-21, 2015 the Royal Society of Medicine sponsored its 11th Jenner Glycobiology and Medicine Symposium. The purpose of this international forum of scientists and clinicians was to examine the relevance of glycobiology to immunology, and to foster and promote more interaction and participation between Glycobiologists and clinicians. The opening speaker was Professor Pauline Rudd, from the National Institute for Bioprocessing Research and Training, Dublin Ireland.

On March 9-11, 2018 the University of San Diego Glycobiology Research and Training Center conducted their 21st annual Glycobiology symposium. The purpose of the symposium was to exchange the latest research in Glycobiology and to foster interaction among those in academics, biotechnology and pharmaceutical. They will conduct their 23rd San Diego Glycobiology Symposium (SDGS) on Friday and Saturday, March 20-21, 2020.

On September 17-19, 2018, the 4th Glycobiology World Congress gathered in Rome Italy. The theme was: Glycobiology: The Study of Sweet Life. This is where scientists from around the world, including the United States, gathered to exchange information, and promote the advances in Glycoscience. Track one of the symposiums entitled, "Glycobiology and Biochemistry." In this session they discussed the various aspects of glycans [glyconutrients], including the structures of carbohydrates and their biological applications. On July 17-18, 2020 the 8th Glycobiology World Congress will gather in Vienna, Austria. Information about upcoming conferences go to their website: https://glycobiology.expertconferences.org/.

There was a time when sugars were credited with magical healing powers but are now seen, like salt, as an evil necessary in small doses but the cause of numerous diseases, such as diabetes, if taken in excess. The latest research suggests that this view ignores the vital role played by more complex sugars, such as those found in the Aloe Vera plant.

The National Cancer Institute (NCI), part of the National Institutes of Health (NIH), spent $15.5 million, five-year initiative to discover, develop, and clinically validate cancer biomarkers by targeting the carbohydrate (glycan) part of a molecule (NCI, 2007).

Scientists have long recognized that certain sugar structures, which are attached to protein and lipid molecules, may be important as markers for cancer development," said NCI Director John E. Niederhuber, M.D. "While this area has compelling scientific interest, its biological, and chemical complexities have often discouraged investigation.

Today with the advent of advanced technologies to conduct protein and carbohydrate chemistry, research into this intriguing area has experienced renewed interest (NCI, 2007).

The Massachusetts Institute of Technology (MIT) profiled the science of glycomics as a new technology that *"...could have an impact on health problems ranging from rheumatoid arthritis to the spread of cancer cells."*

Glycomics is the study of sugars and includes glycobiology-the study of the effects of sugars on living organisms." *If you do not have glycosylation, you do not have life. The medical potential...is absolutely enormous"* (MIT, 2003). Glyconutrients are needed by every cell in your body for it to function in optimal health and wellness, and according to recent research many of these essential sugars are missing or deficient in the American diet. Prior to 1970s the world of glycobiology did not exist. Today, glyconutrients are one of the most phenomenal discoveries since penicillin (https://www.technologyreview.com/s/401227/glycomics/).

If someone were to ask if, you have ever heard of glycobiology or of glyconutrients, the answer probably would be, no, which is not unusual, since the scientific discovery only occurred in the early 1990s. By scientific standards the pivotal role of glyconutrients in human health and well-being is considered one of the most phenomenal discoveries of the 21st century, yet many doctors and naturopaths are still ignorant of their very existence and the numerous roles these sugars play in the facilitation of numerous bodily functions. What are of prime importance are the incredible healing mechanisms, which are built into the human system using these sugar molecules. Until recently their significant role was undetected by scientists.

Glyconutrients are a mixture of ten essential micronutrients (saccharides) once found in abundance in family farms and orchards. These micronutrients do not heal or cure diseases, such as cancer, but rather, facilitate proper biological structure on a molecular level. This is a process of interdependence, where one level of development and function is dependent upon another level of development and function.

The genes control cellular synthesis (the building blocks for the biochemistry of life) using element and nutrient molecules, which are used to assemble bioactive structures and functional compounds that conduct the biochemistry of life. The specific function of a bioactive compound is determined by its molecular structure, which requires specific nutrients to be present in the diet (McDaniel, 2012).

Without the presence of these specific nutrients, genetic coding or communication on a genetic level does not function optimally. Without these essential nutrients regulating immune function becomes dysfunctional. Without these essential nutrients the number of gatekeepers for cellular communication becomes deficient and the long-term repercussions are illness and disease, including the uncontrolled growth of cancer cells. An example of these functions would include immune defense, cellular, and biological repair, recovery, structural restitution, and homeostasis (McDaniel, 2012).

I could have included so much more information on the relevance of glyconutrients and their essential contributions to human health and well-being. If you need more convincing simply Google "Glycobiology symposiums." The advancements in biological research is so phenomenal and the discoveries are overwhelming. Yet, ironically, very few of us have ever heard of a glyconutrient, or even know where to purchase a glyconutrient supplement. I buy my supplements from, WellnessQuest.org. The glyconutrients are called, New Eden. Wellnessquest.org is the website of Dr. Reg McDaniel. You will find an informational video and more information on the phenomenal discovery of Glyconutrients.

I would like to finish this chapter with a quote from Dr. Reg McDaniel. In reference to the addition of glyconutrients to the diet in varying amounts, depending on the person and their specific needs, in a person's quest to eradicate cancerous tumors, he states: *"Utilizing multiple immune mechanisms to identify abnormal cells to specifically destroy only the malignant cells by activity of NK [natural killer cells] lymphocytes and avoid damage to normal cells is the most attractive and desirable capacity for these mechanisms of action to destroy cancer cells while supporting the health of a patient.*

This advance in management of malignancy that is unequal in safety, unparalleled in effectiveness and is economically unmatched, employs natural and innate mechanisms provided in the human genome that is supported by nutrients found in nature. This natural technology as old as life itself achieves a goal sought unsuccessfully by science and medicine for many, many generations."

CHAPTER 16

COMMERCIALISM - CONFRONTING AN OLD ADVERSARY

"...in America it's incurable, but there are natural treatments in other countries that can reverse this problem in a matter of weeks. Unfortunately, the FDA has not approved these treatments. So, yes, in America it is incurable." –Harvard Medical Doctor, Yiwen Y. Yang, founder of the Century Clinic, Reno Nevada

"Convention is a hard and implacable enemy." –Dr. Barry Durrant

William Henry, during the reign of Queen Elizabeth I (1533 – 1603), made the mistake of informing the medical establishment that the heart's main function was to pump blood throughout the body. His dissemination of information resulted in a price being placed on his head. He had to flee the country to save his life, and he could not return for 10 years.

During the Victorian era Ignaz Semmelweiss (1818 – 1865) suggested that the death rate of delivering mothers would be decreased substantially if doctors would simply wash their hands before entering the delivery room. As a result of his outlandish recommendations, he was scorned as an interfering charlatan. It was not until 1961 that Methicillin-Resistant Staphylococcus aureus (MRSA), infections that occur in people who have been in hospitals or other health care facilities, was discovered.

In 1830 a French scientist calculated that the percentage of deaths in Paris France attributable to cancer was approximately 2%. At the turn of the century the cancer rate in the United States was estimated at 4%. Today, cancer accounts for 22.5% of all deaths in America (CDC, 2015), which is a far cry from the, mere, 4% at the turn of the century. In 2012, 8.2 million people died of cancer worldwide and 14 million new cases were diagnosed.

The number of new cases is expected to rise 70% over the next 2 decades (World Health Organization, 2015). According to the Centers for Disease Control and Prevention (CDC), in America, there were 2,596,993 deaths in 2013, of which 584,881 were cancer related (CDC, 2015). In 2018, according to the National Cancer Institute, in the Unites States, an estimated 1,735,350 new cases of cancer will be diagnosed, and 609,640 people will die from the disease, which is from previous records.

Disregarding newly discovered scientific and medical breakthroughs is not historically uncommon, but it comes with a cost, the lives of millions. Even today as researching scientists and doctors attempt to disseminate recent discoveries, they are confronted with convention and commercialism that continues to mitigate, underrate, disregard, and even attempt to cover-up the current data. Physicist, Dr. Otto Warburg, a Nobel Prize recipient, frustrated with the direction of the medical community states, "Science advances one funeral at a time" (Coy, 2017).

Since President Nixon declared war on cancer in 1971 the National Cancer Institute, which maintains 4,000 employees, has spent in excess of 105 Billion dollars on cancer research, not including the countless billions of dollars that have come from various organizations. According to a 2009 article in the New York Times, age-adjusted deaths because of cancer have improved only 5% between 1950 and 2005. In contrast, the death rate for heart disease has decreased 64%, and the rate of death due to the flu or pneumonia has decreased by 58% (Kolata, 2009a; Spector, 2010).

COMMERCIALISM – CONFRONTING AN OLD ADVERSARY

Although there have been some improvements with certain cancers over the last 50 years, prior to metastases, the concern becomes critical when metastases occur, which is true for all types of cancer. For example, with breast cancer using conventional methods, if metastasis occurs, there is only a 20% survival rate that extends beyond five years, and with colorectal cancer that has metastasized, there is only a 10% chance of living beyond five years. For prostate cancer, if metastases occur, there is only a 30% survival rate beyond five years, and the survival rate goes into the single digits for those with lung cancer that has metastasized (Kolata, 2009a; Spector, 2010).

These figures have not changed since 1950, despite all the new drugs that have been introduced. What is just as alarming is that the medical community, along with the pharmaceutical industry, continues to promote a very favorable outlook toward the treatment of cancer using conventional methods. However, the evidence clearly shows that conventional treatments are decades behind, especially when compared to the phenomenal advances in the treatment for heart disease, the flu, and pneumonia (Kolata, 2009a; Spector, 2010).

According to a 2009 article in the New York Times:

> *"Data from the National Center for Health Statistics show that death rates over the past 60 years — the number of deaths adjusted for the age and size of the population — plummeted for heart disease, stroke, influenza, and pneumonia. But for cancer, they barely budged. The cancer death rate, now about 200 deaths a year per 100,000 people of all ages and 1,000 deaths per 100,000 people over age 65 — is nearly the same now as it was in 1950, dropping only 5 percent. But the death rate from heart disease is only a third of what it was in 1950. Even though more people die of heart disease than from cancer, cancer deaths have been edging closer to heart disease deaths each year. Are the statistics lying, hiding major advances because of the way the data is analyzed? No, researchers say"* (Kolata, 2009).

Taking into consideration the current data, what is clear is that cancer is on the rise. The highest rates for the incidence of cancer can be found in the United States and in Europe. Much of this increase has to do with lifestyle, diet, nutrient deficiencies, non-exercise, and the amount of toxic and chemical exposure (Kolata, 2009; ACS, n.d.; Stone, Campbell, & Esselstyn, 2011; Campbell, Parpia, & Chen, 1998). Americans and Europeans who live in urban settings are at higher risk because their environment is a host to tens of thousands of carcinogenic agents that inflict the human body (CDC, 2009; CDC, 2013).

Recent research contends that the average American is inflicted with approximately 700 different toxins that can add an additional 23 pounds of weight. It is estimated that the average newborn baby has approximately 287 chemicals in their umbilical cord blood, of which 217 are considered poisonous to nerves and nerve cells (neurotoxic) (Hyman, 2012).

Country dwellers may be considered at less risk, but their very existence is also threatened by countless environmental condiments that invade the air they breathe, the water they drink, and the soil with which they plant their produce. While genetic links play a role in the onset of some cancers, according to recent research genetics only plays a minor role for the onset of cancer. Of greater concern are a host of environmental factors that include commercial processing, and harvesting of foods, depleted soil, genetically altered seeds, toxins, and chemicals in the soil, contaminated water, and urban stress.

The reason people have been able to survive over the centuries, even though every human being produces cancer cells daily is because the human system was genetically designed for survival, with two elaborate defense systems, the immune system, and the genetic system. However, maintaining a healthy body is a concerted effort that employs all the body's systems.

This concerted effort relies on a multitude of factors, including effective cellular communication and system to system communication, a comprehensive process, which is just beginning to be understood. And all these elaborate systems require a constant intake of raw materials, called nutrients (vitamins, minerals, trace elements, etc.). These raw materials come in the form of unprocessed foods, which, not only promote health, but sustain life. (Burzynski, et al., 2008; Campbell, Parpia, & Chen, 1998; Chen, Campbell, Li, & Peto, 1990; Stone, Campbell, & Esselstyn, 2011; Warburg, 1966).

The human body, in a concerted effort to maintain optimal health also requires a lifestyle that includes daily exercise and minimal amounts of chronic stress, along with the absence of foreign toxins, chemicals, and excessive amounts of pharmaceutical drugs, which inhibit proper cellular function, including the inhibition of oxygen to the cell (Burzynski, et al., 2008; Campbell, Parpia, & Chen, 1998; Chen, Campbell, Li, & Peto, 1990; Stone, Campbell, & Esselstyn, 2011; Warburg, 1966).

In 1970 Dr. Reg. McDaniel and others discovered that carbohydrate molecules known as glycans act as immune system modulators. In 1996 Harper's medical textbook was revised to include eight essential carbohydrates, as essential for optimal health. Recent scientific and medical breakthroughs have advanced the understanding on the etiology of cancer as well as the processes and safeguards the body employs to mitigate the effects of cancer and to eradicate it.

Dr. Warburg, Campbell, Esselstyn, Chen, and countless others could determine, emphatically that health, and the absence of cancer begins with three key factors, nutrition, the absence of foreign toxins, and a stress-free lifestyle. When sufficient nutrients are lacking in the foods we consume, or there is a presence of sufficient foreign toxins and prolonged chronic stress, a disruptive chain reaction occurs that moves in three key directions, genetic disposition, immunological dysfunction, and cellular metabolic breakdown (Burzynski, et al., 2008; Campbell, Parpia, & Chen, 1998; Chen, Campbell, Li, & Peto, 1990; Stone, Campbell, & Esselstyn, 2011; Warburg, 1966).

Dr. Otto Warburg, a Nobel- Prize recipient and renowned scientist, for his exhaustive research on cancer, stated in1966, 33 years after receiving his Nobel Prize for his research on cancer:

> *"These proposals [the eradication of cancer] are in no way utopian. On the contrary, they may be realized by everybody, everywhere, at any hour. Unlike the prevention of many other diseases the prevention of cancer requires no government help and no extra money"* (Warburg, 1966).

Because of the 20th and 21st century scientific and medical discoveries a new cancer paradigm has evolved, based on empirical evidence. James Madison, one of our founding fathers, once said, *"The advancement and diffusion of knowledge is the only guardian of true liberty."*

Jim Morrison once said, *"If you can control the media, you control the mind."* John Swinton, former head of the editorial staff of the New York Times was considered one of America's beloved newspapermen. At a banquet in his honor he stated,

> *"There is no such thing, at this date of the world's history, in America as an independent press. You know it and I know it. There is not one of you who dare to write your honest opinions, and if you did, you know beforehand that it would never appear in print. I am paid weekly for keeping my honest opinions out of the paper I am connected with. Others of you are paid similar salaries for similar things, and any of you who would be so foolish as to write honest opinions would be out on the streets looking for another job.*
>
> *If I allowed my honest opinions to appear in one issue of my paper, before twenty-four hours my occupation would be gone. The business of the journalists is to destroy the truth; to lie outright; to pervert; to vilify; to fawn at the feet of mammon, and to sell his country and his race for his daily bread. You know it and I know it and what folly is this toasting an independent press? We are the tools and vassals of rich men behind the scenes. We are jumping jacks; they pull the strings and we dance. Our talents, our possibilities and our lives are all the property of other men. **We are intellectual prostitutes**"* (Boyer & Morais, 1974).

Thus, the challenge regarding the 20th and 21st century medical and scientific discoveries about cancer is not about knowing what cancer is, where it originates, or how to treat it affectively. The challenge is in the dissemination of information to doctors, oncologists, and the practical application of these phenomenal discoveries in combating cancer. The challenge is in confronting an old adversary and dispelling ago old theories that have given way to current 21st century empirical evidence, and to mitigate the effects of commercialism that influences the flow of information.

CHAPTER 17

THE PROBLEM WITH CURRENT TREATMENTS

CHEMOTHERAPY

"There was a time when the heads of medicine determined that the only acceptable protocol in treating cancer would entail: ablaze it with fire, pour venomous toxins upon it, sever it from the body, or apply other chemical agents, all of which seem to be antithetical to health and well-being."
–Estrada

"And knowing their thoughts Jesus said to them, 'Any kingdom divided against itself is laid waste; and any city or house divided against itself will not stand.'" Matthew 12:25

Ruth's Story

In 1982 Ruth Heidrich (at the age of 47), a marathon runner from Vancouver Canada, was diagnosed with breast cancer. She underwent a mastectomy, but the cancer had metastasized to her lungs and bones, and her doctor's recommended chemotherapy and radiation therapy. What Ruth may not have known, at the time, is that once metastasis occurs, her probability of death, even with chemo and radiation therapy is 80% (Heidrich, 2000).

Instead of pursuing chemo and radiation therapy, Ruth decided to visit Dr. John McDougall. Dr. McDougall had Ruth review several studies showing the reversal of breast cancer by way of diet. Ruth decided to change her diet and refused to use conventional treatments. At the same time, she began to train for a triathlon. She became obsessed and maintained a very difficult physical regiment. In response, many of her friends said, *"You should be resting, you are a cancer patient."*

Because of her modified diet she felt healthy and had plenty of energy. She believed that if she had a healthy body, and consumed the proper foods, she would win her battle against cancer. At the ironman triathlon, Ruth Heidrich won a Gold Medal for her age group and conquered her battle against cancer. Having changed her diet, she also discovered that her arthritis and chronic constipation had also disappeared. Had she decided to pursue chemo and radiation treatments her chances of survival were less than 20%. You can read her complete story in her book, "A Race for Life" (Heidrich, 2000).

What are often not mentioned, or underrated, when someone is diagnosed with cancer are the horrific side effects of chemotherapy radiation therapy and other forms of chemical applications. What is almost always underrated is that many of those who eventually die, do not die of the cancer but of the direct and indirect side effects of chemo and radiation therapy. This is because chemo is a very toxic substance that *"often"* kills cancer cells and at the same time debilitating healthy cells and organs throughout the body.

These side effects can result in damage to the heart, the brain, the blood, the muscles, the digestive tract, the skin, the kidneys, the bladder, the bones, etc., often causing mouth sores, digestive distress, loss of appetite, balding, sexual dysfunction, infertility, the acceleration of menopause, hormonal imbalance, swelling of the hands and feet, anxiety and depression, etc.

I use the word "***Often***" because cancer patients only have three choices while under conventional care, surgery, chemo and radiation. Frequently doctors will recommend a form of chemo, only to find out, **after the fact**, that that particular chemo drug was not effective against the cancer, or, even worse, that the chemo drug was not effective at all, other than to debilitate the body's immune system and create lasting damage to other organs and tissue.

Chemotherapy

What is chemotherapy? It is the introduction of an FDA approved drug or series of drugs that cannot distinguish the difference between a healthy cell and a cancer cell. So, the chemo-drug, when administered, attacks everything it touches. As a result, both good cells and bad cells are destroyed or damaged. Unfortunately, when good cells are attacked by the chemo-drug they, as a result, become damaged and eventually die or become cancerous.

An ironic twist in protocols, since the very drug used to kill cancer cells is also complicit in creating future cancer cells that are often undetected. In many cases these newly formed cancer cells can go undetected for years. If too many good cells are damaged a second crisis occurs, patient survival. If too many of the surrounding good cells are damaged beyond repair, the patient dies.

The first and foremost side effect of these toxic chemo drugs is the damage done to the immune system. The immune system is the body's protective shield against all foreign invaders and mutant cells (viruses, bacteria, cancer, etc.). It is not uncommon for a cancer patient, after having undergone chemotherapy, to die of pneumonia. This is because the immune system has been compromised and is no longer capable of protecting against, even a common cold virus. Chemotherapy results in neutropenia (low white blood count). White blood cells play an intricate role in immune defense by warding off illness and disease. A low white blood count lowers the body's natural defenses, becoming susceptible to viruses, bacteria, fungi, and other germs (Healthline, 2014).

Chemotherapy can also adversely affect the red blood cells produced in the bone marrow, which can result in a host of problems, because it is the red blood cells that carry oxygen to tissue. A lowered red blood cell count results in anemia, and fatigue. Inhibiting the natural flow of oxygen on a cellular level will result in the promotion of new cancer cells, which is self-defeating.

Chemo can also lower the patient's platelet count, which accounts for bleeding easily and bruising. Chemotherapy can also damage the heart muscle, causing cardiac arrest, cardiomyopathy, arrhythmia (Healthline, 2014).

Chemo drugs often affect the gastrointestinal tract. Keep in mind that an intricate part of your immune system is in your intestinal tract. So, anything that affects your intestines can also affect your immune response. This can lead to vomiting, nausea, loose stools or diarrhea, bloating and gas. Conventional remedies for some of the side effects are other prescribed drugs (Vighi, 2008; Castillo, 2015).

Another major side effect is loss of bone mass, which contributes to pre-mature osteoporosis. What they may not tell you is why your body loses large amounts of calcium. When toxic chemo drugs, which are highly acidic, are introduced into the body, the body reacts defensively, which is what it was designed to do, to defend itself against foreign invaders and pursue a balanced pH of 7.35 (1 -14).

Any physiological introduction of acidic toxins triggers a biological reaction that is immediate. The body's first reaction is to neutralize the foreign toxic and acidic substance. The means to accomplish this immediate threat is to douse the highly toxic and acidic substance with large amounts of calcium, which the body obtains from the bone. Any prolonged exposure to acidic substances will result in a calcium deficiency, often referred to as, "brittle bones." After extensive bounds of chemo, it is not uncommon for cancer patients to have brittle bones that are easily fractured or broken (Lipton, et al., 2009).

When chemo drugs are introduced, they are excreted through the kidneys. As a result, both, the kidneys and bladder are damaged. Symptoms of a damaged kidney include swelling of hands and feet, decreased urination, and headaches. Symptoms of a damaged bladder include a burning sensation while urinating, and increased urination (Healthline, 20014).

Another major side effect is infertility in, both, men and women. Chemotherapy drugs can have a negative effect on hormones. In women this equates to hot flashes, and pre-mature menopause, often resulting in permanent infertility. Other symptoms include a dry vagina, which equates to painful or uncomfortable intercourse, fatigue and anxiety. If chemo is administered during a pregnancy, this can lead to birth defects and deformity. In men, chemo drugs can damage sperm or lower sperm count, leading to infertility (Healthline, 2014).

Farrah Fawcett's Story

I am reminded of Farrah Fawcett, who died after contracting anal cancer. Did the cancer kill her or the treatment? After two bouts of chemotherapy her cancer returned three months later. She eventually flew to Germany for a chemo-sensitivity test only to discover that the two bouts of chemo she had undergone were ineffective.

The results of those two bouts of chemotherapy were devastating, destroying her immune system – her only line of defense and hope for survival. The chemotherapy did not just destroy her immune system, it robbed her of her human dignity, and on June 25, 2009 our "Charlie's Angel" died (Somers, 2009).

Why wasn't she administered a chemo-sensitivity test before administering the chemo, and why is not a chemo-sensitivity test standard protocol in America? These are some of the basic questions those who have been diagnosed with cancer should be asking but they cannot ask if they are unaware of the advances in bioscience.

In conventional circles, treatments are often so toxic that the immune system becomes compromised and, in the end, it is not even capable of functioning effectively, leaving the individual vulnerable to the most common of all viruses, the common cold.

Farrah Fawcett discovered this truth, after the fact, and it cost her, her life and her dignity (Somers, 2008).

Kristen's Story

I recall the testimony of Sergeant Rich Schiff, of the San Francisco police department. He was testifying before a congressional subcommittee on February 29, 1996. One of his twin girls (Kristen) had been diagnosed, at the age of four, with a highly malignant brain tumor that had spread throughout her brain and into her spine. The doctors gave him two options, take her home and let her die, or allow her to undergo massive doses of chemo and radiation therapy, to be administered simultaneously.

These recommendations were presented even though she would die, either way. The side effects were horrific. She received second degree burns and the loss of her hair. Her urine was so toxic that they had to use rubber gloves. After six months of treatment her cancer was still present, and she was sent home to die.

After hearing about a non-toxic genetic therapy using antineoplastons he agreed to have them administered. Almost 2 years later her tumors had disappeared, and she was cancer free. However, she eventually died of neurological narcosis.

Simply stated, *"her brain fell apart from the radiation."*

> *"The autopsy showed that she was completely cancer free. Out of 52 cases [at the time of his testimony] of that disease, ever, no one died cancer free, just Chrissie. She didn't die of a terminal illness, she died because of my inability to care for her properly. She died from bad advice. She died because there is a government institution that disseminates false information and is not looking out for the welfare of the people"* (Ryder, 2011).

Another study was conducted in 1999 - 2001 on 30 children (3 – 14 years of age) whose medium age was 8, who were diagnosed with brain stem glioma. The treatment of choice, based on previous research that suggested their effectiveness, was Vincristine and Etoposide (VP-16), both of which are toxic chemotherapy drugs. They were administered in combination with radiation therapy. The chemotherapy consisted of two 28 days cycles, which were concurrent with radiation and continuing for 10 cycles.

All thirty children died. Twenty-seven of the children survived one year, and three survived for two years. The medium survival was nine months. During the treatments the side effects included toxicity to the blood, anemia, neutropenia (suppression of white blood cells; an intricate part of the immune system), gastrointestinal toxicity, constipation, nausea, vomiting, stomatitis/pharyngitis, and grade three infection. One child experienced severe pancreatitis, while another child had a central nervous system hemorrhage.

It was concluded that Vincristine and Etoposide (VP-16), along with standard radiation treatment was ineffective and did NOT improve the survival rate of children with brain stem glioma. Despite this Vincristine is still being used today for those diagnosed with brain tumors (Korones, et al., 2007; Cancer Therapy Advisor, n.d.).

Chemo-Sensitivity Tests

Ironically, throughout Europe cancer patients, before taking a chemo drug, undergo a *"Chemo sensitivity test."* This is a process whereby the patient's cancer cells are subjected to the chemo drug, in vitro, to determine whether that, particular, drug will be effective against that particular form of cancer. Only after it has been determined that that chemo drug will be effective is the patient subjected to the chemo treatment.

In America, chemo sensitivity tests are not administered and when requested they are often shunned as unreliable, often citing outdated data. The reality is, in many European countries chemo sensitivity tests are common protocol. Do they know something we don't, or is commercialism taking precedent over health and well-being in America?

I would recommend that all cancer patients who have decided to have administered chemo drugs insist on a chemo sensitivity test before taking the prescribed drugs. This is a life and death scenario, and in preparing your battle plan it is best to know your enemy – does the current cancer respond to the recommended chemo or not?

If you could know before the fact, this information could save your life and you could avoid untold damage and suffering. Fortunately, today all you have to do is search for "Chemosensitivity testing labs" to find avenues for pre-testing chemo drugs for their effectiveness before being administered a toxic drug that may not be effective against your, particular, cancer (Somers, 2008).

There are numerous other side effects of chemotherapy, not mentioned, fortunately, Ruth Heidrich did not have to experience such horrific circumstances and can function normally, during her time of healing. According to Dr. McDougall, countless men and woman who have changed their diet have reversed their prostate cancer, their breast cancer, and other types of cancer, without any horrific side effects. At the age of 71 (2006) Ruth is still training for triathlons (Stone, Campbell, & Esselstyn, 2011).

RADIATION TREATMENTS

High energy radiation therapy consists of administering doses of radiation to specific locations on the body. Unlike chemo, which is administered via the veins and can travels to all parts of the body, radiation therapy is localized and consists of high intensity radiation, which acts as a burning agent. Because it is localized the side effects are generally specific to that location but can have indirect long-term effects on other organs and tissue, especially the lungs, which are located behind the breasts.

Scientists and researcher have concluded that a woman who undergoes radiation therapy for breast cancer has 10 times higher risk of developing lung cancer. The side effects can be categorized as short-term and long-term. The side effects also differ dramatically per individual. The extent of the damage is also directly correlated to the extent of treatment. Longer treatments result in greater damage, both short-term and long-term (Brownstein, 2017).

Short-term effects have more to with the location of the radiation treatment. For example, for breast cancer, after radiation treatment the breasts are often sore, rough to touch, burned (reddish in color), and swollen. Due to burning some of the outer skin may peel. Fatigue is also very common, since the body is using much of its resources to treat the damaged area (Komen, n.d.).

Long-term effects for women with breast cancer who have undergone radiation treatments include lymphedema, which is a swelling of the lymph node. Lymph nodes are often removed, which permanently inhibits the effectiveness of the immune system. Surrounding tissue may also be damaged because of radiation. Rib fractures can also occur if radiation weakens the rib cage area. Heart problems can also occur, including heart disease, years after treatments were administered. Inflammation of the lungs can also occur, symptoms would include, shortness of breath, dry cough, and fever, and fibrosis. (Komen, n.d.; Brownstein, 2017).

Women who undergo radiation treatment are also at higher risk to develop lung cancer. The lungs are located directly behind the breasts and are subject to radiation when radiation therapy is applied. Worldwide, lung cancer is the leading cause of death among women (Brownstein, 2017).

Because prostate cancer is the leading cause of cancer in men, it is important to include the many side effects of conventional radiation treatments. They include (Seattle Cancer Care Alliance, 2012):

- Incontinence: 50% will need to wear a pad for leakage after treatment.
- Impotence: 50% of those treated with notice a permanent change
- Infertility: With radiation therapy infertility is permanent.
- Bowel Problems: diarrhea, bowel urgency, hemorrhoids, burning during bowel movement. Some symptoms can be controlled with medication, although 20% of all men notice a permanent change.

- Fatigue: External radiation will cause fatigue that can last up to one or two months after treatment.
- Tissue Damage: radiation therapy can inflict damage to the bladder, rectum, and surrounding tissue, which may require surgery to repair.

The short-term and long-term effects of radiation treatments have to do with the areas that have been radiated and the inhibition of their normal daily functions and contributions to homeostatic conditions. I referred to the short-term and long-term effects of radiation treatments as it related to breast cancer and prostate cancer because these are the two leading cancers in women and men.

But the short-term and long-term side effects of radiation treatments, unlike chemo treatments that can affect all part of the body, have everything to do with the location of treatment, thus, the effects of treatment will vary significantly.

CHAPTER 18
21ST CENTURY STRATEGIES IN DEALING WITH CANCER

"The first step in maintaining health is to alkalize the body. The cells of a healthy body are alkaline, while the cells of a diseased body are acidic - below a pH of 7.0. The more acidic the cells, the sicker we become. If the body cannot alkalize the cells, they become acidic and thus disease sets in. Our bodies produce acid as a byproduct of normal metabolism. But our bodies do not manufacture alkalinity, so we must supply it from an outside source to keep us from becoming acidic and dying."
–Arthur C. Guyton, M.D., author of:
Textbook of Medical Physiology

BATTLING CANCER

There are two paths in the battle on cancer. One is prevention, and the other is the eradication of cancer, once it is detected. The answer to the eradication of cancer is more often than not, not found in antiquated commercial treatments. These treatments have reduced the death rate by only 5% since 1950, and often leave their victims without human dignity, without immune function, and susceptible to a common cold and dying of pneumonia.

The answer has been with us for a very long time, and there are hundreds of doctors who are successfully treating the onset of cancer.

For example, Dr. Burzynski, Dr. McDougall, or the Gerson Clinic, to name a few.

The prevention of cancer has everything to do with key nutrient ingredients and specific variables, including lifestyle. Some of those key ingredients are, plenty of oxygen, pure water (absent the fluorides, chlorine, and other toxins) abundant in natural minerals, organic foods, produced from rick volcanic soil, natural organic supplements that contain all of the natural vitamins, minerals, enzymes, and trace elements, glyconutrients, a diet that consists primarily of unprocessed fruits and vegetables, a lifestyle that is primarily stress free, adequate sleep, and daily exercise.

Today, it is becoming more and more difficult, if not impossible, to live in an environment that is toxin-free. We live in a toxic planet, which is why education and the understanding of the cancer paradigm is imperative. The differences between a normal cell and a cancerous cell are vast and the ramifications are not only the difference between life and death, but also the quality of life and death. We are all too familiar with the horrific devastation to body and mind that too many people go through, as they attempt to survive the ravages of cancer and the ravages of various forms of conventional cancer treatment.

The significance and ramifications have everything to do with how the body responds to cancer. The human body functions as one entity, with countless moving parts. When your typical book on biology states that the human body consists of, approximately, 75 trillion individual cells, this does not include all the moving parts contained within every individual cell.

Today, if one were to break down the human body into individual moving parts the actual number would be exponentially close to infinity. On a broader spectrum the human body consists of systems (immune system, endocrine system, nervous system, etc.).

What is unique about the human body is that these systems and every moving part within these systems are not only interdependent they function in concert with one another, a phenomenal feat that boggles even the greatest of minds.

This dynamic rhythm of cellular interdependence flows and adjusts to all forms of stimulation, whether internal or external. The human body was designed to survive by adapting, compensating, and overcoming. The human body is quite resilient and capable of enormous abuse before succumbing to illness and disease.

When the human body detects an *anaerobic* cell (a cancer cell) the first thing that occurs is an immediate system communiqué that goes out to all concerned systems, raising the alarm.

What follows is an array of mechanisms that fall into place to combat the mutant cells. This all occurs automatically and systematically unless there are biological hindrances. When someone goes to the doctor and they perform a few tests and confirm that cancer is present, at this point the human body has already accumulated more than two billion cancer cells, which is when cancer cells becomes detectable. This is when the individual cancer cells accumulate and form small tumors that become visible.

What is essential to understand in reading through this material is that cancer begins on a cellular level. Its etiology is a result of damage in the respiration of cellular function. What causes the damage can consist of a host of elements, all playing a role in preventing cellular metabolism or cellular maintenance.

The cancer paradigm is divided into five key areas of function that play specific roles in human well-being. Cellular metabolism has everything to do with how a cell produces energy and what happens when there are disruptions to that process – the etiology of cancer cells. The immune system is an elaborate system that extends throughout the body, whose main purpose, among other things, is to eradicate all cancer cells.

The genes, often referred to as the second immune system, among other things, has a specific function in the eradication of cancer cells.

X-factors are those elements that assist in the promotion of cancer by assisting in the inhibition of natural biological functions. Stress, also referred to as the "silent killer" is the one variable that can circumvent all attempts to maintain health.

The five points to the cancer paradigm are broad influences that play an intricate role in health and well-being. Only with the advent of chemicals and toxins and with the processing of foods has there been an exponential explosion in the rate of cancer. Unfortunately, only with a proper education and a specific plan of action will individuals be able to reduce and avoid the devastating effects of cancer.

PH

In 1909 a Danish biochemist, named Peter Lauritz Sorensen (1868-1939), came up with a way to measure the acidic/alkaline value of a fluid. PH (pH) stands for "potential hydrogen" or "The power of hydrogen." Simply stated, pH refers to acidic and alkaline value. The pH of a neutral fluid is seven, zero to seven is considered acidic and seven to 14 is considered alkaline.

Based on 21st century research, in human critical care the difference between alkalinity and acidity can mean the difference between a healthy individual and a diseased individual. This is because any acute changes in blood pH bring about potent regulatory effects throughout the human system, including the cells and organs. pH has everything to do with oxygen, or the lack thereof (Kellum, 2000).

Researchers have discovered that any changes in blood pH, are because of three variables, carbon dioxide, relative electrolyte concentrations, and total weak acid concentrations. This becomes a critical variable in the treatment of cancer, especially as it relates to specific methods and approaches used to mitigate and eradicate cancer, especially as it relates to foods, which are either acidic, or alkaline (Kellum, 2000; Lyobebe, 2012).

Our blood maintains a pH level of 7.3 to 7.4. If the blood pH drops below 7.3 acidosis occurs. Acidosis refers to an extended length of time in which the body's pH balance remains in an acidic state. If this occurs it can lead to a variety of illness that includes arthritis, lupus, tuberculosis, osteoporosis, high blood pressure, and most cancers.

If the blood pH goes above 7.5 alkalosis occurs. Alkalosis can occur by hyperventilating, prolonged vomiting or severe dehydration. Prolonged alkalosis may result in irritability, muscle spasms, cramps, or no symptoms at all (Kellum, 2000; Lyobebe, 2012).

Human life is sustained between a pH of 6.8 and 7.8. Any changes that cause the pH balance to become too acidic can affect the distribution of sodium, potassium, and oxygen to the inner cell membrane. It is important to note that when the cell lacks the oxygen necessary for normal cellular metabolism the cells revert to fermentation, an irreversible process that transforms a normal cell into a cancerous cell.

Cancer cells excrete lactic acid, thus promoting a low pH balance. The key ingredient for normal cellular metabolism is oxygen. A slightly alkaline pH promotes the distribution of oxygen into the cell membrane. A slightly acidic pH hinders the flow of oxygen into the cell membrane (Kellum, 2000; Lyobebe, 2012; Warburg, 1956).

The human body goes to great lengths to maintain a normal pH balance by utilizing alkaline minerals found in the diet. Almost half of all acids formed or introduced into the body are neutralized by consuming certain highly alkaline foods, the other half are neutralized through chemical buffers, the respiratory system, and through the kidneys and pancreas.

Despite the body's efforts to maintain an alkaline environment most Americans have a higher than normal acidic pH balance. This is primarily attributable to a highly acidic diet that lacks the alkaline minerals necessary to neutralize acids. Other factors that contribute to an acidic pH balance are emotional stress, environmental toxins, pharmaceutical toxins, and other processes that deprive the cells of oxygen and other nutrients (Kellum, 2000; Lyobebe, 2012).

What does pH have to do with cancer? Dr. Otto Warburg found, without exception that cancer cannot survive in a high oxygen environment. An alkaline environment is, by definition, high in oxygen. On the other hand, cancer thrives in an acidic environment. An acidic environment is, by definition, low in oxygen (Warburg, 1956).

Maintaining a proper pH balance is necessary for:

- Repairing damaged cell.
- The assimilation of vitamins, minerals, enzymes, and other nutrients.
- Proper cellular function.
- Maintaining a high cellular energy.
- The disposal of toxic waste and cellular debris.
- The eradication of pre-cancer cells and cancer cells
- Healing of various illnesses and disease.

No matter what modality one chooses in one's pursuit of healing from cancer or any other illness, healing is not achieved until the pH balance is alkaline. Cancer patients can be 1000 times more acidic than a normal healthy person. In more advanced stages of cancer, it is not uncommon for the body's pH balance to be as low as 6.5. If metastasis occurs, it is not uncommon for the PH balance to be 5.7 or lower.

When your pH gets this low, it becomes almost impossible to fight off diseases and serious illnesses. A blood pH of 6.9, which is considered mildly acidic, can induce coma and death (Kellum, 2000; Lyobebe, 2012).

If you will recall from Dr. Otto Warburg's work, by manipulating the oxygen content by 35% he could affect the outcome of cancer. By increasing the intracellular oxygen level by 35%, cancer died, without exception. Alkaline tissue holds 20 times more oxygen than acidic tissue.

Even though raising the pH balance above normal limits will kill cancer cells, it also affects normal cellular function. In order to maintain a healthy body, the pH balance should range between 7.35 and 7.45 (Kellum, 2000; Lyobebe, 2012; Warburg, 1956).

With the advances in science we can measure our pH balance at home without the need of a doctor. You can easily test your pH balance by wetting a piece of litmus paper with your saliva two hours after a meal. This should give you a fair indication of your body's pH balance. A healthy saliva pH should be around 6.4 to 6.8. After a meal the pH of your saliva should rise to about 7.8 or higher.

The pH balance of saliva, if not tested around mealtime, reflects the pH balance of your blood and the extracellular fluids. If it is lower than 6.4 it is indicative of insufficient mineral reserves calcium and magnesium (Kellum, 2000; Lyobebe, 2012).

Urinary pH will always be more acidic than saliva. A urine pH conveys information regarding body chemistry, reflecting an accurate picture of the body's blood pH. There are a variety of foods considered alkaline forming and among them are almonds, Aloe Vera, apples, apricots, buckwheat, cabbage, cantaloupe, celery, carrots, cucumbers, most dairy products except hard cheese, dates, figs, grapefruit, honey, lettuce, millet, parsley, raisins, peaches, fresh red potatoes, pineapple, soy products, sprouted seeds, spinach, wakame miso soup, azuki beans, rice, and mineral water (Lyobebe, 2012).

Foods that are alkaline include most fruits and vegetables, lentils, peas, beans, seasonings, spices, herbs, nuts, and seeds. Acidic foods would include legumes, poultry, fish, meat, eggs, and grains. In maintaining optimal health, a diet should consist of foods 60% alkaline and 40% acidic. In attempting to restore health a diet should consist of foods 80% alkaline and 20% acidic.

Avoid caffeinated and alcoholic beverages because they dehydrate the body. Coffee has a pH balance of four. For every six-ounce cup of coffee you need to drink 10 to 12 ounces of water to re-hydrate yourself. Beer has a pH balance between 2.5 and 4.2. Coral Calcium has a pH between 10-12. Milk has a pH of 7. After four minutes of eating candy the saliva pH in your mouth drops from 6.5 to 4.5.

Cancer patients are considered 1000 times more acidic than a normal healthy person.

Another health concern has to do with the consumption of sodas. In America, sodas have replaced water as the drink of choice. It is not uncommon to observe an entire family gathered around the dinner table, or an office gathering, and the drink of choice are sodas.

Scientists now know that sodas are highly detrimental to health and well-being and are indirectly responsible for the onset of cancer and other illnesses. This is because sodas are highly acidic, having a pH balance of 2.5, which means every time a person drinks a soda, it takes 32 – 8 ounces of pH balanced water to counterbalance one can of soda.

Every time one's acidic levels drop below normal the body's defensive system uses its calcium deposits to neutralize the acid. Keep in mind that most water is relatively neutral with a pH of 7.2; water with a pH of 10 is approximately one thousand times more alkaline than your run of the mill glass of water.

All chemotherapy drugs are highly acidic, which is why most chemo patients lose their hair and experience calcium deficiencies. Because, as a natural reaction for survival, once an element of chemo enters the body, by default, and in defense of itself, the body extracts calcium from the bones and teeth to neutralize the chemo.

CANCER IMMUNOTHERAPY

Cancer immunotherapy is a cancer therapy that uses the body's immune system to kill cancer cells. The immune system is a complex system designed to protect the body from both internal and external adversaries, such as toxins, bacteria, and cancer cells. To accomplish this comprehensive and ongoing task the immune system maintains are arsenal of weapons such as T-cells, B-cells, macrophages, monocytes, granulocytes, and white blood cells, which circulate mainly in the blood and lymph fluid.

The immune system maintains two specific recognition systems for detecting these adversaries, antibodies, which are designed to target cell surface proteins, and T-cell receptors, which target, human leukocyte antigen- (HLA) presented peptide antigens (HLA-peptide) (Baeuerle, Patrick, & Christian, 2012; Life Extension, 2013; Liddy, et al., 2012).

DUKE UNIVERSITY & THE POLIO VACCINE

Under the heading of cancer vaccines, another phenomenal innovation is the introduction of a modified version of the polio vaccine, which makes it incapable of multiplying in healthy cells. Once the modified polio vaccine is injected into the tumor, it releases a toxin that attacks the cancer cell and dismantles the cancer cells ability to remain hidden. Once exposed to the body's immune system, the immune system begins a revenging attack eradicating the cancer. Ironically, there are no devastating side effects. Non-specific immunotherapies focus on boosting the body's immune system, by activating or stimulating immune response (LifeExtension, 2015; Texas Oncology, n.d.).

Until recently those diagnosed with a glioblastoma (a rapidly growing brain tumor) were essentially given a death sentence. The average life span, once diagnosed, was 15 months and 12,000 people each year died of a glioblastoma. Today, Duke University is accepting those who qualify, for treatment using a re-engineered polio vaccine. It seems that just one application is enough to eradicate the tumor, with no known adverse side effects.

Duke University does maintain a criterion for acceptance, but the criteria may change over time, so it is worth the inquiry. Their current phone number is 919-684-5301 and press option 1. If the number is no longer available call Duke University direct and ask about their polio vaccine clinical trials.

It is so unfortunate that it has taken seven years of bureaucratic hurdles before this phenomenal discovery has been made available. Glioblastomas have always been 100% fatal, until now.

Nathan's Story

A few years ago, I came across a boy named Nathan, who was battling with a brain tumor. He was eight years old and I noticed that his right eye was turned in. I asked Nathan if he was the student with the brain tumor. He said, "Yes." I asked him how long he had been suffering from the brain tumor. He said, "All of my life." I assumed that meant that he had never known a time when he was not battling with the brain tumor. I asked Nathan what form of treatment he was taking. He said, "Chemotherapy."

I asked Nathan if I could talk with his mother, and he said, "ok." As his mother approached me, I introduced myself and said that I had been researching cancer for over decade and asked her if she was aware of the research that was going on at Duke University. She said, "No."

I began to explain to her that Duke University was conducting government approved treatments against brain tumors with phenomenal success, and that they had been successful in eradicating brain tumors for the past seven years. I said, "*go to Google or YouTube and type in, Duke University and the polio vaccine, and you can see for yourself what they have discovered.*"

In the wake of almost a century of conventional treatments, the death tolls are staggering. Because of the Internet it is no longer easy to hide the tide of innovative discoveries in the war against cancer, and Duke University is leading the way. Unfortunately, because of the hold the pharmaceutical companies have, Duke University's phenomenal treatment, that has been going on for over seven years, is restricted, even though they have been successful in using this treatment against other types of cancer, including breast cancer.

FOODS

It stands to reason that an excellent beginning strategy would be to eliminate or substantially reduce commercial foods and bad habits (i.e., drinking, smoking) and to use organic foods, take vitamin supplements, exercise, a low stress lifestyle, and reduce electro-magnetic pollution, and the rate of cancer would fall precipitously. Unfortunately, for most, old habits are difficult to change, and, based on where one lives, making dramatic changes may not be as easy as it seems. But if one is to be effective in fighting uncontrolled cancer growth one must embrace change.

All the body's functions, every nerve impulse, thought, muscular action, brain function, emotion, and cell function begin with a chemical reaction, energy that is initially derived from the foods we eat. Foods contain specific elements such as oxygen, potassium, sodium, calcium, magnesium, phosphorous, chloride, etc., which maintain a specific number of electrons and protons. The interaction between the electrons and protons in the foods we eat, and the electrons and protons, within our bodies, determines the creation of energy.

If you will recall, Nobel Prize Recipient Dr. Otto Warburg was the first to discover that oxygen deprivation damages cellular respiration, which if continued, can result in a normal cell converting into a cancerous cell. On a cellular level oxygen is transported into the cellular membrane with the help of oxidative enzymes. These oxidative enzymes include iron, vitamin A, B2, B3, B5, B12, zinc, selenium, and water.

Whenever these nutrients are inhibited oxygen transport is inhibited and if this inhibition of vital nutrients continues irrevocable cellular damage occurs. If the inhibition of vital nutrients is left unchecked a normal functioning cell (*aerobic*) reverts to an abnormal functioning cell (*anaerobic*) – a cancer cell.

There are foods that are high in alkalinity (oxygen) and low in acidity. Consider adding more oxygen to one's biological environment. There are tables and charts on the Internet that can categorize all foods based on their oxygen level (pH). For example, a soft drink has a pH (114) of 2. Coffee has a pH balance of 4. Beer has a pH balance between 2.5 and 4.2. Coral Calcium has a pH of 10-12, and milk has a pH of 7.

There are specific foods that fight the onset of cancer. For example, Dr. Li presents an age-old remedy that may have been forgotten, that has proven to be effective in fighting cancer. He recommends eating specific foods that prevent the formation of blood vessels that tumors require in extracting nutrients, specifically, berries, cruciferous veggies, green tea, and garlic (Li, n.d.). Because all nutrients aid in health and well-being, it is safe to say that all foods that contain vital nutrients assist in fighting cancer, whether directly or indirectly.

Electrolyte Balance

Electrolytes facilitate the process of re-hydration. Too much pure water dissolves vital nutrients such as salts, which can impede cellular function. Too much pure water without enough salts can lead to water poisoning. This can occur when athletes train, using up vital nutrients such as salt. Waters that contain electrolytes allow the body to replenish without any ill effects (Kellum, 2000; Lyobebe, 2012).

Intracellular function also depends on electrolytes, which facilitate cellular metabolism. Without electrolytes the cell fails to function properly and if left unchecked may contribute to a process known as cellular fermentation. Electrolytes consist of Sodium (Na), Potassium (K), Calcium (Ca, Magnesium (Mg), Chloride Cl), Phosphate (HPO4), Sulphate (SO4) and Bicarbonate (HCO3). The major Intracellular electrolytes, which are part of the "Active group" that Dr. Otto Warburg identified, consist of Potassium and Phosphate (Kellum, 2000; Lyobebe, 2012; Warburg, 1956).

Fruits and Vegetables

While it may be difficult, if not impossible for most Americans to consume the recommended 5-9 servings of fruits and vegetables, an excellent strategy and alternative would be juicing. Juicing allows a large amount of nutrients to enter the body at one time. Juicing also aids in detoxification and promotes healthy cells. To begin with, try juicing one meal a day. One of my long-time friends suffered from Crones Disease for over a decade and illuminated all symptoms by simply juicing one meal a day and changing his diet to primarily, vegetables and fruits.

A diet that is poor in nutrients cannot supply the body with the required vitamins, minerals and enzymes that are pre-requisites to health and well-being. It may take months, years, or even decades before nutrient deficiencies result in illnesses and diseases, especially cancer and autoimmune diseases. But the reality is, three out of four Americans will die from diet related illnesses.

There are those who have embraced change and have moved away from large consumptions of meat and commercial foods, and now consider unprocessed fruits, vegetables, grains, and seed their main source of nutrition, along with adequate exercise, proper sleep, reduced stress, and a reduction in electro-magnetic devices, and as a result have been able to reduce and eradicate cancer.

A good example of this is the Amish. Ohio State University conducted a study on the incidence of cancer, between 1996 and 2003, on an Amish population consisting of 9,993 adults and concluded that they had a much lower incidence of cancer. Their study strongly suggested that a healthy lifestyle reduces the risk of cancer (Westman, 2010).

Sugar is highly acidic, and the preferred food of all cancer cells. Remember, cancer cells only produce 2 ATP (energy) and require more nutrients in order to survive. So, cancer cells develop an elaborate system whose sole purpose is to extract nutrients from the blood in order to feed themselves, and sugar is high on their list. If you will recall, the average child consumes 137 pounds of sugar a year. Too much sugar consumption will lead to poor health. A diet that is primarily vegetable based is high in oxygen and therefore alkaline. Processed foods are fundamentally acidic in nature.

Vitamin C

Nobel Prize recipient, Dr. Linus Pauling and Dr. Chi Dang, professor of Oncology Research at John Hopkins Medical University, and a team of scientists were among the first to discovered that vitamin C or N-acetylcysteine (NAC) can inhibit the growth of tumors (Johns Hopkins Medical Institutions, 2007).

When Dr. Pauling first announced this to the medical community he was ridiculed. Today, eight years later, the National Cancer Institute acknowledges that vitamin C (when administered intravenously, has proven to be more effective, reaching a higher level in the blood) can be effective against various types of cancer including, prostate, pancreatic, liver, ovarian, and colon.

Researchers at Sweden's Karolinska Institute found that women with breast cancer who take vitamin C as a supplement or from foods, in adequate quantities, have a higher survival rate. The article was published in the European Journal of Cancer (NCI, n.d.; Ferlay, 2010).

For those who have been diagnosed with cancer and prefer to go to a clinic that adheres to a natural organic method of healing using foods, there is the Gerson Clinic located in Tijuana Mexico. Dr. Gerson was born in Wongrowitz, Germany in 1881. He would eventually migrate to America and begin practicing medicine in New York in 1938. For the next 20 years he would successfully treat cancer patients, who had no hope after all conventional treatment had failed, using his dietary methods.

He was so successful and had gained such a reputation for eradicating cancer that in 1946 he was asked to speak before a congressional subcommittee on how diet can be effectively used to treat cancer. In 1958, after 30 years of clinical research and documentation, he published, "A Cancer Therapy, Results of Thirty Cases." Dr. Gerson died in 1958 but his method of treatment continues. The Gerson corporate office is in San Diego, California. There website is: https://gerson.org/gerpress/clinics/

Fasting

Cancer cells are poor producers of energy and as a result develop ways to rob the body of their natural nutrients. Fasting prevents cancer cells from receiving those nutrients. While there is more research to be done on the subject, it is believed by many that fasting is a viable way of eradicating cancer.

DR. REG MCDANIEL - GLYCONUTRIENTS AND THE SCIENCE OF GLYCOBIOLOGY

Another food group that has had little or no press is glyconutrients. The need for glyconutrients was first discovered in the 70s and has since spawned an entirely new category of biology called, glycobiology. Harpers medical textbook was revised in 1996 to include eight glyconutrients as essential for optimal health.

Glyconutrients are essential carbohydrates that affect all systems of the human body. For example, they act as immune modulators, and gate keepers to the cell, regulating what enters the cell. These specialized carbohydrates are also responsible for cellular communication and are responsible for a host of other biological functions.

Unfortunately, because of foreign toxins, processing of foods, and green picking most foods purchased commercially are deficient these vital nutrients, which is why supplements are important in maintaining optimal health. Unfortunately, these complex carbohydrates are difficult to find in supplement form. There is one website that carries these essential nutrients at a reasonable cost, Wellness Quest, and the glyconutrient brand name is "New Eden." The website is: http://www.wellnessquest.org/

If you were to go to YouTube.com and type in, "Dr. Reg McDaniel, glyconutrients," several videos would appear. My favorite, is: "Pass It On." To locate it type, "Reg McDaniel, Pass It On." Dr. Reg McDaniel was part of the first government study on glyconutrients. When you go to his website you can read about how this amazing science was first discovered.

The University of California, San Diego maintains a Glycobiology Research and Training Center, and will be sponsoring their 23rd Annual Glycobiology Symposium on March 20-21, 2020. They invite scientists and researchers from all over the world to exchange information on the latest discoveries.

For no less than 23 years, scientists, doctors, and researchers have been exchanging their findings. Yet, it seems that the local doctor is unaware of this phenomenal field of study, and the need for glyconutrients in order to maintain optimal health, or the long-term effects on the human body when there are gross deficiencies.

In January 2021 there will be an international conference on Glycobiology and Glycosciences in Rome Italy, and another International conference on May 18-19, in Montreal Canada. The Society for Glycobiology recently sponsored their annual symposium on November 2-5, 2019, in Phoenix Arizona.

Yet, if you were to ask your local doctor if he has ever heard of glyconutrients, or the science of Glycobiology he would, more than likely say, "no."

Glyconutrients are effective nutrients in the fight against cancer, both in the eradication of cancer cells and the prevention of cancer. For more information refer to my chapter on Glyconutrients.

CHAPTER 19
PULSATING ELECTRO-MAGNETIC FIELD THERAPY

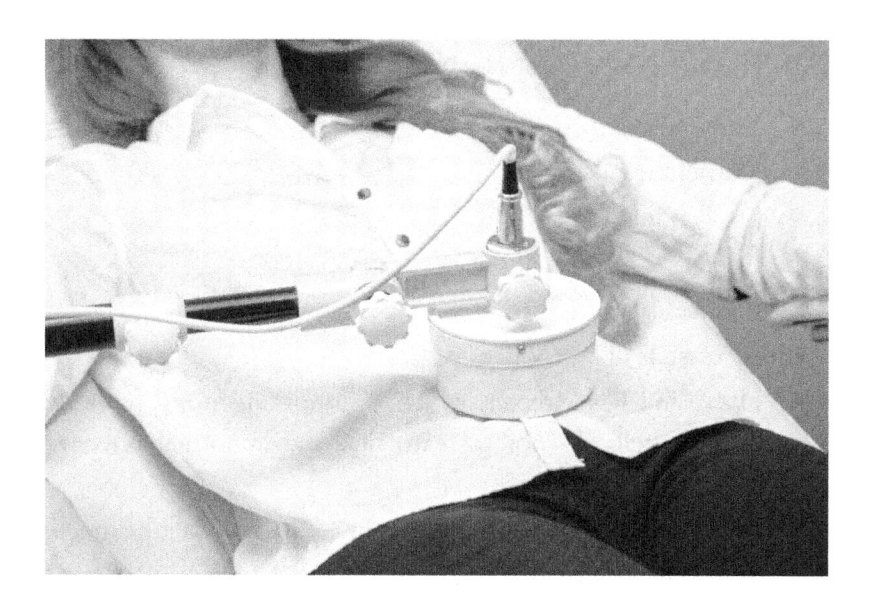

In 1979 The FDA approved Pulsating Electro-Magnetic Field (PEMF) devices for the use in non-union bone fractures. In 1998 the FDA approved PEMF devices they were approved for use in depression and anxiety. In 2011 PEMF therapy was approved for the treatment of cancer and tumors (FDA, 2005).

Since its introduction PEMF therapies have been effective in treating pain, inflammation, multiple sclerosis, carpal tunnel syndrome, arthritis, and most importantly, certain types of cancer. PEMF therapies have also been effective in restoring and enhancing the efficiency of mitochondria as well as the production of ATP, increasing cellular alkalinity, de-bunching of red blood cells, providing for easier flow and enhancing their ability to transport oxygen to the cell membrane; reducing blood pressure by 20% to 30% within minutes of treatment; restored electro-charge, allowing for an increased flow of lymph fluids, making them more efficient in delivering nutrients to the cell and extracting toxins and waste; restoring sodium potassium levels, which acts to reduce pain and increase the healing process by 30% (Bowers, 2015; Khurana, et al., 2009; The Interphone Group, 2010; Lehrer, 2011).

PEMF Therapy causes ions to be charged, which leads to increased:

- Immune health,
- Nutrient uptake
- Oxygen intake
- Decreases inflammation
- Reduces pain
- Increased ATP production,
- DNA and RNA repair, which is important in cell replication. Healthy cells do not recreate sick and abnormal cells. They replicate in like form.
- Stimulating the release of endorphins (positive well-being),
- Stimulates Antioxidant regulation

Re-differentiation of cells is vital in preventing cancer. It is important to note that most cancer cells are NOT instantaneously created. There are stages whereby a normal cell goes through before becoming cancerous.

The transformation of a healthy cell to a cancer cell is progressive. For example, a strong healthy cell becomes weakened, lacking energy (ATP production is limited). Eventually the weakened cell becomes inflamed, going from mild inflammation to heavy inflammation, becoming more and more deteriorated, eventually transforming into a cancer cell, from which there is no reversing. But, prior to this transformation, it is possible for a weakened and inflamed cell to become healthy, referred to as, cellular redifferentiation (Bowers, 2015; Khurana, et al., 2009; The Interphone Group, 2010; Lehrer, 2011).

Recharging of cellular energy can be accomplished in several ways. One simple way is through exercise. The constant movement of every cell in your body creates friction, which creates energy. Another way is using pulsating electro-magnetic field therapy (PEMF therapy), which has been FDA approved.

All PEMF devices are ion transporters, which stimulates the movement of protons, which in turn recharge and re-polarize the cell membrane, thus promoting a healthy energized cell. Scientists have discovered that when a cell membrane's electro-charge is less than 70 micro-volts then nutrients and oxygen intake is blocked. When the micro-volts are between 70 and 90 then nutrients and oxygen can penetrate the cell (Bowers, 2015; Khurana, et al., 2009; The Interphone Group, 2010; Lehrer, 2011).

While PEMF devices are not a cure all, they have proven to be an effective tool in re-establishing health and promoting a homeostasis. Life exists because of energy, and energy is created by way electro-magnetic frequencies, and the human body is composed of trillions of electro-magnetic impulses that allow for thoughts, motion, a heartbeat, and the movement of an eyelid.

It seems clear that our daily interaction with an ever-increasing number of electromagnetic instruments and devices has played havoc with the body's natural electro-magnetic impulses facilitating a host of problems and concerns, including illness and disease.

Recent scientific research has led to one of the most innovative instruments whose sole purpose is re-establishing the body's natural electro-magnetic (EM) rhythm, and in so doing stimulating, and accelerating the healing process, as well as reversing the effects of EM pollution. This new and innovation form of therapy is referred to as:

Pulsating Electro-magnetic Field (PEMF) Therapy. PEMF devices have FDA approval, and you can find PEMF mats on Amazon.com for approximately $795.00. They were also introduced to the American public via the Dr. Oz show. You can go to YouTube and type Dr. Oz, PEMF, to view the show.

CHAPTER 20

TWO KEY ORGANS – THE LIVER AND THE COLON

It is currently estimated that there are over 100,000 foreign toxics that pollute the air we breathe, the food we eat, and the water we drink. Once these toxins enter the human body a regiment of responses immediately go into effect and a key player is the liver. One of the key roles of the liver is to filter out poisons and toxins. So, maintaining a healthy liver is imperative. Here are a few tips on how to maintain a healthy liver.

Twice a day, just before mealtime, drink a cup of warm water with the juice of a half a lemon (fresh and preferably organic) or a tablespoon of apple-cider vinegar. This will aid in bile formation and efficient fat metabolism. It also helps to cleanse the liver.

With each meal add a little protein. Protein contains the amino acids that the liver requires in order to produce bile and to manufacturer the necessary enzymes needed for detoxifying the body of those harmful chemicals. Eggs are a great source of, both, protein and lecithin, which the liver uses to produce bile.

A daily source of fatty acids is also important, which can be found in Omega-3 (3,000 mg daily), walnuts, flaxseed oil, salmon, fish-oil supplements, and cod-liver oil.

A daily serving of essential minerals is also important, such as magnesium, zinc, and copper. They play a key role in detoxifying the liver from the massive amounts of foreign chemicals that invade the human body daily. Vitamin C, most B vitamins, folic acid, and flavoids also play an important role.

In researching other examples of scientific research that promote vitamins, minerals, and various other elements in fighting I was overwhelmed with the amount of research on the subject. There are literally thousands of research reports, which makes it almost impossible to document within the pages of this book. But to give you an idea here is a brief example:

Metformin: In January 2015, the Proceedings of the National Academy of Sciences, along with the journal of European Oncology (2014), published the findings of the antidiabetic drug, metformin and its ability to reduce cancer (Spratt, 2013; Rothermundt, 2014).

Calcium: In the February (1999) issue of Reader's Digest published an article entitled, "The Superstar Nutrient," stating that according to the Journal of the American Medical Association, colon cancer patients who consumed 1500 milligrams of calcium per day reversed the uncontrolled growth of cancer cells. Calcium not only aids in the production of bone, but it also assists in the transfer of oxygen into the cell. It is estimated that calcium is responsible for 147 body functions. In a recent study, published in the International Journal of Cancer, they concluded that calcium, by foods or supplements, reduced the risk of colorectal cancer.

Curcumin: On October 2012, the journal, Carcinogenesis, published an article stating that, "curcumin" helps in preventing metastasis (Killian, et al., 2012).

Soy Foods: In August 2013, The University of Illinois published an article stating that "soy foods" protect against colon cancer (University of Illinois, 2013).

Aspirin: August 2014, the journal, Cancer Research published an article stating that "Aspirin" may help delay breast cancer recurrence (Gaut, 1993; Giovannucci, 1995). (LifeExtension, 2014).

Vitamin D: In 2012 the Proceedings of the National Academy of Sciences of the United States of America, published an article that states that the intake of vitamin D reduces the risk of cancer. In December 2012 McGill University published an article stating that vitamin D helps prevent cancer. Another study in the journal, Endocrinology, concluded that vitamin D, helps in the reduction of prostate cancer (Tabar, et al., 2012; McGill, 2012; Qadan, 2000).

Saffron: Recent research into the Mediterranean diet have found that the spice saffron reverses and slows tumor growth (Provos, 2015).

CHAPTER 21
ACEROGENIN THERAPY

Types of Cancer: gastrointestinal, lung, breast, prostate, liver, colon, cervical, kidney, gastric, bronchial, and others.

Acetogenin is a natural substance found in one of the largest groups of plants (annonaceae) in the world. The name of the plant would depend on who you asked. In Brazil it is called, chirimoya. In Latin America it is called, guanábana. In America, it is called the pawpaw tree. It also goes by the name, custard apple, also known in English as, graviola.

In 1977 researchers from Purdue University narrowed the plant substance with the anti-cancer agents to annonaceae acetogenin. In 2011 the Journal of Nutrition and Cancer published the results from Virginia Tech in Blacksburg, VA. Their findings stated that acetogenin inhibits the growth of breast cancer cells, while having no ill effect on normal cells. Researchers found that acetogenin killed cancer cells by inhibiting their ability to produce energy (ATP).

As noted, earlier cancer cells only produce 2 ATP while a healthy cell will produce 32 ATP. Deficient the amount of energy to survive, cancer cells develop a higher metabolism. Absent their ability to produce the needed energy for survival, they simply die (Liu, 2012; Dai, Schmelz, Ju, Canning, & Zhou, 2011; Oberlies, Chang, & McLaughlin, 1997; Oberlies, Jones, Corbett, Fotopoulos, & McLaughlin, 1995).

It is fascinating to note that acetogenin accomplishes this by using oxygenated groups of chemicals, which aligns itself to the "Warburg

Effect," which states that if you can increase the oxygen content a cancer cell will, invariably, die (Warburg, 1966). In 2012 a group of researchers substantiated its anti-cancer fighting ability. You can find pawpaw and graviola supplements (a natural herbal supplement) from several online stores. They are one of the most potent dietary additives in fighting cancer (Liu, 2012; Dai, Schmelz, Ju, Canning, & Zhou, 2011; Oberlies, Chang, & McLaughlin, 1997; Oberlies, Jones, Corbett, Fotopoulos, & McLaughlin, 1995).

The number of research articles that validate the need for vitamins, minerals and herbs in the battling cancer are overwhelming. Proper nutrition is a key player in cancer prevention and mitigation.

CHAPTER 22

OXYGEN THERAPIES: PHOTODYNAMIC THERAPY (PDT), OR BLUE LIGHT THERAPY

Types of Cancer, USA: skin, lungs, bladder, esophageal

Types of Cancer outside USA: skin, bladder, esophageal, mouth, gastric, colon, & bronchial

Photodynamic Therapy (PDT), or **Blue Light Therapy** uses oxygenated molecules to preferentially destroy only cancer cells. The FDA approved the use of PDT in 1996. Within the mainstream medical community PDT is considered the fifth acknowledged form of treatment (surgery, chemotherapy, radiation therapy, bio-immune therapy).

PDT therapy consists of three parts, light, photosensitizer, and oxygen. A photosensitizing drug is administered intravenously into the body up to 48 hours before treatment is administered. Once it is absorbed, normal cells with excrete the drug. Since cancer cells do not excrete the photosensitizer the cancer cells become the target.

Thus, the photosensitizer is used to identify the target cells. The light is used to activate or turn on the killing power of the oxygen molecules through oxidation. Because PDT only target cancer cells, it does not damage adjacent tissue and there is minimal trauma to the patient. Unfortunately, PDT works better with those with lighter skin. The darker the skin the less effective they are to the light administered.

HYDROGEN PEROXIDE THERAPY (HPT)

Types of Cancer: Skin

Hydrogen Peroxide Therapy (HPT) is made up of two parts hydrogen and two parts oxygen (H_2O_2), which has proven to be an ideal therapy for certain skin cancers. Since hydrogen peroxide carries an extra oxygen molecule, it can wreak havoc on cancer cells that are easily accessed, such as within the skin.

The therapy is quite simple, simply apply 4 to 8 ounces of 35% Food Grade hydrogen peroxide to a full bath of, moderately, hot water, and soak for approximately, 30 to 45 minutes. The heat from the bath water will open the skin pours and allow the oxygen molecules to penetrate. This process should be continued two to three times a week for about six weeks.

After six weeks there should be substantial improvement or even total eradication of the skin cancer cells. 35% Food Grade hydrogen peroxide can be purchased online, including Amazon.com. Since HPT is non-invasive the side effects are re-oxygenated skin, and healthier skin. If you have very sensitive skin or thin skin, you may want to apply only 4 ounces or less. It is important to note that the killing agents are the oxygen molecules.

HYPOBARIC THERAPY

Hypobaric Oxygen Therapy is a process whereby the body is exposed to 100% oxygen at pressures above normal. It increases the oxygen levels in the blood, which is then circulated throughout the body, effecting cellular tissue.

Wounds require oxygen to heal. By exposing the body to large sums of oxygen at one time, the body heals quicker. Hypobaric oxygen therapy is a well-established therapy for decompression sickness. This is a condition that occurs when scuba divers return to the surface of the water too rapidly. Hypobaric oxygen therapy is also used for a variety of illnesses, including wounds that refuse to heal due to too much radiation.

It is well established that cancer cells die when exposed to high amounts of oxygen. Thus, using this form of oxygen therapy has proven to be a viable therapy.

TESTOSTERONE REPLACEMENT THERAPY

Prostate cancer is one of the leading killers for men over 50. It was once believed that the introduction of testosterone as a treatment for prostate cancer would only exacerbate the problem. Today scientists now know that testosterone therapy helps in preventing cancer as well as reducing and eradicating cancer.

Dr. Morgentaler, a hormone researcher from Harvard Medical School was one of the first doctors to go against convention and successfully treat those who were diagnosed with prostate cancer with testosterone replacement therapy (Morgentaler, 2008).

In June of 2014 the Journal of Urology, published an article that concluded that testosterone replacement therapies do not increase the risk of cancer, but in fact prevent, reduce and eradicate prostate cancer. Another recent study published in the, Annals of

Pharmacotherapy, concluded, for men age 66 and older, testosterone replacement treatments also provide a protective agent against heart attacks (Gaylis, et al. 2006; Baillargeon, 2014).

GENE TARGETED THERAPY

For those who have been diagnosed with inoperable brain tumors, as well as other forms of cancer, there is the Burzynski clinic, Houston Texas, which acquired its reputation for successfully treating inoperable stage four brain tumors, which were considered 100% fatal.

Initially, those who could participate in these trials consisted solely of those who had undergone chemo and radiation therapy, which had proven to be ineffective, leaving the cancer patient with no hope of survival. After participating in Dr. Burzynski's therapy over 30% survived. Dr. Burzynski pioneered gene targeted therapy.

He takes your medical insurance, unfortunately, the FDA will not allow him to export his therapy and it is currently restricted to his one location, in Houston, Texas. If you have Netflix, there are two documentaries on Dr. Burzynski. You may also be able to find these documentaries on YouTube. For an extensive review of his findings refer to my chapter on Dr. Burzynski. His website is: http://www.burzynskiclinic.com/

IMMUNOTHERAPY

The immune system and its effectiveness in combating cancer were underrated by scientific research until recently. Today's most innovative and effective cancer therapy designs centers on the immune system. The 21st century will probably be remembered as the time of exponential multiplication of information. This would include a new form of cancer therapy, referred to as: immunotherapy.

There are four common forms of immunotherapy, **monoclonal antibodies**, **adoptive cell therapy**, **cancer vaccines**, and **non-**

specific immunotherapies. Monoclonal antibodies assist in the activation of lymphocytes, which then seek and destroy cancer cells. Adoptive cell therapy differs from monoclonal antibodies, in that the lymphocytes are extracted from the patient's tumor, then they are modified, augmented, and multiplied in vitro, before reinserting back into the tumor area (Texas Oncology, n.d.).

TARGETING T-CELLS

A new form of non-specific immunotherapy involves T-cells. An ongoing concern in fighting cancer has to do with the location of cancer cells. T-cells often find it difficult to distinguish between normal cells and cancer cells. This is because cancer cells can hide from the body's immune system. Realizing this, researchers at the University of Pennsylvania's Abramson Cancer Center and Perelman School of Medicine developed a protocol for fighting certain types of cancer.

They remove T-cells from cancer patients and genetically altered them, reprogramming them to attack chronic lymphocytic leukemia (a B cell cancer), and then infusing them back into the cancer patient. The results of their pilot studies, which initially involved three patients whose only other option would have been a bone marrow transplant with only a 20% survival rate, are in stark contrast to conventional therapies (Kalos, et al., 2011; Penn Medicine, 2011; Williams, 2011).

"Within three weeks, the tumors had been blown away, in a way that was much more violent than we ever expected, it worked much better than we thought it would," said senior author Carl June, MD, director of Translational Research and a professor of Pathology and Laboratory Medicine in the Abramson Cancer Center (Penn Medicine, 2011).

One of the positive side effects is that the T cells develop a memory. This was evident as the cells multiplied and months later were still vigilant against cancerous cells throughout the body. Further studies involve using the same process with other forms of cancer, including acute lymphocytic leukemia and non-Hodgkin's lymphoma (Kalos, et al., 2011; Penn Medicine, 2011; Williams, 2011; Texas Oncology, n.d.).

Dr. Bent Jacobsen, a Danish scientist with Immunocore, a privately owned, clinical-stage, UK-based biotechnology company, developed a unique approach, that is radically different, in working with T-cells. Because T-cells find it difficult to recognize cancer cells Immunocore engineered a T cell receptor-based targeting system that develops small protein molecules, called ImmTACs (Immune mobilizing mTCR Against Cancer), which acts much like glue.

These glue-like protein molecules glue themselves to cancer cells and then glue themselves to T-cells, while leaving healthy cells alone. Once the T-cell is attached to the cancer cell via these protein molecules (ImmTACs) the T-cell receptor binds to the cancer cell and destroys it.

You can view a video of these T-cells, activated by protein molecules, killing cancer cells, on the company website (www.immunocore.com). To date, there is no other company in the world that is actively working with T-cells in this manner (Baeuerle, Patrick, & Christian, 2012; Life Extension, 2013; Liddy, et al., 2012).

WHAT TO AVOID

Hopefully, this small list of research articles validating nutrition will lead you in the right direction. In creating an effective battle plan for the eradication of cancer it is not always about what to do or take, but what not to do or to avoid or minimize, if possible.

For example, avoiding or limiting the use of: CT scans, living under or near electro power stations or electric cables, vaccines, sodas, excess amounts of sugar, fluorinated water, electric devices (including microwaves), and avoiding conventional chemotherapy and radiation therapy.

If you should decide that chemo is a viable option, proceed only after completing a "Chemo sensitivity test."

We now live in a toxic planet and the proliferation of illnesses and diseases is one of the consequences, which is why every individual needs to be proactive. Unfortunately, much of the information presented in this book has been dismissed by the mainstream media, even though it is readily available on the Internet for those diligent enough to seek it out.

CHAPTER 23
ORGANIZATIONS

The following is a list of a few of the more renown or recognized organizations that provide the most advanced treatments in the world.

The Gerson Clinics are in America, Mexico, and Hungry. In America they are in San Diego, California and you can be seen by appointment only. You can obtain all their information on their website: http://gerson.org

Other important contacts are as follows:

Burzynski Clinic
Dr. Burzynski
9432 Katy Freeway
Houston, TX 77055
(800) 714-7181
International Calls +1 (713) 335-5697
Website: http://www.burzynskiclinic.com/Burzynski

Exsalus Health & Wellness Center
Dr. Lederman & Dr. Pulde
Category: Family Practice
532 1/2 N Vista St
Los Angeles, CA 90036 (323) 876-3600 http://www.exsalus.com

Dr. McDougall's Health and Medical Center
Dr. John & Mary McDougall
PO Box 14039

Santa Rosa, CA 95402
(800) 941-7111
(707) 538-8609
(616) 874-8155 - Skype
(707) 538-0712 -Fax
Website: http://www.drmcdougall.com/about.html

EDUCATIONAL VIDEOS

The following list is some of the educational videos that I came across, which helped in understanding what has happened to our foods and why organic consumption is imperative, and some of the alternative approaches in treating cancer. You can find them on YouTube, and Netflix:

- Knives over Forks
- Foods Inc.
- Supersize Me
- Dr. Reg McDaniel and Glyconutrients, video, "Pass it On."
- Fat, Sick, and Nearly Dead
- PEMF & Dr. Oz
- Jeff Novick, RD, MS – Dietician

CHAPTER 24

THE GREAT PHYSICIAN

"Daughter, take courage; your faith has made you well."
–Jesus of Nazareth

And Jesus said to him, "Go; your faith has made you well."
–Jesus of Nazareth

"Science without religion is lame; religion without science is blind."
–Albert Einstein

Einstein was a brilliant man who, after developing the theory of relativity realized that his equation inherently concluded that the universe had a beginning. The work of Edwin Hubble (of the Hubble telescope) confirmed that the universe was expanding, which also inherently concluded that there was, at some point, a beginning.

For Einstein, this meant that there had to be a creator. When Einstein was later interviewed, he was asked, *"Do you accept the historical existence of Jesus?"* Einstein responded, *"Unquestionably! No one can read the Gospels without feeling the actual presence of Jesus. His personality pulsates in every word. No myth is filled with such life"* (Viereck, 1929).

While Einstein may have never had a personal relationship with God, he disapproved of those who did not believe there was a God who created everything. He stated, *"In view of such harmony in the cosmos which I, with my limited human mind, am able to recognize, there are yet people who say there is no God. But what really makes me angry is that they quote me for the support of such views*" (Lowenstein, P. H., 1968).

Tihomir Dimitrov's book (2007), "50 Nobel Laureates and Other Great Scientists Who Believe in God" lists fifty Nobel Prize recipients who believe in God, which would include, Winston Churchill, Albert Schweitzer, Johannes Kepler, Theodore Roosevelt, Nelson Mandela, Martin Luther King, Sir Isaac Newton, Galileo, Copernicus, Descartes, Pascal, and Pasteur, et al. (Dimitrov, T., 2007).

I am far from brilliant, but even in my humble mind, I acknowledge that there is a God, who sent "Jesus" to redeem me of my sins and to restore my fellowship with the God who created me, and who healed me of my ailments. So, I would be remiss if I was to publish a book on cancer and I did not introduce you to the "Great Physician" – Jesus of Nazareth.

I would be the first to tell you that I am a far cry from someone who has lived a pristine Christian life. In fact, I lived much of my life in rebellion. My life is riddled with countless sins, indiscretions, and wild living.

In 2005, I remember sitting in my living room, alone, coughing up blood, and thinking to myself, *"if I were to die, right here, right now, no one would find me for days, and what a sad death it would be, what an unfortunate legacy I would leave."* I ended up driving myself to the emergency room, barely able to breathe, and a body covered with anxious perspiration. I did not follow hospital protocols, I forced myself into the examiner's room, ripped off my shirt, and said, *"I can't breathe or cease from coughing, and with each cough I spew up blood."*

They immediately admitted me and the next thing I know, I was on a bed, with doctors and nurses hovering over me. After a brief examination my emergency room doctor said that I was literally hours away from death. She said that my body had a problem starting and that they needed to help it start. I was administered what seemed to be a continuous flow of steroids, that slowly dripped into my veins. The steroids allowed me to breathe by reducing the inflammation of my bronchiole tubes.

After a week I was released and put on a prescription of drugs. Soon thereafter I noticed lumps underlying my abdomen. First there was just one, and then two appeared. At first, I didn't think much of it, but then they continued to grow. After talking with a close friend, I naturopathically healed myself and I began my research on cancer.

But the real story in my experience with near death, my wake-up call, was that realized most of my life was filled with regret, and I did not want to continue down that road. I wanted to change directions, find peace, and rest from all the troubles my past life had brought. I wanted to restore my relationships with my children and family. But more importantly, I wanted to find peace with God, and to feel His presence.

I will never know your circumstances, your illness or disease, but I do know that whatever it is, there is a merciful God who earnestly desires to heal you. Understanding God's Christ and accepting Him into your life will open the doors to peace, forgiveness, healing, and most of all, an eternal relationship with the God who created you.

Does this mean that when you accept Jesus as your personal savior you will automatically be healed? God's priority is to heal your broken relationship with Him. God has said "your faith has made you well." What I do know is that the God of creation is merciful, and He has a purpose for your life – which is to be in fellowship with Him. God is also a God who desires for you to prosper and to be in good health. The following is the story of God's provision.

THE GOSPEL ACCORDING TO GOD'S DIVINE TEACHINGS

God created mankind in His own image for one purpose, to be in an intimate, loving, and obedient relationship with Him. But mankind rebelled and decided to follow his/her own thoughts and beliefs, which continues to this day. Such rebellion is referred to as sin, and the penalty for sin is death. In this instance, "death" refers to physical death, meaning that mankind will not live forever, and spiritual death, meaning that mankind, because of sin, is eternally separated from the God who created him/her.

However, God is quite merciful and just and earnestly desires to save anyone, who is willing, from this eternal separation. So, God, in His wisdom promised to bring "Christ," through which God would reconcile mankind to Himself.

Jesus Christ is a real historical person who was born, lived and died. However, Christ was unlike any other man, for he had no earthly father, was born from a virgin, named Mary, and he had never sinned against God. Christ died for one purpose, to redeem everyone who believes in Him, from their sins, providing a pathway for eternal fellowship with the God who created them. Finally, unlike other men, Christ was resurrected and lives today. He sits at the right hand of God, in heaven.

To accept His provision all you must do, is say the following words,

> *"God forgive me for my sins, I accept Christ as my savior, your provision for my life, and today, I choose to follow you and turn away from my past life. Today, I choose to be eternally bound to you, as your servant, please come into my life and become my Lord and savior."*

If you need healing you can pray the following, but before you do, you need to believe that the God who created you is able to heal you. You must also be free from all your past sins, having turned away and forsaken them. If this is the case, you can pray the following:

> *"God, I ask for your divine healing over my life [be specific about your illness or disease], and ask Christ Jesus, who died for me, will cleanse my body of its illness. I pray this believing that you are the "Great Physician" and able to cleanse me completely. I pray this in the name of Jesus, for there is no greater name in all of heaven who can heal my body. Amen."*

If you prayed this prayer, expect divine intervention. I am reminded of the following verse of scripture that I have always found comfort in. *"I will lift up mine eyes unto the hills, from whence cometh my help, my help cometh from the Lord, who neither slumbers nor sleeps"* Psalms 121:1(King James Version).

If you prayed and asked Christ into your life, you are now a child of God. If you prayed for physical healing expect a miracle. But I am reminded of the various ways that God chooses to heal. "...Their fruit will be for food, and their leaves for healing." Ezekiel 47:12. "...The leaves of the tree were for the healing of the nations." Revelation 22:2. God often used herbs to heal His people.

As I wrote this book on cancer I have been reminded of the doctors and scientists who used foods and herbs to heal their patients. The Gerson Clinic is a prime example, and the number of people who have been healed from cancer are numerous, too numerous to count. In the greatest study ever done on cancer, "The China Study," where 880,000 people participated, they concluded that diet was the central theme.

Dr. Reg McDaniel was the first to discover Glyconutrients (monosaccharides), and in doing so, expanded the world of science to include the science of, Glycobiology. Glyconutrients are extracted from the leaves of the Aloe Vera plant. "Their fruit will be for food, and their leaves for healing" Ezekiel 47:12.

It is estimated that, no less than 10,000 research papers are published each month on the healing power of these monosaccharides. These simple monosaccharides have been linked to the healing of cancer, autoimmune disease, and a host of other illnesses and ailments. They are also responsible for a host of biological functions. The introduction of these monosaccharides can accomplish something far greater than any drug can offer. There is no doctor on this earth that can prescribe something more powerful and life changing than the introduction of these simple monosaccharides. When they are present in the body, it functions far more optimally, when they are found to be deficient in the body, there is a breakdown in biological function.

Fat, Sick, and Nearly Dead is a documentary about a man by the name of Joe Cross. You can find his documentary on Netflix, and or YouTube. Joe was obese and had a crippling autoimmune disease. Desperate, Joe decided to go on a 60-day juice fast, under the supervision of a physician. Deciding to allow natural foods to cleanse him changed his life forever. He not only lost weight, he was healed from his autoimmune disease. He no longer had to deal with prescription drugs. He no longer had to deal with an autoimmune disease that had crippled his ability to function normally. He was healed.

Joe's story is not unusual, but far more common than we have been led to believe. He had eliminated the bad foods, that debilitated him, and re-introduced himself to the natural foods that God created for healing. You can find Joe's story at: www.rebootwithjoe.com/.

The Bible says, "My people perish for a lack of knowledge…" (Hosea 4:6). I believe this is just as true today as when it was first written. When it comes to cancer, the lack of knowledge can cost you your life, which is why I wrote this book. For too long we gave too much credit to conventional methods, dictated by pharmaceutical companies, as they have influenced the medical community. We, as a society, have moved away from the natural methods of herbs and organic foods, and replaced them with conventional methods, that have proven to be more deadly and debilitating than ever imagined.

But the tide is changing. With the advent of the Internet, is far more difficult to dismiss the massive amounts of research and discovery on cancer. As the death tolls mount, and the debilitating side effects of conventional treatments become real, people are beginning to ask the question, "Are there viable alternatives to conventional methods, in the treatment of cancer?" And the answer is, "Yes."

God, in His wisdom, provided a natural way to heal the nations from their illnesses and diseases, using natural remedies. Joe Cross discovered the healing power of foods, and the list of others is countless. Hopefully, you will allow God's natural resources to heal you.

CHAPTER 25
SUMMARY

"...nobody today can say that one does not know what cancer and its prime cause be. On the contrary, there is no disease whose prime cause is better known, so that today ignorance is no longer an excuse that one cannot do more about prevention."
– Revised lecture at the meeting of the Nobel-Laureates on June 30, 1966, at Lindau, Lake Constance, Germany, by Nobel Prize recipient, Dr. Otto Warburg, Director, Max Planck-Institute for Cell Physiology, Berlin-Dahlem.

The Watchman has been examining the truth and declares, "My people perish for a lack of knowledge." Hosea 4: 6

This exhaustive collection of information is not the end but the beginning in cancer research. Even as I write these concluding remarks, there is ongoing research and discoveries that are currently being published.

Having said that, let me remind you that the contents of this book are meant to be a light of information and a road map, and chronology of cancer, from the first doctor and scientist to discover its origins, and the variables that cause it to grow (Dr. Otto Warburg), to those innovative scientists and doctors whose tireless research have brought about cures and remedies, ranging from prevention to eradication.

At the turn of the 20th century cancer in America accounted for 4% of all deaths. Today cancer accounts for approximately 25% of all deaths in America (CDC, 2017), and this figure has not changed since 1950, despite all the new drugs that have been introduced over the past 70 years (Kolata, 2009a; Spector, 2010).

According to the national Cancer Institute, in 2019 it is estimated that 606,880 Americans will die of cancer and 1.8 million Americans will be diagnosed with cancer for the first time (NCI, 2019). Historically the proliferation of cancer at epidemic proportions is a 20th and 21st century phenomenon. So, what has changed that would cause the rate of cancer to climb exponentially?

Based on 21st century science what is cancer? How does it originate? What are some of the factors that allow it to grow? Why has it become a major killer of adults and children? Has the perception of cancer changed based on new information? Is there any cohesive data that brings this together?

THE PRIMARY CAUSE OF CANCER

The primary cause, as defined by Nobel-Prize Recipient, Dr. Warburg, is because a cell has a damaged respiration (anaerobic respiration) – the inability to utilize oxygen in the production of energy, a process referred to as fermentation. It is important to note that all cancer cells produce energy anaerobically but not all anaerobic cells are cancerous.

Once a normal cell is converted into a cancer cell the process is irreversible (Warburg, 1956). Based on 21st century science, scientists have not only validated the work of Dr. Otto Warburg for his exhaustive research and discoveries but have added to his research without compromising his findings (Kellum, 2000; Campbell, et al., 2008).

Producing energy anaerobically creates a host of problems. To begin with, the amount of energy created is insufficient to maintain cellular life. To compensate these mutant cells, which are cancerous, evolve, losing all specialized function and increase in their metabolic rate producing more mucus, circumventing apoptosis, and begin to reproduce uncontrollably.

To compensate for energy deficiencies, these cancerous cells release growth factors that cause blood vessels to branch out and form new blood vessels that grow into the cancerous tumor, which supplies the cancer cells with the required nutrients necessary for survival, and at the same time starving the individual.

Dr. Warburg discovered that oxygen was the key variable in the propagation and termination of cancer cells. This truth is as viable a discovery today as when it was first discovered, in the late 1920s. Dr. Warburg demonstrated that cancer begins when a cell produces energy (ATP) without the use of oxygen, in the same way plants produce energy. He also demonstrated that by increasing the oxygen level by 35% all cancer cells invariably die. This forgotten fact of science and biology has had enormous repercussions in treating cancer. This valuable piece of information is a cornerstone in the world of health and well-being.

SECONDARY CAUSES

So, what has changed in the last 100 years to cause such an exponential increase in the rate of cancer in America? In a nutshell, everything relating to food, environment, and lifestyle has changed. What has also changed is the overwhelming introduction of foreign chemicals and toxins, many of which are carcinogenic that have polluted our oceans, streams, foods, and the produce we consume daily. We all live in a toxic planet.

What exactly caused a damaged respiration can also be a result of multiple variables working in concert or solo. An example of a variable working solo would be the introduction of radiation. An example of multiple variables could be chronic stress, which suppresses the immune system, and long-term exposure to commercial foods that deprive the body of essential nutrients required for proper cellular metabolism. The two in combination allow for the unchecked growth of cancer cells. The secondary causes of cancer that are directly and indirectly responsible for the proliferation of cancer are countless.

Changes in Environment

Currently there are more than 100,000 foreign chemicals and toxins in our atmosphere, many of which are carcinogenic and excitotoxic. Even the lifestyle of the average American has changed dramatically over the past 100 years, evolving from a lifestyle that included daily exercise to a lifestyle predominantly sedentary. This is evidenced by the dramatic increase in childhood obesity (Riely, 2011).

The air we breathe contains less oxygen and is often filled with a host of chemicals and toxins. This is especially true for those living in highly congested urban dwellings, such as New York City, Los Angeles, Chicago, etc. Our oceans are so contaminated that people run the risk of mercury poisoning if they consume too much tuna or sword fish.

Changes in Food

Most of the foods Americans consume are a product of genetically altered seeds, produced on soil depleted of many of its natural nutrients. To keep up with the demands of an expanding urban population, foods are now "Green picked," laced with chemicals that delay maturation then just before they are displayed, they are sprayed again with chemicals that promote maturation. In the processing of foods preservatives are added to delay decay, promote shelf life, and enhance flavor, such as Thimerosal, which is a version of mercury (FDA, 2012).

According to Senate Bill #264, Published in 1936, foods produced, consumed by Americans are deficient in nutrient values. In a study conducted between 1936 -1992 researchers found that several fruits and vegetables were deficient in vitamins and minerals (Bergner, 1997). Today, it is estimated that one would have to consume 50 peaches to receive that same nutrient value of a peach produced in 1950. The water Americans drink is no longer safe for drinking unless it has been filtered and even then, researchers have discovered trace elements of pharmaceutical drugs in many major cities and metropolitan areas (Donn, Mendoza, & Pritchard, 2008; Mendoza, 2008).

What is also of major concern are the secondary causes of cancer, which have everything to do with how commercial foods are processed, diet, and environmental influences. These cumulative adverse influences inhibit the "Active Group," (first coined by Nobel Prize recipient, Dr. Otto Warburg, a, in the late 1920s), which refers to a specific list of natural ingredients, found in foods required for normal cellular metabolism and the creation of energy.

The procedures of processing American foods destroys all of the natural nutrients, including six of the eight essential carbohydrates (glycans) found in wheat, oats, rice, etc.; that these eight carbohydrates are essential for an array of human functions, and that their absence would play out on a grand scale resulting in all forms of cancer, autoimmune disease, and other types of illnesses.

Only in the last 120 years have economies promoted large farming with no regard to natural soil enrichment, but rather, the addition of certain synthetic nutrients, not taking into consideration the overall nature of soil composition, creating a soil imbalance. Only is the last few decades have commercial fish farms produced commercially grown fish that have been fed foods unnatural to their normal diet resulting in nutrient deficient fish.

Only since 1949 have commercial food manufacturers introduced flavor enhancers referred to as excitotoxins, which are responsible for the onset of cancer, its propagation, and the destruction of neurons that leads to autoimmune disease, and to damaged DNA.

Historically, the consumption of meat, as a major part of a diet, is primarily a 20th and 21st century phenomenon. In past generations the over consumption of meat was considered a luxury that few could afford. Dr. Campbell, et al., could demonstrate, emphatically that casein, a natural substance found in all dairy products, is toxic to the liver. When incorporated as part of a normal diet (20%) it overwhelms the liver with toxicity, inhibiting the production of antineoplastons, which are required in the modulation of our cancer genes.

Changes in Culture

Urban living has spawned a new breed of killers, coined, "The silent killer" or "Urban stress" Psychological stress not only depresses the immune system, it inhibits the flow of oxygen and other vital nutrients from getting to the cell. Psychological stress has a direct effect on the reproductive system, the endocrine, immune, and nervous systems (Barry, 2011; Baum, Revenson, & Singer, 2007; Brydon, et al., 2007; Reiche, Nunes, & Morimoto, 2004; Cohen, Tyrell, & Smith, 1991; Wright, 2010; Abbott, Blazek, & Foster, 2010; Gourounti, et al. 2010).

Environmental influences also extend psychologically in relation to urban stress, which has a direct impact on immune function and DNA replication. Urban stress depletes our supply of vitamins and essential nutrients, which results in individuals becoming susceptible to illness and disease.

Commercialism

Commercialism never took into consideration the impact processed foods would have on the human system. Realizing that the procedures in processing foods resulted in killing all active natural nutrients, there was some attempt to replace natural nutrients with synthetic nutrients, such as those found in cereals (vitamin K, Vitamin A, B, etc.) and milk (vitamin D).

There were countless consequences that commercialism and the procedures of processing American foods did not foresee. Including the harsh reality that synthetic nutrients are not assimilated by the human body in the same way natural ingredients found in unprocessed foods are assimilated by the human body.

Cellular Communication and Glycobiology

What has been of interest is how the human body communicates comprehensively between systems. Scientists assumed that it all began with the nervous system by way of neurotransmitters.

We now know, through 21st century breakthroughs in science that there is an active communication system that extends beyond the nervous system and directs human function on a cellular level. The process is called cellular communication, which was discovered in the last 25 years and falls under the science of glycobiology, which prior to the 1990s did not exist as a science.

The process of cellular communication not only plays a pivotal role in the health and well-being of every cell, cellular communication also regulates cellular access and system functions, including the regulation of the immune system, and its significance in the battle against cancer cannot be overstated.

There are eight essential glycans (sugars) only recently discovered (1970s) by modern scientists. What modern science has discovered is that these eight essential sugars are prerequisites to optimal human health, and cellular function. These simple sugars are also responsible for countless other human functions including, cellular communication, and immune modulation.

The Science of Glycobiology is so new that Harper's Medical textbook was revised in 1996 to include these eight essential sugars as necessary ingredients for optimal health. This little-known fact is probably one of the greatest scientific discoveries of the 20th century. It is estimated that 10,000 research papers are published each month about glycobiology, and many esteemed universities now maintain a glycobiology department.

When a diet is absent or deficient in these essential nutrients (vitamins, minerals, glyconutrients, trace elements, enzymes, amino acids, etc.) the body lacks optimal health. Over time this lack of enough nutrients will play a toll on health and lead to illness.

For example, if one is lacking enough glyconutrients the immune system becomes unbalanced and incapable of communicating efficiently on a cellular level as well as properly regulating immune function. This can result in either an overactive or underactive immune system. An overactive immune system results in autoimmune disease. An underactive immune system results in unchecked cancer growth.

It is important to note that these glyconutrients are not, in themselves, healing agents, but rather, catalysts, which promote health and well-being, by regulating, and stimulating immune function and cellular communication. They are also responsible for countless other biological functions.

CHAPTER 26

THE CANCER PARADIGM SHIFT

Based on the culmination of research and empirical data, a paradigm shift has occurred in the perception of cancer and in the progressive treatment of cancer. To align with these scientific discoveries and to coincide with the paradigm shift on cancer a new definition of cancer is required. It is as follows:

> *"Cancer is not a disease but a symptom or a condition of an efficient biological system whose daily production of three billion new cells also produces defective cells, from which 'Spontaneous cancers' originate. This efficient biological system can be compromised due to a lack of adequate nutrition, oxygen, overwhelming exposure to foreign toxins, excessive amounts of prolonged stress, lack of adequate sleep, or electro-magnetic imbalance.*
>
> *The guardians of this biological system are genetically and immunologically linked. Once this biological system has been compromised and the genetic and immunological links have been severed or substantially inhibited cancer is allowed to grow unchecked or inadequately checked. The result is, uncontrolled growth, and the spread of abnormal cells with no physiological function other than to cause bodily harm, destroy healthy tissue, and multiply, causing death or serious disablement unless effectively treated."*

THE CURE REQUIRES KNOWLEDGE

But the precursor to cures and remedies is a complete understanding of a cancer cell, which includes the characteristics of a cancer cell. Once we have a comprehensive understanding of the life of a cancer cell, we can develop effective treatments, and strategies for its eradication.

Because all cancers are unique, there is never a single strategy that is suitable for every cancer. For example, strategies depend on a variety of variables, such as, the stage of cancer, its location, its aggressive or subtle nature, and whether it has metastasized. Then you need to take into consideration the human element, lifestyle, which includes diet, stress, geographic domicile, etc.

There are unnumbered variables that need to be evaluated before deciding on an effective treatment, which is why choosing the right doctor is imperative. For example, if one had a stage four inoperable brain tumor, there are few options, other than the Burzynski Clinic, located in Houston, Texas (1 800 714-7181). If you have stage one or stage two breast cancer, there are many options, including the Gerson Clinic, located in Tijuana Mexico, whose corporate office is in San Diego, CA (1 888 447-7357). These are just a few of the many locations and doctors who are successfully treating cancer.

The Gerson Clinic also has a prevention clinic called; The Sedona Wellness Retreat that has several programs designed to meet your medical conditions. At this retreat you have the option of being under the care of a licensed doctor and having a prevention program designed specifically for you (www.wellnesretreat.com/Gerson). Their phone number is, 928 239-4589.

There are countless stories of *"Healthy individuals who one day discover they have cancer"*. So, how is it that a seemingly healthy individual, with no history of cancer or genetic disposition to cancer, contracts cancer?

THE CANCER PARADIGM SHIFT

The answer is quite simple, yet complex. As you may have discovered when it comes to cancer, there is no "smoking gun."

Contracting cancer is a very complex process that involves a variety of variables, over an extended period. And any one or, often, a combination of variables creates an environment for the onset and propagation of cancer. Hopefully, the following illustration will help you to understand.

How an Individual Contracts Cancer – Illustration:

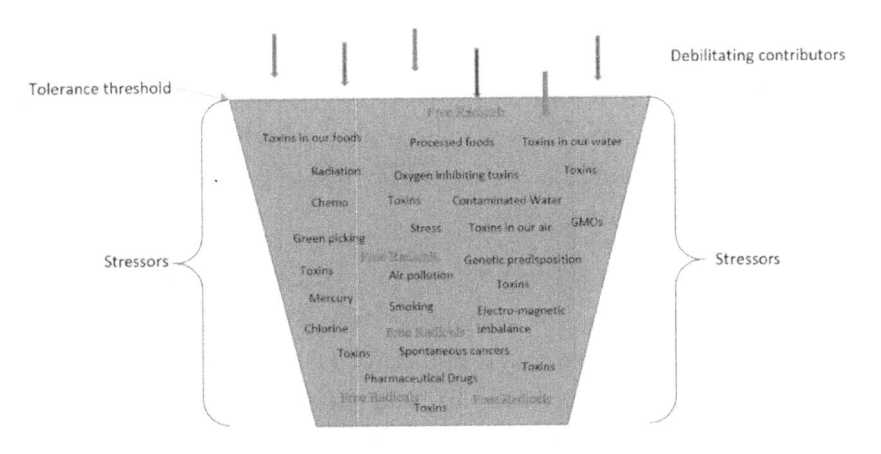

[Figure: A cup-shaped diagram labeled "Tolerance threshold" on the left and "Debilitating contributors" on the top right, with "Stressors" on both sides. Inside the cup are listed: Toxins in our foods, Processed foods, Toxins in our water, Radiation, Oxygen inhibiting toxins, Toxins, Chemo, Toxins, Contaminated Water, Green picking, Stress, Toxins in our air, GMOs, Free Radicals, Genetic predisposition, Toxins, Air pollution, Mercury, Smoking, Electro-magnetic imbalance, Chlorine, Toxins, Spontaneous cancers, Toxins, Pharmaceutical Drugs, Free Radicals, Toxins]

By: Estrada

In the above illustration, the cup represents the human body, and what goes into the cup (debilitating contributors) represents the foreign elements that contribute, on a cumulative scale, to the onset of cancer. Once the body reaches its tolerance threshold death is immanent. The stressor is what triggers the proliferation of cancer cells, which can be any combination of elements that have accumulated to the point of onset.

As you can see, the number of variables is countless, especially if you take into consideration the 100,000 foreign toxins that have been introduced into our environment (soil, water, foods, and air), and the extent of processed foods in our diet. But it's not just these variables, but rather, the combination of variables that makes it impossible to determine the exact cause of cancer, and when you add the element of time, and the damage done by free radicals, which can range from months to decades, the exact cause becomes incalculable.

But there is hope in fighting and successfully eradicating cancer. This is because now that we understand cancer, we have also gained tremendous insight on how the human body has been so successful in eradicating cancer.

There are so many books and websites on cancer offering vast amounts of information. As I read through them it seems that something is missing. What I have discovered is that most of these books and websites are missing the mark and are, at the very least, conveying only half of the story. The truth is some doctors are on the cutting edge of the medical and scientific breakthroughs that are tilting the scales in favor of the patient.

The truth is there are doctors successfully treating cancer today using the latest scientific and medical discoveries; The truth is cancer is a common occurrence that every human being experiences daily, from which the body has successfully arrested and is far more prepared for than any conventional approach.

The truth is the human body has one of the most sophisticated and comprehensive defense mechanisms already in place combating cancer and other diseases, viruses, and foreign elements. In fact, the human defense system is so elaborate that it would take several volumes just to describe it in detail. Based on current research and scientific discoveries the human defense network is far more sophisticated and extensive than scientists ever imagined, causing all other man-made therapies to pale in comparison.

So, what went wrong? Why isn't it working affectively, as before? The truth is, our defense system didn't fail us, we failed it. We circumvented a natural and effective system and replaced it with conventional methods that only derail the natural process. To add insult to injury, we have also disabled the supply link that provides the necessary elements (nutrients) in order to facilitate the process of seeking and destroying cancer cells, along with other diseases. In other words, we messed with Mother Nature, and are reaping the consequences, which is why cancer should be viewed from two points of concern, prevention and onset.

Prevention has everything to do with lifestyle and onset has everything to do with methods of eradication. Prevention is predicated on a comprehensive understanding of biological functions, as it related to healthy cellular life and what it takes to maintain homeostasis. This would involve maintaining a stress-free lifestyle, drinking lots of clean water, eating organic foods, taking the proper supplements (vitamins, minerals, glyconutrients, selenium, NAC., etc.), exercise, proper sleep, and oxygenating your cells. A glimpse of physical evidence of health can be seen by a healthy pH, lack of inflammation, normal bowel movements, a healthy weight, and clean arteries, etc.

Have you ever noticed that the older we get the more prone to illness we become? For example, I have never heard or read about a 21-year-old with prostate cancer. The truth is as we age our body chemistry changes. We produce less calcium, our metabolism slows down etc., etc. So, maintaining a healthy body at 65 is different than maintaining a healthy body at 21. Quite honestly, at 65 we need some extra help, which is why a healthy lifestyle becomes a vital link to longevity.

With the onset of cancer all is not lost. Based on cutting edge scientific and medical breakthroughs it is possible to intervene on a genetic level (gene therapy), as well as on a cellular level (glycans, immunotherapy, PEMF therapy, proper supplementation, etc.) to assist our vast defense network in its efforts to conquer the cancer dilemma.

Based on these cutting edge scientific and medical breakthroughs one would think that the best approach and strategy in fighting cancer would include a plan that enables our vast defense network and embraces it as an alley. It would seem logical that such an elaborate and effective defense system was supported and fortified, especially given the scientific and medical understanding of just how effective our immune system can be in eradicating all cancers. One would assume that the entire medical community would come together and develop an effective strategy that includes these scientific and medical breakthroughs.

The truth is the medical community is not united and remains divided and often, ignorant, of most of these cutting-edge scientific discoveries. As a result, current conventional treatments are often based on outdated therapies, which are debilitating, ineffective, and robbing the human spirit of its dignity. The irony is that the information about these innovative scientific breakthroughs is readily available over the Internet. All you have to do is search for them.

As I speak to people in America most have never heard of the protocols, procedures methods, discoveries, and doctors whom I take for granted. It seems that the door of information has been closed to most families and when faced with a crisis, there is no venting of information other than what is commercially acceptable.

It is so easy for doctors and individuals alike to disregard information that follows a different path then the one they are most comfortable following. This is a common commercial trait, one that has played out well for those who profit from traditional methods. Unfortunately, for those in dire need of the latest scientific breakthroughs and the new choices that follow, it could mean death, and for many this equates to, death without dignity.

As I have pieced the cancer puzzle together, over the course of a decade, you may have noticed that I often refer to "functions that occur on a cellular level." This is because I want you to understand the what, why, and where of cancer, fundamentally.

As I introduced you to these phenomenal doctors and scientists, along with their incredible discoveries as well as the latest biological discoveries, my hope is that you will begin to understand several fundamental principles.

THE CANCER PARADIGM SHIFT

- First that cancer begins and ends on a cellular level.
- Second, the successful treatment for cancer has already been discovered, in fact, it was there all along.
- Third, the eradication of cancer is a common occurrence, given the appropriate atmosphere and biological functions.
- Fourth, there are doctors and scientists successful at treating cancer or who have successfully treated cancer and have a success rate far greater than conventional methods, and with little, or no adverse side effects.
- Fifth, the successful treatment of cancer is a contingent process.

These contingencies, though fundamental can be inhibited by countless variables or combination of variables, which is where modern medicine, along with countless external factors have exasperated the problem.

What is so ironic and often maddening, is that modern protocols often interfere with the body's natural, and phenomenal, ability to eradicate cancer cells. The human body has a tolerance threshold from which there is no longer any hope of survival. Once cancer has spread too far, and the body is no longer capable of regaining its health, that threshold has been reached.

It is possible, however, to prevent the onset of cancer. In fact, there are many places around the globe where cancer is extremely rare, or where certain types of cancer are far less prevalent then in America. Also keep in mind that if thirty percent of all Americans will contract cancer, 70 percent will not.

It is my hope that as you read this book and review its material, you will begin to understand these fundamental concepts, and you will begin to see how cancer, and the body are forever intertwined; that cancer and the environment are forever interwoven; that cancer and how the body responds has everything to do with our current state of health.

Our current state of health has everything to do with how the body reacts on a cellular level to not only cancer cells but also to any form of treatment that is administered. It is all contingent on the current state between one's biological system and the current relationship it maintains with the environment from which the biological system gains its sustenance.

Adding foreign toxins, especially, in the form of therapy (chemo and radiation), completely changes the biological system often titling the scales against the patient. After all, once a chemo molecule enters the human system the body must, by necessity, use all its resources to neutralize these chemicals.

This is why the entire process (the contracting of cancer and the path to healing) is so dynamic, complex, and often convoluted because of all the internal and external variables that play pivotal roles. These countless intersections, between internal variables and external variables, are so varied, unmappable, and unpredictable that it makes it impossible for scientists to even begin to forecast the outcome of anyone approach to the healing of cancer, which is why so many different approaches have had some form of success, including traditional methods. The key word here is "some form of success."

Today's scientists are constantly adding to the pool of cumulative information so comprehensive that it has forever changed the cancer paradigm, which equates to a revised perception that is far more comprehensive and informative than past generations. Today's scientists know exactly how and why cancer begins.

Scientists also understand specifically how and why cancer grows uncontrollably. Scientists have also become aware of the countless variables that work in concert in promoting the onset and propagation of cancer. These combinations are so varied that at any time several variables can come together and affect cancer, and while these variables are in play the onset of cancer may not reveal itself for decades. This scenario, alone, describes why it is impossible to determine exactly, which variables cause the onset of cancer and which variables promote the propagation of cancer.

In dealing with a life and death scenario, which is exactly what cancer is, there needs to be more than just protocols, convention, and a way of doing things, and "some form of success" should be a last resort not a first resort. In the equation of life and death, the quality of one's death is a scenario that has been underrated, or not taken into consideration.

I was listening to a man speak before a committee about his daughter's physical experience with conventional treatments. In the end her brain had absorbed so much radiation that it laterally fell apart and she died, not from the cancer but from the treatment. All too often cancer patients die of pneumonia, an easily treated illness because their immune system was compromised by the massive amounts of chemo and radiation, and in the process, they lose all human dignity. All too often after several bounds of chemo or radiation therapy the only thing left, is a skeletal figure, a shell of what once was a fully functioning person, absent any human dignity.

CHAPTER 27

BREAST CANCER

Since 1975, the rate of breast cancer among women has gone up 30% (Nachman & Hardy, 2015). Throughout the world breast cancer is the most commonly diagnosed cancer, and the leading cause of cancer death in women. In 2008 there were 1.4 million new cases of breast cancer and 458,000 deaths worldwide. In 2017, within the United States, 252,710 women will be diagnosed with invasive breast cancer and 63,420 of non-invasive breast cancer. Over 40,000 women will die of breast cancer in 2017. To date it is the second leading cause of death for women in America (Breastcancer.org, n.d.; Brownstein, 2017).

Fortunately, because of the advances is diagnostics and treatments most women with early onset breast cancer will not die as a direct result of the cancer. What is of grave concern are those who die as a result of the side effects of conventional treatments. While early stage detection of breast cancer is 100% curable, women with stage four breast cancer have only a 25% survival rate that extends beyond five years.

Another concern is the disparity in incidence and mortality of cancer throughout the world. For example, the highest rates of breast cancer are found in Switzerland, the United States, Italy, and many other European countries. The lowest rates of breast cancer can be found in Africa, Asia (including Japan), and South America (Jemal, Center, DeSantis, & Ward, 2010). These discrepancies assist scientists in determining the secondary causes of cancer in American women.

In America, each year over 252,000 women are diagnosed with breast cancer and 40,000 die annually (Breastcancer.org, n.d.; Brownstein, 2017). The risk of contracting breast cancer only increases with age. The American Cancer Society (ACS) states that one in eight women run the risk of developing breast cancer in their lifetime (ACS, 2011). The etiology of breast cancer, or the primary cause of cancer was well documented by Nobel Prize recipient, Dr. Otto Warburg, back in the 1930s.

Regarding the secondary causes of breast cancer, there is no smoking gun. This is because the dynamic flow of internal biological functions and external environmental variables are so fluid and intertwined that no one factor is ever a standalone cause, making it impossible to determine with absolute certainty.

However, there is a cumulative effect that takes place over time, along with certain factors that increases one's risk of getting cancer, which this chapter will attempt to explain. What makes this a formidable task is that the scientific discoveries are happening so quickly that it is impossible to keep up with all the current research.

If cancer is diagnosed early there are far more options and a greater chance for survival, so early detection is imperative. The ACS and other advocacy groups encourage annual screening for those over the age of 40 who are at average risk and clinical breast examinations every three years beginning at the age of 20 and every year after the age of 40.

It is also important to know your own breasts, to conduct breast self-examinations (BSE) to determine what is normal, getting to know one's own breasts is a major part of prevention and early detection. The Susan G. Komen website provides an excellent educational video on breast cancer, which includes how to perform a proper self-exam. Health care providers are also excellent sources in learning how to conduct a proper BSE. If there are any indications of abnormalities, it is imperative to contact a healthcare provider and conduct a thorough examination.

Cancer prevention begins with education but also includes making healthy lifestyle choices, which include maintaining a healthy weight, regular exercise, limiting the amount of alcohol one consumes, healthy eating habits, knowing one's risk potential (Komen, 2011), and limiting one's exposure to toxins and chemicals.

Once one is diagnosed with breast cancer conventional treatments only include, hormone modulators, surgery, chemotherapy, and radiation. What doctors fail to say, is that these conventional treatments do not meet the goal of prolonged life. If you were to take the age adjusted mortality rates from 1930 to 2014, the rates of death for woman with breast cancer are virtually unchanged. In other words, all the current therapies over the past 75 years have not reduced the death rate of woman with breast cancer (Brownstein, 2017)

Dr. Conley, an Assistant Clinical Professor of Medicine at Michigan State (2004), in referring to 21st century advances in research states that one of the most valuable assets in the war against cancer is one's own immune system. Until recently, the Lymphatic System had been generally ignored by most medical research studies, as if it had nothing to do with health, when in reality researcher recognize it as the most critical asset in a women's ability to fight breast cancer, and a major part of immune function.

Symptoms

According to Susan G. Komen (2011) symptoms or indications of breast cancer can include the following:

- Lumps, hard knots, thickening
- Swelling, warmth, redness, darkening
- Change in the size or shape of the breast
- Dimpling or puckering of the skin
- Itchy scaling sore or rash in the nipple
- Pulling in or the nipple or other parts of the breast
- Nipple discharge that starts suddenly
- New pain in one spot that does not go away

Risk Factors

The possibilities of getting breast cancer increases when certain risk factors are involved, and the medical community has developed an informal list that includes the following:

- Family history of breast cancer (genetics)
- Stress
- Hormones (estrogen & progesterone) extracted from horse Urine
- Toxins (how chemicals increase one's risk for breast cancer)
- Alcohol
- Melatonin
- Antibiotics
- Nutrition
- Cultural Effects and Country of Origin
- Age
- Not having children
- Obesity

Some of these factors increase the risk of breast cancer a great deal while others increase the risk minimally (Komen, 2011). The medical community believes that this information is key in helping women to avoid breast cancer and to encourage procedures that can help detect breast cancer early.

Genetics

Most breast cancers are *not* inherited. This information is collected from the New England Journal of Medicine. They studied 44,000 sets of twins and discovered that only 27% of all breast cancer is genetically linked. This means that 73% of all women who have a family history of breast cancer never got breast cancer. Other studies contend that the percentage is as low as five to seven percent. According to Newman et al., (1988), "Inheritance of Human Breast Cancer," only 4% of breast cancer is genetically linked.

So how do genes get damaged, since most women are born with normal breast genes? Researchers realize that as one progresses through life genes become damaged, and one of the primary villains is free *radicals*. *Free-radicals* damage healthy cells and genes and the more *free-radicals* the greater the damage, another cause is carcinogens, especially from cigarettes (Conley, 2004).

For many women the genetic link, regardless of percentage, is a major concern and often wonder if there anything that can be done to prevent or reduce the likelihood of getting breast cancer? The answer is, yes. One can up-grade one's genes through, natural foods, natural organic supplements (vitamins, minerals, glyconutrients, enzymes, etc.), mental disposition, and lifestyle adjustments. It is important to keep in mind that one's genes are fluid and can be either improved or downgraded.

Stress

Another culprit is stress. Stress results in excessive adrenalin, which is permissible when running away from a hungry tiger, but urban stress relates to our jobs, divorces, mortgage payments, etc. Stress is also a major contributor to a reduced immune system. Stress is responsible for releasing certain chemicals that damage our genes. The body normally counteracts these elements with antioxidants, which one receives from proper nutrition or from the natural productive processes of the body (Conley, 2004).

However, because of "green picking," soil depletion, chemical agents, etc., foods no longer contain many of the vital nutrients necessary for optimal health, which is why, in the 21st century, natural supplements are pre-requisites to optimal health. It is imperative that everyone understand that the earth has become a toxic planet, and there is a dire need to alter one's lifestyle, to preserve and maintain one's health.

Estrogen, Progesterone & Testosterone

In the past the role of hormones was not fully understood. Today, 21st century science has confirmed that hormones are key players for optimal health. Unfortunately, the production of hormones begins to decline in our early 20s by one-to-one and a half percent per year creating an imbalance that can wreak havoc. This is especially true after menopause.

The optimal estrogen level for women is 90 to 250 pg/mL, testosterone levels for women should range from 1.0 to 2.2 pg/mL, and progesterone levels for women should be between 2.0 and 6.0 pg/mL. To determine whether one is out of balance one should have a hormone panel test (Somers, Men vs. Women, n.d.).

Many women are not aware that the body produces many types of estrogen and the three most common types of estrogen are estrone (relatively potent), estradiol (the most potent), and estriol (a weak form of estrogen). Two of these are potent version of estrogen while the third type, estriol is produced more frequently, is not cyclic and is the least potent and most helpful in aging women.

The Journal of the American Medical Association (2002), the women's health initiative, conducted a study where women who were on conjugated estrogens and a synthetic progesterone were a higher risk of getting breast cancer. Based on this information the study was terminated and the taking of estrogen became taboo. Recent research shows that the synthetic estrogen, which is extracted from horse urine, is a prime culprit in breast cancer (Brownstein, 2017).

The reality is estrogen is a natural function of the body. Recent scientific discoveries have disclosed that natural estrogen (bioidentical estrogen) protects the cerebral cortex and is a powerful inhibitor of excitotoxicity. It is important to note that excitotoxins are found in food enhancing additives (Somers, 2008; Brownstein, 2017).

The problem is physicians, as far back as the 1950s, became obsessed with the two most potent forms of estrogen, and the protocol was to prescribe estrogen extracted from horse urine. Physicians knew that estrogen protected bone density and helped to regulate menopausal symptoms, so they prescribed the most potent forms of estrogen.

Unfortunately, the body was not designed to maintain a constant flow of certain estrogens day in and day out, month in and month out, year in and year out. There is, however, a weak form of estrogen, estriol, which the body produces more often than the others that controls menopausal symptoms but does not stimulate the breast and uterus as much as those previously mentioned (Conley, 2004).

So, who should use estrogen and who should not? There is a growing argument that everyone living in America should take supplements. It all has to do with how with aging. As we get older our bodies produce less estrogen, progesterone, and testosterone. Recent research has found that female hormones has a multitude of functions, including regulating body functions, reducing the risk of cancer, and as an anti-aging mechanism. Some of the most common symptoms of deficiencies are sagging skin; sleep disorders, "flu" like symptoms, and low libido.

It is important to note that most women have been introduced to synthetic hormones, such as Premarin, which is taken from horse urine and can lead to cancer. With hormones, the key word is: "Bio-identical." This means that the hormones have the same chemical structure as human-produced hormones. It is also important to note that hormone replacement requires monitoring for balance. Too much can be as harmful as too little.

The way American farms grow its products have changed dramatically over the past 50 years. Today, there is a tremendous amount of pressure to produce bigger and faster and as a result farmer have begun to inject strong amounts of estrogen into their cows to help them produce more milk, which increase our health risks.

According to The American Journal of Epidemiology women low in progesterone have a five times higher risk of developing breast cancer. Why? Progesterone helps to balance out estrogen. Some studies indicate that by age 35 half of all women may not be producing enough progesterone (Conley, 2004). Some of the symptoms of low progesterone are irregular periods and PMS.

Progesterone is more than just a hormone. If a woman has had a hysterectomy, she is no longer producing progesterone and should be taking bioidentical progesterone cream. PMS is a neurological disorder not a uterine disorder and progesterone is important for nerve function, muscle strength, and energy production (Conley, 2004).

There are three ways to determine if one's hormone levels are low, a blood test, urine test, or saliva test (the best way) but make sure that the test indicates your free progesterone, because it is the free progesterone that works in the body.

Take the time to locate a doctor who specializes in anti-aging and have them run the appropriate, saliva, blood, and urine tests necessary to determine your hormone levels. It is important that you balance your estrogen with your progesterone. Keeping your estrogen and progesterone levels balanced is vital because too much or less of one or the other can also create problems, such as weight gain.

Finally, play close attention to your estriol levels, if your levels are too low, you are at a greater risk of getting cancer. If you need to take estrogen take it in cream form and not by pill. Pills need to go through the liver and are broken down into metabolites (unhealthy) while creams enter the bloodstream directly (Conley, 2004).

Chemicals & Toxins

There are certain chemicals found in the American diet that increase a women's risk of developing breast cancer. According to the Journal of the National Cancer Institute dichlorodiphenyldichloroethylene (DDE) is a chemical that increases a women's risk of developing breast cancer. Women who have high levels of DDE have a 400% higher risk of developing breast cancer. Polychlorinated biphenyls (PCB) are chemicals once widely used in the United States banned in 1979 but are still in use in other countries. PCB is linked to breast cancer and liver cancer.

It enters the environment as a breakdown of dichlorodiphenyltrichloroethane (DDT), which is a pesticide once used to control insects. Its use was banned in the United States in 1972 but is still used in other countries.

DDT takes anywhere from two to 15 years to breakdown and is stored in the fatty tissue of fish, birds, and other animals. It is also found in roots and in leafy vegetables. It also can be air-born and be found in drinking water. DDT and DDE exposure are primarily because the import of vegetables and meats from other countries. DDT not only increase the risk of developing breast cancer it also affects the nervous system and women who have had exposure to large amounts of DDE have an increase chance of premature babies.

Cooking reduces the amount DDT in fish and washing fruits and vegetables removes most of the DDT on the surface. There are laboratory tests that can detect DDT and DDE in fat, blood, urine, semen, and in breast milk. Because the United States relies on imported product's DDE and PCBs have been found in pizza, fried chicken, ice cream, and hamburger. Essentially, these contaminants have been found in most of our foods, including our water, air, and our soil.

Alcohol

According to the Iowa Women's Health Study (Conley, 2004) women who consumed two grams of alcohol had a 60% higher risk of developing breast cancer when they were in the lower 25% of folic acid (vitamin B). Women in the higher 25% level of folic acid and who consumed more than four grams of alcohol had no increased risk or were at the same risk as those women who did not consume alcohol. Folic acid can be found in green leafy vegetables, beans, peas, flour, and in multi-vitamins. Unfortunately, three of five women are low in folic acid.

Melatonin

According to the British Medical Journal, blind women had a 36% lower risk of breast cancer than women with site (Conley, 2004). The study revealed that blind women had a higher level of melatonin. Melatonin is a natural hormone produced by the pineal gland used biologically to regulate sleep and reproductive cycles. Melatonin is also a strong antioxidant, found in warm milk, turkey, chicken, and tuna. Many of those over the age of 40 have a problem making melatonin. Melatonin is produced in the dark, so if one sleeps in light it hinders the production (light pollution). Hugging, touching, and sex also helps to produce melatonin.

Antibiotics

According to the Journal of the American Medical Association, the use of antibiotics kills not only harmful bacteria but also healthy bacteria. First, antibiotics kill all bacteria and women often have yeast infections. It is necessary for your intestines to have good bacteria present. If the level of good bacteria is very low, it hinders the body from properly detoxifying estrogen. It produces an enzyme, which hinders the detoxifying of estrogen.

It is important to avoid antibiotics if possible. Also avoid antibiotics for viral infections such as flues and colds. If one does have low bacteria an easy way to boost one's level of good bacteria is to eat foods that contain good bacteria, such as organic yogurts and kefir or a good supplement called probiotics (with live cultures).

Seidman, in his book, "A Different Perspective on Breast Cancer Risk Factors" states that, "all of the risk factors can account for only about 30% of breast cancer causes – leaving 70% unexplained by established risk factors."

Nutrition – Vitamins & Minerals, Antioxidants, and Sugars

There are certain vegetables, vitamins, and glyconutrients (please refer to our chapter on glyconutrients) linked to the prevention of cancer and to breast cancer, specifically. Cruciferous vegetables such as broccoli, cauliflower, cabbage, kale, Brussel sprouts, bok choy, are high on the list. Researchers believe that the Endol three carbinol (I3C), which is contained in these vegetables, is responsible for assisting the liver in properly detoxifying estrogen and therefore reducing the risk of developing breast cancer. There are also I3C supplements (Conley, 2004). There is also an active ingredient of a spice called curcumin, which is an extract from turmeric, which is often used in spicy chicken and can be found in food supplements that lower a women's risk of developing breast cancer (Conley, 2004).

According to the Journal of the National Cancer Institute women in the highest 25% of vitamin E, which they received in food form had a 60% less risk of developing breast cancer. Women who took vitamin E by supplement had no reduction in the risk of breast cancer (Conley, 2004). The reason for these conflicting results is that vitamin E is made up of eight structural compounds (alpha, beta, delta, and gamma tocopherol) and the corresponding tocotrienols 21 (Himmelfarb, et al., 2003). Most commercial vitamin E supplements consist ONLY of one vitamin E, alpha tocopherol (Conley, 2004; Shintani & DellaPenna, 1998).

Vitamin E is a fat-soluble antioxidant, which fights cancer, and breasts are approximately 70%- 80% fat. Vitamin E can be found in organic nuts, whole grain bread, rice bran, wheat germ, canola oil, and olive oil. It is important to note that vitamin E has been known to thin the blood slightly. If one is will take an organic and natural vitamin E supplements one should make sure that the entire family of vitamin E is present. For those who have enough amounts of vitamin E studies indicate that they have up to a 90% reduction in risk of contracting breast cancer.

According to the American Journal of Epidemiology (2001) women highest in two antioxidants, lutein (found in spinach) and carotenes (found in carrots, broccoli, cauliflower, squash, yams, pumpkin, melon, and cantaloupe) have a reduced risk of developing breast cancer

(Toniolo et al., 2001). Other studies indicate that another antioxidant, lycopene significantly reduces the risk of developing breast cancer (Giovannucci, 1999).

There are several studies that indicate Curcumin (obtained from turmeric) and Genistein (obtained from soybeans) applied to the diet can prevent hormone induced cancers (Verma, Salamone & Goldin, 1997). Another study by the journal, Carcinogenesis, where they induced breast cancer to two sets of rats, through radiation, of which 70% of the rats contracted breast cancer.

The second group of rats who were also subjected to high doses of radiation had been given Curcumin and of these rats only 18% contracted breast cancer (Conley, 2004). Curcumin is a very potent antioxidant that has been used in India for centuries. Curcumin, as an antioxidant, helps to protect the cells from damage. When Curcumin was applied directly onto cancer cells in vitro, the cancer cells died (Conley, 2004). Curcumin also prevents toxins and pesticides from attaching to the breast tissue. It is believed that Curcumin helps prevent cancer in the G2 stage.

Recent research has found that green tea contains substances that help in preventing breast cancer. The substance is EGCG (epigallocatechin-3-gallate), which prevents cancer by inhibiting or blocking the interaction of tumor promoters, hormones, growth factors, and estrogen with its receptors in breast tissue. The tea extracts also inhibit the growth of cancer cells in breast tissue (Komori, et al., 1993). Do not use green teas without caffeine; the caffeine is needed for the green tea extracts to work.

Most individuals are lacking enough amounts of these and other vitamins, which is why supplements are so vital to health. This, along with exercise is vital to the reduction of breast cancer. Exercise is directly related to the flow of the lymphatic system, which is a major part of the immune system. The lymphatic system plays a key role in the removal of toxins and waste material from the breast tissue (Please refer to our chapter on the immune system).

BREAST CANCER

Americans consume more than 50 pounds of soda each year, which contain corn syrup and sugar. Large amounts of sugar not only spike our insulin levels and encourage our bodies to store energy as fat, which causes us to gain weight, too much sugar also depresses the immune system making us more susceptible to illness and disease.

Diet sodas may be compared to, "going from the frying pan into the fire." Diet sodas may be worse because they are filled with foreign chemicals, which cause cancers and brain tumors.

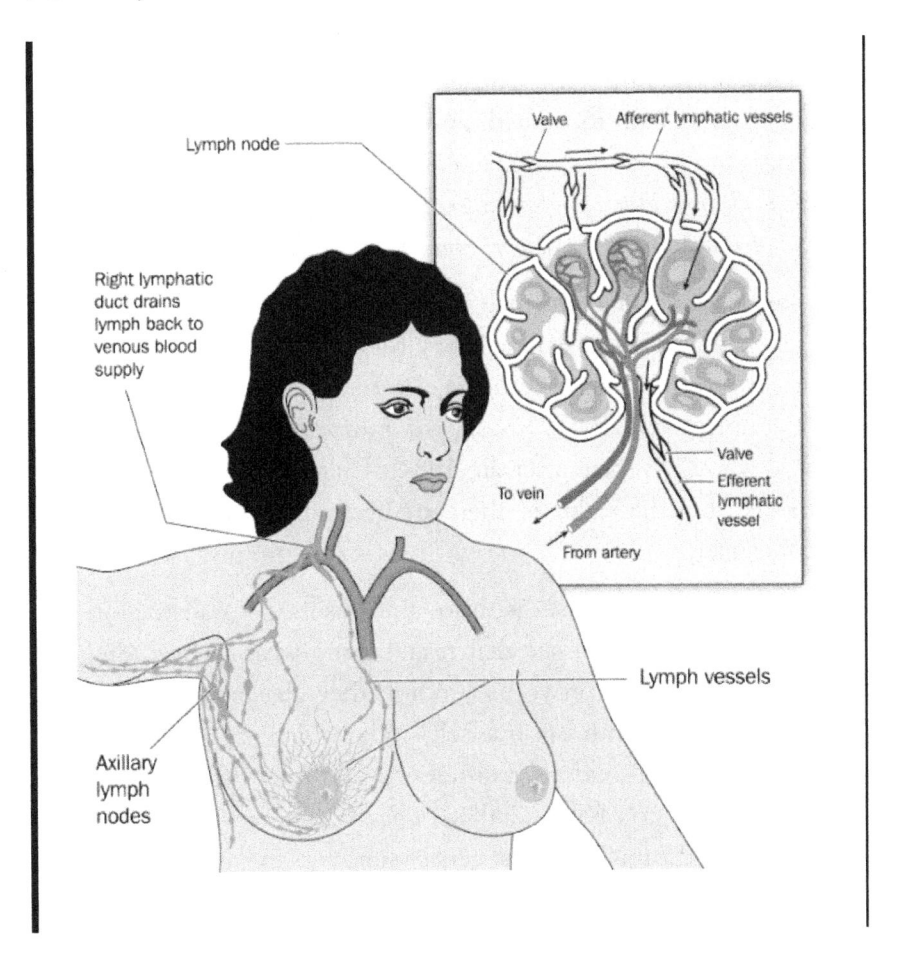

A Cultural Effect

Based on several research articles bras may be a major risk factor responsible for the onset of cancer. This is because of their inherent ability to hinder the lymphatic system preventing it from cleansing the breast tissue of foreign toxins and waste material. According to several research articles, the use of bras is more of a cultural influence.

In an article by Regina Ziegler (1993) entitled, "Migration Patterns and Breast Cancer Risks in Asian American Women", she noted that Asian women born in the West experience a rate that is 60% higher than that of women born in the East. Those of Japanese rural background had a lower incidence than those with an urban background. She concluded that *"exposure to Western lifestyles had a substantial impact on breast cancer risk in Asian migrants to the United States during their lifetime… this study should provide new insights into the secondary causes of breast cancer"* (Ziegler, 1993).

This study is further confirmed by a previous study by Thomas and Karagas (1987). Nasca, et al. (1981) found that woman from Great Britain, Ireland, Germany, Austria, Poland, Italy, Russia, from their native country. *"This rise in risk suggests a major environmental component for cancers of these sites"* (Nasca, et al., 1981). Cultural influences are often overlooked, but the reality is, there are geographical differences in the rates of cancer.

Fibrocystic breast disease is also the result of constriction and compression of breast tissue that results from wearing bras (Singer & Grismaijer, 2006). To prove their point, they challenge all women to conduct the one month bra-free self-study, which is cost free and risk free to see if there is, indeed, a difference, and refer their readers to the book: Dressed to Kill, (2006). The good news is there are approximately 2.5 million breast cancer survivors in America.

Age

While cancers occur at all ages, most cancers occur in people age 50 and older. There are numerous reasons for this, a major contributor are age related events that occur within the human body. While these events are numerous there are two that stand out, immune senescence, and an aging thymus gland.

The medical dictionary defines Immune senescence as:

> Immune: *"highly resistant to a disease because of the formation of humoral antibodies or the development of immunologically competent cells, or both, and as a result of some other mechanism, as interferon activities in viral infections."*

> Senescence: *"the process of growing old, especially the condition resulting from the transitions and accumulations of the deleterious aging processes"* (www. http://medical-dictionary.thefreedictionary.com/).

In essence "Immune senescence" refers to an aging immune system. The repercussions of an aging immune system are the inability to adequately protect the human body against cancer and other diseases. Instead of protecting the immune system generates excessive inflammatory reactions that affect every cell in our body.

These inflammatory reactions are the precursors to a host of diseases that are age related, including dementia, atherosclerosis, and uninhibited cancer growth. Another reason why older individuals are more likely to contract cancer is because they have had decades to accumulate toxins, along with decades of inadequate nutrients, together with an aging immune system. An exhausted immune system also inhibits the effectiveness of vaccines (Faloon, 2015).

As we age our thymus gland begins to atrophy. An aging thymus gland is exacerbated with extended vitamin deficiency, especially zinc. The thymus gland is responsible for programming immune cells into functional T-cells. Natural killer (NK) cells are the bodies first line of defense against all forms of disease including cancer. Unfortunately, as we age the number of NK cells also decline, making us more vulnerable to illness and disease (Faloon, 2015; Posnick, 2015).

Obesity

According to the journal, Cancer Research (2014) obesity and inflammation, the precursor to disease, seem to go together, which results in a worst-case scenario for breast cancer. Inflammation stimulates the production of estrogen, which promotes the progression of breast cancer. Antidotes are nonsteroidal anti-inflammatory drugs, which inhibit estrogen production.

Testing for Cancer

The Estrogen Tests – EMI & EQ

There are tests that can predict whether you will get breast cancer. One test is called the estrogen metabolite index (EMI), which is a simple urine test. All estrogen whether taken or produced naturally is detoxified in the liver. EMI lets one know how the liver is detoxifying estrogen is a strong indicator of whether one will get breast cancer.

There are two pathways in the EMI the two pathway and the 16 pathways. Women should have an EMI of two or slightly above. If a women's EMI is at 1.5 studies indicate that a woman is at a 30% higher risk for developing breast cancer. This is an important test for those women who have a history of breast cancer, have had breast cancer in the past, or currently on estrogen.

The last thing a woman wants to do is to take the pill forms of estrogen if the liver is not detoxifying estrogen properly (Conley, 2004). For those women who have a family history of breast cancer it is recommended to take the test as early as in one's teens. Because the earlier one's knows that their EMI is low the better off they are and can take the necessary steps to improve one's EMI.

Another simple urine test is called EQ (estrogen quotient). EQ is equal to the amount of estriol (the weaker form of estrogen and preferred estrogen) divided by estrone and estradiol (the two stronger estrogens). EQ is an important predictor of whether women will develop breast cancer. One can improve their EQ by taking soy and flax.

Breast exams

Currently clinical breast exams consist of Mammograms (x-rays), Thermal scans, CT scans, and MRIs. Currently Mammograms are the primary procedure doctors rely on for breast screening. Mammograms are essentially x-rays (low doses of radiation) used to identify cysts, calcifications, and tumors.

The controversy over mammograms is the radiation used to detect tumors damages DNA. With each mammogram, the tissue of the breast is damaged, and the body's immune system is required to remedy the damage. Unfortunately, not everyone's immune system is working properly. If an individual's immune system is not up to the task those damaged cells continue to grow, unhindered.

Unfortunately, damaged cells will replicate themselves as damaged cells and eventually or several generations, those damaged cells can become cancerous. Current research indicates that the radiation from a mammogram increases the risk of breast cancer from 1% to 3%, while some oncologists believe that it may be as high as 10%.

X-rays require breast tissue suppression, which adds trauma to the tissue and may cause an existing tumor to rupture, leading to metastasis, while the majority of breast cancers are in the upper outer quadrants of the breast, which is not always covered by an x-ray, thus avoiding detection. When a thermography is used in conjunction with an x-ray (used as an affirming tool), the chances of detection increase by 10%.

Another concern over mammograms is the false-positive readings that can account for 8% to 10% of all mammograms. A false-positive reading results when a test designed to find cancer, comes back positive when in fact, there is no cancer (Lynge, 1998).

One of the most common non-invasive forms of breast cancer is ductal carcinoma in situ (DCIS), which accounts for 20% of all breast cancers. Prior to the introduction of mammograms DCIS only accounted for 1-2% of all breast cancers. Exposing yourself to ionizing radiation (mammograms) damages healthy tissue and causes cancer.

Another concern is that the lungs, which are located behind the breasts, are also being exposed to radiation. Several studies conclude that woman who undergo mammograms are at greater risk (10 times greater) for lung cancer. (Brownstein, 2017).

An alternative procedure that does not require radiation and serves the same purpose is Thermal scans. The Thermography was approved by the FDA for breast cancer screening in 1982. Thermography's use thermal imaging to detect for tumors and is based on the concept that cancer cells have a higher metabolic rate and therefore generate more heat than a normal cell.

Thermography's can detect the formation of cancer cells up to 10 years earlier than any mammogram. The procedure is a non-invasive test that takes about 10 minutes. The following is an example of a thermal scan with no indications of cancer.

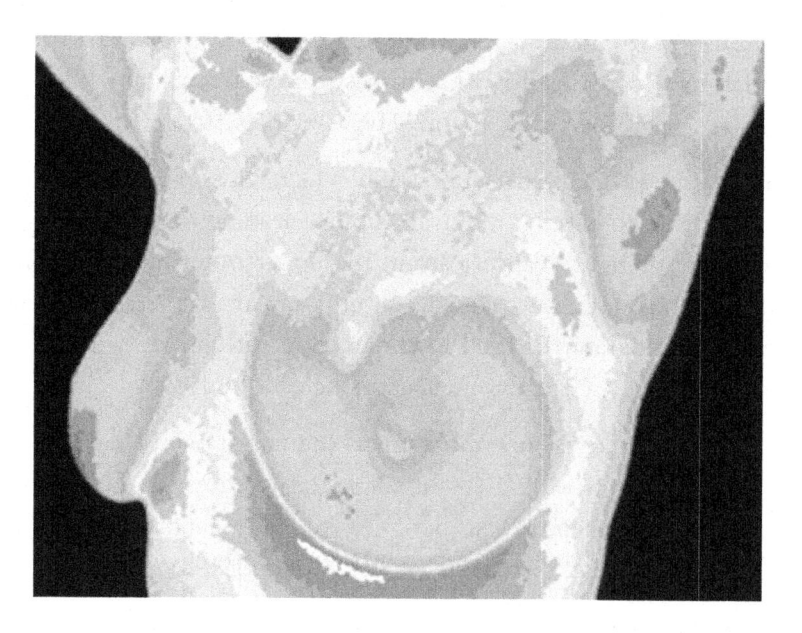

With the advances in technology, the new ultra-sensitive, high-resolution digital infrared cameras are available today and are becoming more accessible. A thermography is a physiologic test that detects heat patterns indicative of breast abnormalities. This ultra-sensitive procedure can detect the subtlest changes in breast temperature indicative of a variety of breast abnormalities, such as cancer, fibrocystic disease, vascular disease, Paget's disease, and infections, etc.

Recent research indicates that the infrared imaging of breast cancer can detect the minutest changes in temperature related to blood flow, which is indicative of abnormal patterns directly related to the progression of tumors. The Thermal scans have been shown to be positive for 83% of breast cancers compared to 61% for clinical examinations and 84% for mammography.

A third procedure is referred to as a CT scan. CT (computerized tomography) scans and the increased risks of developing cancer were in the news recently. In a recent Wall Street Journal (2009) article CT scans, which use higher doses of radiation than a Mammogram, could be responsible for an increase in cancer according to two new studies published in the Archives of Internal Medicine (Wang, 2009).

CT scans are used to detect tumors and injuries. Their use has tripled since the early 1990s to more than 70 million in 2007. A well-documented fact is that radiation increases a person's chances of developing cancer and CT scans use more radiation than a typical mammogram. In one study where 1,000 patients, at four hospitals, projected that the amount of from just one heart scan, at age 40 would result in cancer in one out of 270 women and one out of 600 men. For those who had their heads scanned the results were much lower, one out of 8,100 women and one out of 11,080 men (Wang, 2009).

A second study, which analyzed data from several databases, concluded that 29,000 new cases of cancer could be related to CT scans received in 2007. The study also found that the younger the individual being exposed the greater the risk. For example, a child at the age of three who received a CT scan had a one in 500 chance of developing cancer because of the radiation received from the CT scan. At age 30, the chances dropped to one out of 1,000 and one out of 3,333 at age 70 (Wang, 2009).

Overuse of radiation-based tests is a concern, especially when used to diagnose known abnormalities. The concern is even greater when they are performed for screening tests. According to Amy Berrington, an investigator at the National Cancer Institute, and an author on both studies "*You're exposing a lot of healthy people to radiation.*" It seems clear from these recent investigations that CT scans should be avoided if possible, especially for screening purposes (Wang, 2009).

Another device first brought onto the market in 1984 is Magnetic Resonance Imaging (MRI). Unlike CT scans or X-rays, MRIs do NOT use radiation to create internal images of the body and are non-invasive. MRIs use strong magnetic fields to produce internal images. The procedure usually lasts anywhere from 30 to 90 minutes.

The MRI is especially useful in studying the brain, spinal cord, joints, and the soft tissue of the body. Because of its capabilities of showing contrasting views between normal and abnormal tissue, is it often seen as more superior than CT scans and other imaging methods in evaluating tumors, tissue damage, and blood flow. What is equally important is that MRIs have no known long-term risks. Because MRIs use magnetic imaging, those who have pacemakers, electrical devises, or metal implants should avoid MRIs.

Based on the available data is seems obvious that MRIs and Thermal Imaging are the two known technologies that provide the most information with no known side effects or increase in risk of developing cancer.

The Immune System's Role in Reducing Risk of Cancer

One of the best ways to reduce the risk of developing breast cancer that incorporates much of what has been discussed is by improving the immune system. Ironically, it is never too late to change one's lifestyle and reduce the likelihood of developing cancer or breast cancer. The human body can rejuvenate itself and heal itself.

Ironically, everyday each body produces approximately 200 cancer cells and the role of destroying those cancer cells is the function of the body's immune system (Conley, 2004). The immune system's job is to destroy all the viruses, cancer cells, bacteria, parasites, pollens, etc. There is a blood test that can check the immune system for one's level of natural killer cell. Natural killer cells are part of the immune system and their job is to search for all foreign bodies and destroy them. It is imperative that one's immune system have sufficient numbers of killer cells. Without them all human beings would succumb to the simplest virus.

The Immune system is a vast system made of organs and cells. Within this vast community each organ and cell have a major function. They communicate back and forth using glycans (sugar molecules), which are attached to proteins and lipids and dominate the outer surface of all cells. Harpers Medical textbook (1996) includes eight essential glycans or sugars essential for maximum health. Glycans are referred to as the gatekeepers, policing what does and does not enter the cell membrane. Glycans are also responsible for cellular communication (Murray, Granner, Mayes, & Rockwell, 1996).

The body stores toxins in fatty tissue and breasts consist of fatty tissue, fibrous tissue, milk glands, and milk ducts. The lymphatic system, a major part of the immune system, is active in removing toxins and other elements from the cells of the breast and any hindrance to the flow of the lymphatic system will increase the risk of getting cancer. Examine the following:

The Lymphatic System Surrounding the Breast Tissue

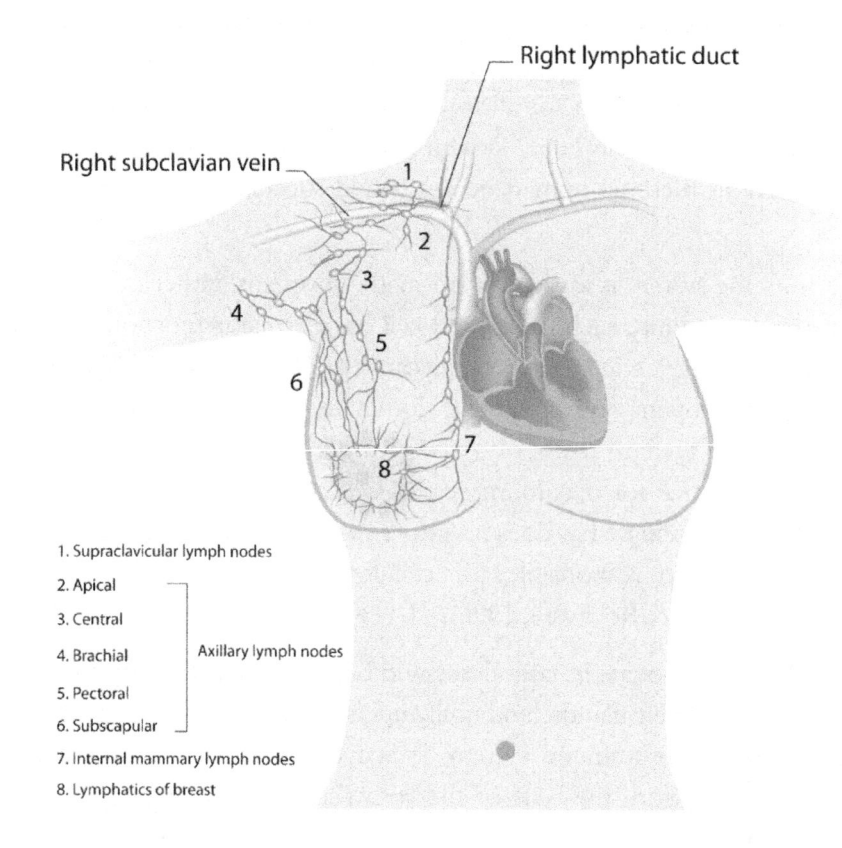

1. Supraclavicular lymph nodes
2. Apical
3. Central
4. Brachial
5. Pectoral
6. Subscapular

Axillary lymph nodes

7. Internal mammary lymph nodes
8. Lymphatics of breast

Please note the green lymph nodes, which are part of the lymphatic system and used to drain toxins and other foreign material and waste from the breast tissue. Also note the series of veins that run to and from the breasts, which carry lymph fluid to the breasts and carry away toxins, waste, and other debris from the breasts. Any hindrance to this flow of fluid (the use of bras) can cause a backup of toxins and waste creating a contaminating environment for cells. The long-term effects can lead to cancer.

Any removal of these lymph nodes reduces the lymphatic system's ability to cleanse the breast tissue. While the blood provides oxygen and nutrients to the breast tissue, the lymphatic system is the body's defense system used in removing harmful elements from the breast tissue. Unfortunately, conventional treatments often remove lymph nodes, thus disabling the body's only line of defense against disease.

What Causes Breast Cancer

It could be that we are asking the wrong question. If could be that the real culprit is anything that interferes with the body's natural ability to police itself. If this is the case the list of possible causes is long, and the possible variables creating a cause and effect could stagger any mathematical probability.

For example, it is estimated that there are more than 100,000 toxins roaming this globe not only foreign to the human body, but highly toxic, and in direct opposition to the normal functions of the human body. Much of the earth's water is considered polluted and even the air most of us breathe is toxic. Cultural values and attitudes have also contributed to this epidemic. Urban living contributes to high anxiety, stress and an un-natural living environment made of concrete and electro-magnetic fields that interfere with normal biological function.

Based on the current 21st century research we know that the body stores toxins in our fatty tissue. Also, the wearing of anything that inhibits the lymphatic system prevents the body's ability to clean out toxins and waste materials. We also know that if metastasis occurs the likelihood of survival with radiation and chemotherapy drops to 20%. Scientists and researchers have concluded that a woman treated with radiation therapy has a 10 times higher risk of developing Lung cancer. This is because the lungs are located behind the breasts and when the breasts are radiated the lungs also receive some of that radiation (Brownstein, 2017).

According to the National Cancer Institute the death rate has not changed much since 1930. In other words, for the last 80 years approximately the same percentage of women are dying of breast cancer, yet the incidence rate has increased, which means that more women are dying today of breast cancer than ever before (Singer & Grismaijer, 2006). To date, it is estimated that 40,000 women die of cancer and another 200,000 new cases will be diagnosed. In 2017 it was estimated that more than 46,000 women would die of breast cancer and over 182,000 new cases would be diagnosed. Since 1950, it is estimated that conventional treatments have stemmed the tide of cancer recovery by only 5%.

The Side Effects of Conventional Treatments

According to a recent study of 100 college educated women who survive conventional treatments, 92% maintain, several untreated symptoms, which include, achy joints, fatigue, weight gain, anxiety and depression. And when you factor in 92% of the 2.8 million breast cancer survivors, the number of women with unattended physical and mental side effects is staggering (Palmer, 2016). According to Dr. Adelson, an oncologist at Yale-New Haven Health, these long-term side effects are what doctors referred to as the "cost" a woman pays for the treatment administered.

According to another recent study, as the cancer progresses medical centers administer too much treatment, which not only adds to the medical cost, but also increases the side effects and toxicity levels of the patient (Harrison, 2016). The side effects of conventional chemotherapy are (Breastcancer.org, 2017):

- Increasing the risk of developing other cancers
- anemia/low red blood cell counts
- diarrhea
- fatigue
- fertility issues
- hair changes
- infection
- memory loss
- menopause and menopausal symptoms
- mouth and throat sores

- nail changes
- nausea
- neuropathy (problems with hands and feet)
- taste and smell changes
- vaginal dryness
- vomiting
- weight changes
- bone loss/osteoporosis
- heart problems
- vision/eye problems

One of the most alarming side effects of chemotherapy is "chemo brain." It is the mental fog that women experience after undergoing chemotherapy, which can last for six months or longer. The symptoms include lapse in memory, difficulty processing information, and attention issues (Doheny, 2017; Janelsins, 2016).

In one of the largest study's ever conducted, involving 100's of women, six months after chemotherapy, researchers found that 36% of all women experienced a reduction in cognitive abilities. For example, while driving women won't remember the way to a friend's house, they forget the names of friends and colleagues, and have trouble writing down numbers. Similar results were also found in women who received hormone therapy and radiation therapy. The decline in cognitive ability is exacerbated with younger women, black women, and those who experienced depression and anxiety (Doheny, 2017; Janelsins, 2016).

It is important to note that many of the side effects of conventional treatments are debilitating and dehumanizing, which is why it is imperative to consider the latest tests, screenings, and procedures, such as those conducted at the Burzynski Clinic, and the Gerson Clinic, to name a few, before proceeding with outdated therapies whose results have not changed much since the 1950s. One of the best places to go to get the latest information on breast cancer is: http://www.breastcancerchoices.org/

CHAPTER 28

PROSTATE CANCER

Prostate cancer is the number one cancer for older men. As men age, their production of testosterone decreases substantially. In young man age 20, whose testosterone levels are at their peak, prostate cancer is unheard of. Prostate cancer usually begins in men after 30 (NCI, 2012; Morgentaler, 2008).

Dating back to 1940 doctors and scientists were under the impression that high levels of testosterone contributed to cancer. As men age their testosterone levels decrease but doctors were always fearful of recommending testosterone treatments, because they assumed these treatments would trigger the onset of cancer, and if a man was previously diagnosed with cancer the testosterone treatments would cause the cancer to multiply rapidly (Morgentaler, 2008).

Dr. Abe Morgentaler, in his book, "Testosterone for Life," disagrees with these outdated assumptions. Dr. Morgentaler, a hormone researcher from Harvard Medical School, states that this theory (high levels of testosterone contributed to cancer) is based on a 1941 study, which consisted of only three cases, and to date there are no legitimate recent studies that confirm this theory (Morgentaler, 2008).

Testosterone is a hormone produced by the testicles, which the body uses to maintain bone density, fat distribution, muscle strength, muscle mass, production of red blood cells, sex drive, and sperm production. Testosterone levels peak during adolescence or early adulthood and begin to gradually decline 1% per year somewhere after the age of 20. Up to this point prostate cancer is unheard of. Only after the age of 30 does prostate become an issue, and of concern after the age of 50 (Mayo Clinic, n. d.).

The sexual symptoms of low testosterone are (Morgentaler, 2008).

- Problems with erections
- Lower sex drive
- Difficulty in obtaining an orgasm
- There is no longer the drive or need for sex (absent the electricity)

The non-sexual symptoms are (Morgentaler, 2008),

- The lack of energy,
- More tired than normal.
- Irritability
- Osteoporosis (low levels of testosterone contributes to osteoporosis)

In a recent scientific study 13 men were selected who had low levels of testosterone, were diagnosed with prostate cancer (early stages), and had not undergone any radiation of chemotherapy. They were treated with testosterone and examined over the course of treatment via biopsies. In an average of two ½ years in all 13 men:

- Their PSA (prostate-specific antigen) levels did not increase.
- The size of their prostate did not increase.
- Symptoms decreased.
- No progress of prostate cancer.
- 54% of the biopsies revealed no cancer.

Some of the men in this study continued with testosterone treatment for eight years with the same results (Morgentaler, 2008).

In diagnosing prostate cancer doctors use a prostate specific antigen (PSA – a protein produced exclusively by the prostate) test, where the blood is tested for elevated levels of PSA. If present, they are indicative of benign enlargement of the prostate (benign prostatic hyperplasia). According to the National Cancer Institute there is no specific normal or abnormal level of PSA in the blood. Today's doctors consider a PSA blood level of four (ng/mL - nanograms of PSA per milliliter of blood) or lower as normal.

If the PSA rating is higher than four most doctors would recommend a prostate biopsy to determine if cancer is present. According to the NCI, certain men are at higher risk, including African American men and men whose brother or father has had prostate cancer (NCI, 2012). Until recently, this was considered the most reliable form of testing.

With the advances of science there may be a more reliable test, Magnetic Resonance Imaging, (MRI). According to a recent European study published in the European Association of Urology, MRI testing may be superior than standard PSA testing. According to the recent research MRI testing may reduce over diagnosis by 50 percent, and overtreatment of prostate cancer by, at least, 70 percent, especially as it relates to biopsies (Pokorny, 2014).

Surveillance

Another recent approach to prostate cancer is called "Active Surveillance." This procedure is initiated when there are no signs of symptoms, when the cancer is slow growing, and when the cancer is growing is small and contained within the prostate. With this procedure PSA tests occur every three months and biopsies are taken every 15 months. If conditions change, then the patient and doctor opt for a more direct therapy (Cancer Treatment Centers of America, n.d.).

Proton Therapy Versus Intensified Modulated Radiation Therapy (IMRT).

With the advances in the science of conventional radiation therapy, proton therapy has evolved into a precise science, especially when you consider "Pencil Bean Proton Therapy." Conventional radiation therapy has a multitude of side effects that relate directly to its application. For example, with IMRT the radiation dosages are higher, and the field of radiation is more difficult to control, which results in non- cancerous tissue being radiated (Rengan, n.d.)

In contrast, proton therapy provides a specific amount of radiation energy that releases its energy at a specific point. This, in effect, spares the surrounding non-cancerous tissue from the effects of radiation. Pencil beam proton therapy adds a more precise element to the procedure, a specific dosage, along with a specific area, where the proton is discharged. This results in killing off the tumor, but sparing the good tissue, which results in reduced side effects (Rengan, n.d.).

Of major concern is the cost of proton therapy, which is estimated to be approximately $100,000 per patient, compared to the average cost of approximately $50,000 per patients who opt for IMRT therapy (Konski, 2007).

Keep in mind that this procedure is so innovative that the research data comparing proton therapy with traditional radiation therapy has not been compiled. But the reality is, prostate patients experience substantially reduced side effects.

Once diagnosed with cancer the conventional approach to prostate cancer is usually radiation therapy (internal or external), surgery, and chemotherapy. Radiation therapy is usually administered to shrink the tumor. The side effects include (Seattle Cancer Care Alliance, 2012):

- Incontinence: 50% will need to wear a pad for leakage after treatment.
- Impotence: 50% of those treated with notice a permanent change
- Infertility: With radiation therapy infertility is permanent.
- Bowel Problems: diarrhea, bowel urgency, hemorrhoids, burning during bowel movement. Some symptoms can be controlled with medication, although 20% of all men notice a permanent change.

- Fatigue: External radiation will cause fatigue that can last up to one or two months after treatment.
- Tissue Damage: radiation therapy can inflict damage to the bladder, rectum, and surrounding tissue, which may require surgery to repair.

As an alternative, by choosing testosterone therapy the patient experiences no known adverse side effects. The positive side effects are listed above. This medical breakthrough by a leading hormones researcher from Harvard Medical School can mean the difference between life and death as well as dealing with lifelong side effects versus no documented negative side effects.

Patients who opt for testosterone therapy can have it administered by injection, pellets, patches, gel or cream. Pellets taken orally probably would be the last choice because it must go through the liver first (Morgentaler, 2008). To learn more about hormones or to order a hormone test go to: www.zrtlab.com.

WHY I WROTE THIS BOOK

The purpose of this book is to educate and inform you, the reader, of the phenomenal scientific and medical breakthroughs on cancer that have taken place in the 20th and 21st centuries, and to introduce you to those unspoken heroes whose dedication have forever changed the outcome in favor of the patient. To expose you to a paradigm that has existed for thousands of years and introduce you to a paradigm shift that occurred for the first time in the 20th century.

The intent of this book is to inform and offer hope and direction to families who have been stricken with cancer. The purpose of this book is to be a light of information to those in need. The purpose of this book is to, if possible, save lives.

I would be well satisfied if just one child, whose parents read this book, could avoid the horrific side effects, and humiliating consequences that befall millions of cancer victims. My heart grieves every time I see a child in a mall or supermarket whose head is absent any semblance of hair. I am appalled at the insensitivity, ignorance, and pride within the medical community who fail to embrace the vast amount of research and scientific discoveries that have reshaped the very definitions of cancer and the processes from which cancer should be approached. It is my hope that this book, at its very least, offers hope to the bewildered, direction to the desperate, and life with dignity to all who reach out.

As you have read through the pages of this book, I hope that you not only obtain a comprehensive understanding of cancer but also are able to grab onto the names of these phenomenal doctors and institutions and their cutting-edge procedures. Names like Dr. Burzynski, the

Burzynski Clinic, the Gerson Clinic, Duke University, and Dr. Brownstein, to name a few.

Finally, even though this book ends at this juncture the stream of scientific information doesn't stop. There is so much more that can be added. Even as I write there are areas of investigation that need to be investigated. Areas that will have to wait until next time, hopefully, and I will add a revision or another volume that includes these areas, or topics that beg the question.

I would love to expand on the topic of prevention. For example, how specific foods and remedies help in the prevention of cancer. Another question that begs my attention is: Can you starve a cancer cell?

I believe you can, but I need the time to investigate. Given the characteristics of a cancer cell, I can see this as a possible solution. What about juicing? Can juicing help kill off cancer cells?

We have talked a lot about how oxygen kills cancer cells, so what about oxygen therapies, how effective are they? And finally, what can we do to create a healthy environment when we live in an unhealthy environment? In our homes, which is where most of us spend most of our time, what changes can we make to extend our health and longevity? These are just a few of the questions I am examining and will write about in my next revision or the next volume. Until then, I hope that this book made a difference in your life. If you would like me to lecture to a group of 50 or more, just email me at: srmsenior@gmail.com. If you can pay for my ticket and lodging, I would be happy to come and present my PowerPoint version of this book. Email me and ask me for more information about my lecture.

God Bless you, your family, and your universe of friends and associates.

Garry Estrada, M.S.
srmsenior@gmail.com

APPENDIX

Exhibit A

The Cancer Paradigm – Flow Chart

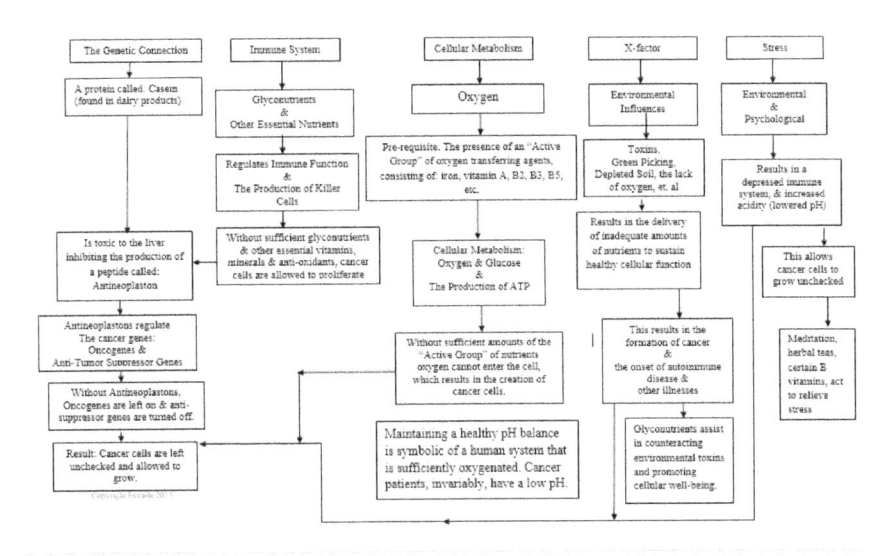

The Genetic Connection

A protein called: Casein (found in dairy products)

Is toxic to the liver inhibiting the production of a peptide called: Antineoplaston

Antineoplastons regulate The cancer genes: Oncogenes & Anti-Tumor Suppressor Genes

Without Antineoplastons, Oncogenes are left on & anti-suppressor genes are turned off.

Result: Cancer cells are left unchecked and allowed to grow.

Immune System

Glyconutrients & Other Essential Nutrients

Regulates Immune Function & The Production of Killer Cells

Without sufficient glyconutrients & other essential vitamins, minerals & anti-oxidants, cancer cells are allowed to proliferate

Cellular Metabolism

Oxygen

Pre-requisite: The presence of an "Active Group" of oxygen transferring agents, consisting of: iron, vitamin A, B2, B3, B5, etc.

Cellular Metabolism: Oxygen & Glucose & The Production of ATP

Without sufficient amounts of the "Active Group" of nutrients oxygen cannot enter the cell, which results in the creation of cancer cells.

Maintaining a healthy pH balance is symbolic of a human system that is sufficiently oxygenated. Cancer patients, invariably, have a low pH.

X-factor

Environmental Influences

Toxins, Green Picking, Depleted Soil, the lack of oxygen, et. al

Results in the delivery of inadequate amounts of nutrients to sustain healthy cellular function

This results in the formation of cancer & the onset of autoimmune disease & other illnesses

Glyconutrients assist in counteracting environmental toxins and promoting cellular well-being.

Stress

Environmental & Psychological

Results in a depressed immune system, & increased acidity (lowered pH)

This allows cancer cells to grow unchecked

Meditation, herbal teas, certain B vitamins, act to relieve stress

---

Exhibit B

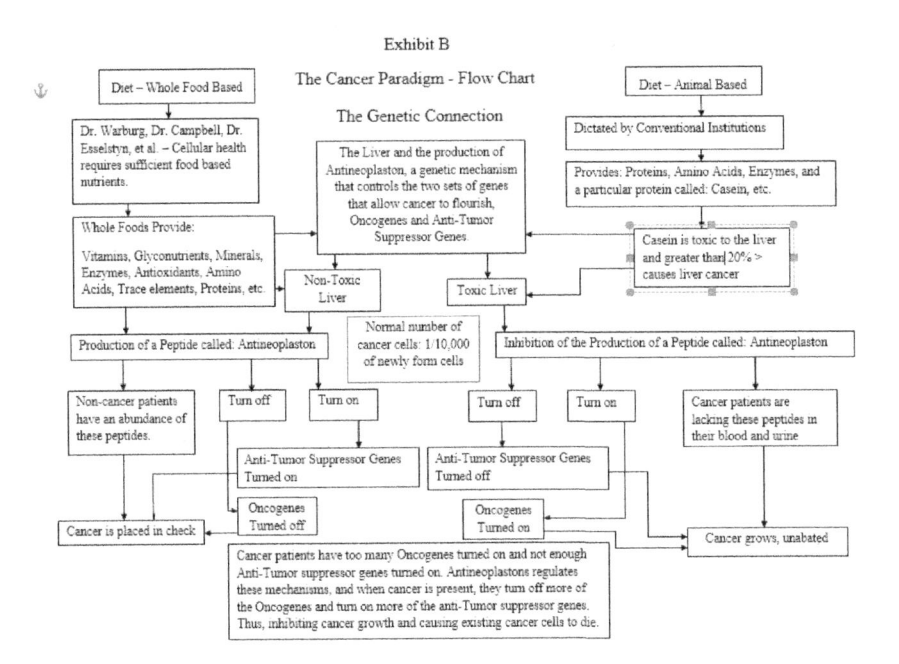

The Cancer Paradigm - Flow Chart

The Genetic Connection

Diet – Whole Food Based

Dr. Warburg, Dr. Campbell, Dr. Esselstyn, et al. – Cellular health requires sufficient food based nutrients.

Whole Foods Provide:
Vitamins, Glyconutrients, Minerals, Enzymes, Antioxidants, Amino Acids, Trace elements, Proteins, etc.

Production of a Peptide called: Antineoplaston

Non-cancer patients have an abundance of these peptides.

Cancer is placed in check

The Genetic Connection

The Liver and the production of Antineoplaston, a genetic mechanism that controls the two sets of genes that allow cancer to flourish, Oncogenes and Anti-Tumor Suppressor Genes

Non-Toxic Liver

Toxic Liver

Normal number of cancer cells: 1/10,000 of newly form cells

Turn off — Anti-Tumor Suppressor Genes Turned on — Oncogenes Turned off

Turn on — Anti-Tumor Suppressor Genes Turned off — Oncogenes Turned on

Diet – Animal Based

Dictated by Conventional Institutions

Provides: Proteins, Amino Acids, Enzymes, and a particular protein called: Casein, etc.

Casein is toxic to the liver and greater than 20% > causes liver cancer

Inhibition of the Production of a Peptide called: Antineoplaston

Cancer patients are lacking these peptides in their blood and urine

Cancer grows, unabated

Cancer patients have too many Oncogenes turned on and not enough Anti-Tumor suppressor genes turned on. Antineoplastons regulates these mechanisms, and when cancer is present, they turn off more of the Oncogenes and turn on more of the anti-Tumor suppressor genes. Thus, inhibiting cancer growth and causing existing cancer cells to die.

REFERENCES

Abbott, S., Blazek, N., Foster, M., (2010). Stress during pregnancy alters immune systems of child. Infectious Diseases in Children, 23 (4) 47.

ACS, (2011). *American Cancer Society.* Retrieved from http://www.cancer.org

ACS, (2013). Cancer Facts & Figures, 2013. American Cancer Society. Retrieved from: http://www.cancer.org/acs/groups/content/@epidemiologysurveilance/documents/document/acspc-036845.pdf

ACS, (2015). Cancer Facts & Figures 2015. American Cancer Society, 2015. Retrieved from: http://www.cancer.org/research/cancerfactsstatistics/cancerfactsfigures2015/

ACS, (n.d.). *The History of Cancer.* American Cancer Society. Retrieved from: http://www.cancer.org/acs/groups/cid/documents/webcontent/002048-pdf.pdf

Allan, S., (2004). Pylon Ambient Energy Lights Fluorescent Bulbs. *Pure Energy Systems News Service.* Retrieved from: http://pesn.com/exclusive/2004/pylon_ambience/

Aihara, Herman, (1986). *Acid & Alkaline.* George Ohsawa Macrobiotic Foundation

Aplin, Harrison, Rycroft, (2008). Investigating Earth's Atmospheric electricity: A Role Model for Planetary Studies. *Space Science Review,* 137,1: pp. 11-27

Anthony C., & Thibodeau, G., (1979). *Anatomy & Physiology*, 10e. Mosby Elsevier, MO.

Baeuerle, A., Patrick, P., & Christian, I., (2012). Clinical Experience with Gene Therapy and Bispecific Antibodies for T Cell-based Therapy of Cancer. *Current Pharmaceutical Biotechnology*, 13 (8), pp. 1399-1408(10).

Bansal B., Rhoads, J., Bansal S., (1978). Effects of Diet on Colon Carcinogenesis and the Immune System in Rats Treated with 1,2-Dimethylhydrazine. *Cancer Research*, 1978;38:3293-3303. Downloaded from: http://cancerres.aacrjournals.org/content/38/10/3293.full.pdf+html

Bailar, J., & Gornik, H. (1997). Cancer Undefeated. *New England Journal of Medicine*. Vol. 336, No. 22, pp. 1569-1574

Baillargeon, J., Urban, R., Kuo, Y., Ottenbacher, K., Raji, M., Du, F., Lin, Y., Goodwin, J., (2014). Risk of Myocardial Infarction in Older Men Receiving Testosterone Therapy. *Annals of Pharmacotherapy*, 48,9, pp. 1138-1144.

Barendse, S., (2013). The Truth About Salt. Natural News & HCBL. Retrieved from: http://drleonardcoldwell.com/the-truth-about-salt/

Barry, M., (2011). *The Forgiveness Project: The Startling Discovery of How to Overcome Cancer, Find Health, and Achieve Peace*. Kregel Publications, pp 77-105.

Baum, A., Revenson, T., & Singer, J., (2007). *Stress, Health, & Illness. Handbook of Health Psychology* (2nd Ed.). Psychology Press, New York, NY.

Beach, R., (1936). *United States Senate Document #264, "MODERN MIRACLE MEN."* United States GPO, Washington, D.C., 1936. Retrieved from: http://www.healthenlightenment.com/document264.shtml

REFERENCES

Benagiano, A., (1965). The Effect of Sodium Fluoride on Thyroid Enzymes and Basal Metabolism in the Rat. *Annali Di Stomatologia*, 14, pp. 601-619

Bergner, P., (1997). *The Healing Power of Minerals, Special Nutrients, and Trace Elements.* Prima Publishing USA

Bowers, L., (2015). *EMF pollution - What is EMF?* Sott.net.

Boyer, R., & Morais, H., (1997). *Labor's Untold Story.* United Electrical, Radio & Machine Workers of America.

Brewer, K., (1984). The High pH Therapy for Cancer, Tests on Mice and Humans. *Pharmacology Biochemistry & Behavior*, 21 (1), p. 1-5.

Brody, J., (1990). Huge Study of Diet Indicts Fat and Meat. *New York Times*, May 8, 1990.

Brownsey, A., (2012). November Is Pancreatic Cancer Awareness Month. *American Society for Gastrointestinal Endoscopy.* Retrieved from: http://www.asge.org/WorkArea/showcontent.aspx?id=16050

Bryant, H., Brasher, P., (2005). Breast Implants and Breast Cancer — Reanalysis of a Linkage Study. *The New England Journal of Medicine.* Vol. 332, No. 23, pp. 1535-1539

Brydon, L., Walker, C., Wawrzyniak, A., Whitehead, D., Okamura, H., Yajima, J., Tsuda, A., & Steptoe, A., (2009). Synergistic effects of psychological and immune stressors on inflammatory cytokine and sickness responses in humans. *Brain, Behavior, & Immunity*, 23 (2), 217-224. Retrieved from: http://www.ncbi.nlm.nih.gov/pmc/articles/PMC2637301/

Brydon, L., Walker, C., Wawrzyniak, A., Chart, H., & Steptoe, A., (2009). Dispositional optimism and stress-induced changes in immunity and negative mood. *Brain, Behavior, & Immunity*, 23 (6), 810-816. Retrieved from: http://www.ncbi.nlm.nih.gov/pmc/articles/PMC2715885/

Budinger, M. (2011). Sir Isaac Newton -- You Lost the War on Cancer: News from the 9th Annual International IPT/IPTLD Conference. *Townsend Letter*, (337/338), 60-65.

Burzynski, (2004). The Present State of Antineoplaston Research (1). *Integrative Cancer Therapies*, 3 (1), pp. 47-48.

Burzynski Clinic, (n.d.). Retrieved from: http://www.burzynskiclinic.com/sr-burzynski-mdphd.html

Burzynski, (2008). Burzynski Research Institute, Inc. (BRI) Presents Promising Phase II Data on Malignant Glioma. Phase II Clinical Study in Anaplastic Astrocytoma Shows Objective Responses to Antineoplaston Therapy. *Business Wire*, 11/21/2008, 09:27 AM ET. Retrieved from: http://www.businesswire.com/news/home/20081121005076/en/Burzynski-Research-Institute-BRI-Presents-Promising-PhaseInstitute-BRI-Presents-Promising-Phase.

Butcher, J.N., Mineka, S., & Hooley, J.M. (2010). *Abnormal Psychology* (14the ed): Pearson Education, Inc.

Campbell, C., Parpia, B., & Chen, J., (1998). Diet, lifestyle, and the etiology of coronary artery disease: the Cornell China Study. *The American Journal of Cardiology*, 82 (10), 2, p. 18-21.

Campbell, N., Reece, J., Urry, L., Cain, M., Wasserman, S., Minorsky, P., Jackson, R., (2008). *Biology* (8th ed.). Benjamin-Cummings Publishing Co

Chen, J., Campbell, C., Li, J., & Peto, R., (1990). *Diet, Lifestyle, and Mortality in China: A Study of the Characteristics of 65 Chinese Counties*. Oxford University Press. CDC, (2007). Center for Disease Control and Prevention. Retrieved from: http://www.cdc.gov/nchs/fastats/deaths.htmr

CDC, (2009). Fourth National Report on Human Exposure to Environmental Chemicals. *Center for Disease Control*. Retrieved from: http://www.cdc.gov/exposurereport/pdf/FourthReport.pdf

REFERENCES

CDC, (2013) Fourth National Report on Human Exposure to Environmental Chemicals Updated Tables, March 2013. *Center for Disease Control.* Retrieved from: http://www.cdc.gov/exposurereport/pdf/FourthReport_Updated Tables_Mar2013.pdf

CDC, (n.d.). Chronic Diseases: The Leading Causes of Death and Disability in the United States. Center for Disease Control and Prevention. Retrieved from: http://www.cdc.gov/chronicdisease/overview/

Calbom, J., & Mahaffey, M., (2006). *The Complete Cancer Cleanse.* Thomas Nelson Inc. Psychological Stress and Susceptibility to the Common Cold. Carnegie Mellon University Research Showcase, Department of Psychology, 263.

Cancer Therapy Advisor, (n.d.). Brain Cancer Treatment Regiments, Brain Cancer Advisor. Retrieved from: http://www.cancertherapyadvisor.com/brain-cancer/brain-cancertreatment-regimens/article/218165/

Castillo, S., (2015). Digestive Health and The Immune System: Good Gut Bacteria Relieves Inflammatory Bowel Conditions. Medical Daily. Retrieved from: http://www.medicaldaily.com/digestive-health-and-immune-system-good-gut-bacteriarelieves-inflammatory-bowel-318976

Cohen, S., Tyrrell, D., Smith, A., (1991). Psychological Stress and Susceptibility to the Common Cold. *Carnegie Mellon University Research Showcase, Department of Psychology*, p. 263.

Conley, E. J., (2004). *Secrets for Reducing Your Breast Cancer Risk.* Detroit Educational Television Foundation & Dr. Edward J. Conley.

Connor, T., (2008). Don't stress out your immune system – Just relax. *Brain Behavior and Immunity*, 22, (8), pp. 1128 – 1129. ISSN 0889-1591

Consumer Report, (2012). Arsenic in your food. *Consumer Reports*, ConsumerReports.org. Retrieved from: http://www.consumerreports.org/cro/magazine/2012/11/arsenic-in-yourfood/index.htm

Coplan, M., Patch S., Masters R., & Bachman M., (2007). Confirmation of and Explanations for Elevated Blood Lead and Other Disorders in Children Exposed to Water Disinfection and Fluoridation Chemicals. *Neurotoxicology*. Sep;28(5):1032-42. Epub 2007 Mar 1. PMID: 17420053.

Coy, Peter, (2017). Science Advances One Funeral at a Time. The Latest Nobel Proves It. Bloomberg Businessweek.

Cromie, W., (2004). Mucus Plays Key Role in Cancer. *Harvard University Gazette*.

Dai Y, Hogan S, Schmelz EM, Ju YH, Canning C, Zhou K. Selective Growth Inhibition of Human Breast Cancer Cells by Graviola Fruit Extract in Vitro and In Vivo Involving Downregulation of EGFR Expression. Nutritional Cancer. 2011 Jul;63(5):795-801. Epub 2011 Jun 22. Retrieved from http://www.ncbi.nlm.nih.gov/pubmed/21767082

Decelles, (2002). Environment Canada, EPA. Retrieved from: http://www.sciencebuddies.org/science-fairprojects/project_ideas/Chem_AcidsBasesphScale.shtml

Devesa, S., Blot, W., Stone, B., Miller, B., Tarone, R. & Fraumeni, J. (1995). Recent Cancer Trends in the United States. *Journal of the National Cancer Institute*, 87 (3), pp. 175-182.

Dimitrov, T., (2007). 50 Nobel Laureates and Other Great Scientists Who Believe in God. Nobelist.net. Retrieved from: http://nobelists.net/

Donn, J., Mendoza, M., Pritchard, J., (2008). AP: Drugs found in drinking water. *USA Today*, 9-12-2008.

Douglas, W., (2007). The Fluoride Myth Busted. *The Douglas Report.* Baltimore, MD.

Durrant-Peatfield, (2006). The Effects of Fluoride on the Thyroid Gland. *The Environmental Illness Resource.*

Durrant-Peatfield, (2006). *Your Thyroid and How to Keep it Healthy: The Great Thyroid Scandal and How to Survive It.* Hammersmith Press Limited, UK.

Edsall JT., (1986). Nature: Albert Szent-Gyorgi (1893-1986). 12(324), 6096, 409.

Elbendary A., Cirisano F., Evans A., Davis P., Iglehart J., Marks J., Berchuck A., (1996). Relationship between p21 expression and mutation of the p53 tumor suppressor gene in normal and malignant ovarian epithelial cells. *Clinical Cancer Research,* 2 (9), pp. 1571-1575. Retrieved from: http://www.ncbi.nlm.nih.gov/pubmed/9816335

EPA, (n.d.). Basic Information About Drinking Water. Retrieved from: http://water.epa.gov/drink/contaminants/basicinformation/fluoride.cfm

Faloon, W. (2015). How Immune Decline Hastens Aging. *Life Extension Magazine.*

FDA, (2005). Reclassification Petition - Non-invasive Bone Growth Simulator. Federal Drug Administration. Retrieved from: http://www.fda.gov/ohrms/dockets/DOCKETS/05p0121/05p-0121-ccp0001-03-Petitionvol1.pdf

FDA, (2012). Vaccines, Blood & Biologics, Thimerosal in Vaccines, FDA. Retrieved from: http://www.fda.gov/BiologicsBloodVaccines/SafetyAvailability/VaccineSafety/UCM096228.

Ferlay, J., Parkin, D., Steliarova-Foucher, (2010). Estimates of cancer incidence and mortality in Europe in 2008, 46,4, pp. 765-781.

Epstein, L., (2014). A New Perspective on Child Development in the Wireless Age. Earthcalm. Retrieved from: http://www.earthcalm.com/child-development-wireless-age

Flanagan, P., (1995). Hydrogen... Longevity's Missing Link. *Nexus*.

Folk, et al., (2007). Fetal methylmercury exposure as measured by cord blood mercury concentrations in a mother–infant cohort in Hong Kong. *Environmental International*, 33 (1), pp. 84-92.

Galleti, P., & Joyet, G., (1958). Effect of Fluorine on Thyroid Iodine Metabolism and Hyperthyroidism. *Journal of Clinical Endocrinology and Metabolism*, 18, pp. 1102-1110

Gaut, Z., (1993). Aspirin Use and the Risk of Cancer. *The Journal of Cancer Research*, 53: 1322–1327, 1993

Gaylis, F., Lin, W., Ignatoff, J., Amling, C., Tutrone, R., Cosgrove, D., (2006). Prostate Cancer in Men Using Testosterone Supplementation. The journal of Urology, 175,4, pp. 1572-1574

Gerson, C., (2010). *Healing the Gerson Way*. Sheridan Books.

Gerson, M. (2002). *A Cancer Therapy* (6 ed.). Whittier Books., New York.

Gandhi, O., Morgan, L., Salles, A., Han, Y., Herberman, R., Davis, D., (2011). Exposure Limits: The underestimation of absorbed cell phone radiation, especially in children, Electromagnetic Biology and Medicine, 1-18. Retrieved from: http://electromagnetichealth.org/wp-content/uploads/2011/10/EBM_Final_v4_10-13-11-1.pdf

Giovannucci, E., Egan, K., Hunter, D., Stampfer, M., Colditz, G., Willett, W., Speizer, F., (1995). Aspirin and the Risk of Colorectal Cancer in Women. The New England Journal of Medicine, 333:609-614.

Giovannucci, E. (1999). Tomatoes, Tomato-Based Products, Lycopene, and Cancer: Review of the Epidemiologic Literature.

Journal of the National Cancer Institute. Issue 91, Volume 4, pp. 317-331. doi: 10.1093/jnci/91.4.317

Glyconutrition For Life, (n.d.). Research. Retrieved from: http://www.glyconutritionforlife.org/research.php

Gourounti, K., Kapetanios, V., Paparisteidis, N., Vaslamatzis, G., Anagnostopoulos, F., (2009). Psychological stress, immune system and IVF outcome. *Journal of Reproductive Immunology*, 81, (2), 9/2009, pp. 157-158, ISSN 0165-0378, 10.1016/j.jri.2009.06.220. (http://www.sciencedirect.com/science/article/pii/S0165037809003532)

Grens, K., (2012). Mercury, oils from fish at odds in heart health. *American Journal of Clinical Nutrition*. Retrieved from: http://www.nlm.nih.gov/medlineplus/news/fullstory_128813.html

Greviskes, A., (2014). Dehydration: Not just a summer thing. *CNN.com*. Retrieved from: http://www.essentiawater.com/news/wp-content/uploads/Dehydration_-Not-just-asummer-thing-CNN.pdf

Hall, I. HA., Coates, R. J., Uhler, R. J., Brinton, L.A., Grammon, M. D., Brogan, D., Swanson, C. A., (1999). Stage of Breast Cancer in Relation to Body Mass Index and Bra Cup Size. *International Journal of Cancer*. 82 (1), pp. 23-27.

Hammarsten, E., (1931). *Physiology or Medicine 1931 - Presentation Speech*. Nobelprize.org. Retrieved from: http://www.nobelprize.org/nobel_prizes/medicine/laureates/1931/press.html

Harada, M., (1995). Minamata Disease: Methylmercury Poisoning in Japan Caused by Environmental Pollution. *Informa Healthcare*. Retrieved from: http://informahealthcare.com/doi/abs/10.3109/10408449509089885

Hillman, D., et al., (1979). Hypothyroidism and Anemia Related to Fluoride in Dairy Cattle. *Journal of Dairy Science*, 62 (3), pp. 416-423

Himmelfarb, J., Kane, J., Mcmonagle, E., Zaltas, E., Bobzin, S., Boddupalli, S., Phinney S., and Miller, G., (2003). Alpha and Gamma Tocopherol Metabolism in Healthy Subjects and Patients with End-Stage Renal Disease. *Kidney International.* 64, pp. 978–991; doi:10.1046/j.1523-1755.2003.00151.x

Holistic-research.org, n.d. Water. Retrieved from: http://www.holistic-research.org/

Howlader N, Noone A.M., Krapcho M., Neyman N., Aminou R., Altekruse S.F., Kosary C.L., Ruhl J., Tatalovich Z., Cho H., Mariotto A., Eisner M.P., Lewis D.R., Chen H.S., Feuer

E.J., Cronin K.A. (eds). *SEER Cancer Statistics Review*, 1975-2009 (Vintage 2009 Populations), National Cancer Institute. Bethesda, MD. Retrieved from: submission, posted to the SEER web site, April 2012.

Hsieh, C. & Trichopoulos, D. (1991). Breast Size, Handedness and Breast Cancer Risk. *European Journal of Cancer and Clinical Oncology*, 27(2), pp. 131-135.

Hsu, P., & Sabatini, D., (2012). *Cancer Cell Metabolism: Warburg and Beyond.* Whitehead Institute for Biomedical Research and Massachusetts Institute of Technology Department of Biology, Cambridge, MA 02142, USA.

Hsu, P., & Sabatini, D., (2012). Cancer Cell Metabolism: Warburg and Beyond. *Cell*, 134(5), pp. 703-707. doi:10.1016/j.cell.2008.08.021. Retrieved from: http://www.sciencedirect.com/science/article/pii/S0092867408010660

Hyman, M., (2012). How Toxins Make You Fat: 4 Steps to Get Rid of Toxic Weight. Retrieved from:

http://drhyman.com/blog/2012/02/20/how-toxins-make-you-fat-4-steps-to-get-ridof-toxic-weight/#close

Imats, R., (1966). Applications of the Coanda Effect. Scientific America, June 1966.

Infoplease, (2013). Life Expectancy for Countries, 2013. Retrieved from: http://www.infoplease.com/world/statistics/life-expectancy-country.html

Interdisziplina re Gesellschaftfur Umweltmedizine. V., (2002). Freiburger Appeal. IGUMED, Bergseestr. 57, 79713 Bad Sackingen IUPUI Biology (2004). Biology N100. IUPUI Department of Biology. Indiana University, Purdue University, Indianapolis Retrieved from: http://www.biology.iupui.edu/biocourses/n100/2k4ch7respiration notes.html

Ivarsson U, Nilsson H, Santesson J, (eds). (1992). A FOA briefing book on chemical weapons: threat, effects, and protection. Umeå, National Defense Research Establishment. Retrieved from: http://www.opcw.org/about-chemical-weapons/types-of-chemicalagent/nerve-agents/

Jacobson, J., Jacobson, S., (1990). Effects of exposure to PCBs and related compounds on growth and activity in children. Neurotoxicology and Teratology, 12 (4), 319-326.

Jemal, A., Center, M., DeSantis, C., Ward, E., (2010). Global Patterns of Cancer Incidence and Mortality Rates and Trends. Cancer Epidemiology, Biomarkers & Prevention. Doi: 10.1158/1055-9965.EPI-10-0437

Jessup, (2008). RX on Tap? Drugs Found in Drinking Water. CBS News.

Johns Hopkins Medical Institutions (2007, September 10). How Vitamin C Stops Cancer.

ScienceDaily. Retrieved February 26, 2012, from http://www.sciencedaily.com/releases/2007/09/070910132848.htm

Johnson, D. (2006). Home Test pH Kit (5th Edition). New Page Productions, Inc.

Kemeny, M., & Schedlowski, M., (2007). Understanding the Interaction Between Psychological and Immune Related Diseases: A Stepwise Progression. Brain, Behavior, and Immunology, pp. 1009-1018.

Kalos, M., Levine, B., Porter, D., Katz, S., Grupp, S., Bagg, A., & June, C., (2011). T Cells with Chimeric Antigen Receptors Have Potent Antitumor Effects and Can Establish Memory in Patients with Advanced Leukemia. Science Translational Medicine, 3 (95), p. 95ra73.

DOI: 10.1126/scitranslmed.3002842

Kellum, J., (2000). Determinants of blood pH in health and disease. Critical Care, 4: 6-14. Current Science Ltd.

Khurana, V., Teo, C., Kundi, M., Hardell, L., Carlberg, M., (2009). Cell phones and brain tumors: a review including the long-term epidemiologic data. Surgical Neurology, 72,3, pp. 205-214

Killian, P., Kronski, E., Michalik, K., Barbieri, O., Astigiano, S., Sommerhoff, C., Pfeffer, U., Nerlich, A., Bachmeier, B., (2012). Curcumin Inhibits Prostate Cancer Metastasis in vivo by Targeting the Inflammatory Cytokines CXCL1 and -2. Carcinogenesis, p.1-36

Kolata, G., (2009a). Forty Years' War: Advances Elusive in the Drive to Cure Cancer. New York Times, April 23, 2009. Retrieved from: http://www.nytimes.com/2009/04/24/health/policy/24cancer.html?pagewanted=all&_r=0

Kolata, G., (2009). As Other Death Rates Fall, Cancer's Scarcely Moves. New York Times, April 24, 2009. Retrieved from:

http://www.nytimes.com/2009/04/24/health/research/24cancerside.html?ref=policy

Komen, S. G. (2011). Breast Cancer, Your Guide to Breast Self-Awareness. Retrieved from: http://ww5.komen.org/ShareStory.aspx?itc=emoentpnt:4

Komen, S. G. (2015). Side Effects of Radiation Therapy. Retrieved from: http://ww5.komen.org/BreastCancer/SideEffectsofRadiationTherapy.html

Komori, A., Yatsunami, J., Okabe, S., Abe, S., Hara, K., Suganuma, M., Kim, S. J., Fujiki, H., 1993). Anticarcinogenic Activity of Green Tea Polyphenols. Japanese Journal of Clinical Oncology. Issue 23, Number 3, pp. 186-190.

Korones, D., Fisher, P., Kretschmar, C., Zhu, T., Chen, Z., Kepner, J., & Freeman, C., (2007). Treatment of Children with Diffuse Intrinsic Brain Stem Glioma with Radiotherapy, A Children's Oncology Group Phase II Study Vincristine and Oral VP-16: Pediatric Blood Cancer. DOI 10.1002/pbc

Lehrer, S., Green, S., Stock, R., (2011). Association between number of cell phone contracts and brain tumor incidence in nineteen U.S. States. Journal of Neuro-Oncology, 101, 3 pp. 505-507. Retrieved from: http://search.proquest.com.contentproxy.phoenix.edu/docview/845871696?pqorigsite=summon&accountid=458

Liddy, N, Bossi, G., Adam, K., Lissina, A., Mahon, T., Hassan, N., Gavarret, J., Bianchi, F., Pumphrey, N., Ladell, K., Gostisk, E., Sewell, A., Lissin, N., Harwood, N., Molloy, P., Li, Y., Cameron, B., Sami, M., Baston, E., Todorov, P., Paston, S., Dennis, R., Harper, J., Dunn, S., Ashfield, R., et al., (2012). Monoclonal TCR-redirected tumor cell killing. Nature Medicine, 18, pp. 980–987, doi:10.1038/nm.2764

Liede, A., Karlan, B.Y., Narod, S.A., (2004, February). Cancer Risks for Male Carriers of Germline Mutations in BRCA1 or BRCA2: A Review of the Literature. Journal of Clinical Oncology. Vol. 22, No. 4, pp. 735-742

Life Extension, (2013). A cure for cancer may be a step closer. Life Extension, Daily News, July 15, 2013.

Life Extension, (2014). Meta-analysis links greater calcium intake to lower colorectal cancer risk. LifeExtension. Retrieved from: http://www.lifeextension.com/newsletter/2014/3/Meta-analysis-links-greater-calciumintake-to-lower-colorectal-cancer-risk/page-01?utm_source=eNewsletter_EZX400E&utm_medium=email&utm_term=Article&utm_content=Button&utm_campaign=2014Wk12-1

Lipton, A., Uzzo, R., Amato, R. J., Ellis, G. K., Hakimian, B., Roodman, G. D., & Smith, M. R. (2009). The Science and Practice of Bone Health in Oncology: Managing Bone Loss and Metastasis in Patients with Solid Tumors. Journal of the National Comprehensive Cancer Network: JNCCN, 7(Suppl 7), S1–S30.

Litzka, M., & Von Mundy, V., (1963). Influence of Fluorine and Iodine on the Metabolism, Particularly on the Thyroid Gland. Muenchener Medicische Wochenschrift, 105, pp. 182-186.

Liu Y-Q, Cheng X, Guo L-X, Mao C, Chen Y-J, Liu H-X, et al. (2012) Identification of an Annonaceous Acetogenin Mimetic, AA005, as an AMPK Activator and Autophagy Inducer in Colon Cancer Cells. PLoS ONE 7(10): e47049. doi: 10.1371/journal.pone.0047049

Lowenstein, P. H., (1968). Towards the Further Shore: An Autobiography. Victor Gollancz, London, 1968, p. 156.

Lustig, R., (2013). Fat Chance, Beating the Odds Against Sugar, processed Foods, Obesity, and Disease. Plume publishing

REFERENCES

Lynge, E., (1998). Mammography screening for breast cancer in Copenhagen April 1991-March 1997. Mammography screening evaluation group. APMIS. 83, pp. 1-44.

Lyobebe, S., (2012). Healthy Eating & Lifestyle. Trafford Publishing.

Madhavan TV, Gopalan C. The effect of dietary protein on carcinogenesis of aflatoxin. Arch Pathol. 1968 Feb;85(2):133-7. PubMed PMID: 4294825.

Mandell, L., Kadota, R., Freeman, C., Douglass, E., Fontanesi, J., Cohen, M., Kovnar, E., Burger, P., Sanford, R., Kepner, J., Friedman, H., Kun, L., (1999). There is no role for hyperfractionated radiotherapy in the management of children with newly diagnosed diffuse intrinsic brainstem tumors: results of a pediatric oncology group phase III trial comparing conventional vs. hyperfractionated radiotherapy. International Journal of Radiation Oncology * Biology * Physics, 43(5), 959-964.

Manikkam M, Tracey R, Guerrero-Bosagna C, Skinner MK (2013). Plastics Derived Endocrine Disruptors (BPA, DEHP and DBP) Induce Epigenetic Transgenerational Inheritance of Obesity, Reproductive Disease and Sperm Epimutations. PLoS ONE 8(1): e55387. doi: 10.1371/journal.pone.0055387

Mayo Clinic, (n. d.) Testosterone therapy: Key to male vitality? Retrieved from: http://www.mayoclinic.com/health/testosterone-therapy/MC00030

McDaniel, (2012.). Glyconutrients - Dr. McGee Interviews Dr. Reg. McDaniel. Retrieved from: http://www.youtube.com/watch?v=3T5Vl189GfI

McDougall, J., (n.d.). A Revelation: Your Health is Not Determined by Heredity. Dr. McDougall's Health & Medical Center. Retrieved from: http://www.drmcdougall.com/free_2c.html

McLaughlin, J.K., Blot, W. J., Yin, O. N., Jossefsson, S., Adami, H. O., Fraumeni, J. F., (1998). Cancer Risk Among Women with Cosmetic

Breast Implants: A Population-Based Cohort Study in Sweden. Journal of the National Cancer Institute. Vol. 90, Issue 2, pp. 156-158.

McNally Institute, (2000). Commercial and Industrial use of Carcinogens. The McNally Institute. Retrieved from: http://delloyd.50megs.com/hazard/carcinogens.html

Mendoza, (2008). Water Probe Prompts Senate Hearings. Associated Press, 3-11-2008.

Mondoa, E., & Kitei, M. (2001). Sugars That Heal: The New Healing Science of Glyconutrients. The Random House Publishing Group, N.Y.

Montazeri, A., Jarvandi, S., Ebrahimi, M., Haghighat, S., & Ansari, M. (2004). The Role of Depression in the Development of Breast Cancer: Analysis of Registry Data from a Single Institute. Asian Pacific Journal of Cancer Prevention. Vol. 5, pp. 316–319.

Morgentaler, A., (2008). Testosterone for Life: Recharge Your Vitality, Sex Drive, Muscle Mass, and Overall Health. McGraw Hill.

Morishita, K., (1976). Hidden Truth of Cancer. Dr. Morishita Keiichi.

Mundy, V., (1963). Influence of Fluorine and Iodine on the Metabolism, Particularly on the Thyroid Gland. Muenchener Medicische Wochenschrift, Vol. 105, pp. 182-186

Murray, R., Granner, D., Mayes, P., & Rockwell, V., (1996). Harper's Biochemistry Volume 24

Nachman, D., & Hardy, D., (2015). The Human Experiment.

National Science Foundation, (n.d.). Contaminant Guide, Fluoride. Retrieved from: http://www.nsf.org/consumer/drinking_water/contaminant_fluoride.asp

Nasca, P. C., Greenwald, P., Burnett, W. S., Chorost, S., and Schmidt, W., (1981)

REFERENCES

Cancer Among the Foreign-born in New York State. Cancer. Vol. 48, Issue 10, pp. 2323-2328.

National Geographic, (n.d.). U.S. Life Expectancy Map: The Gender Gap. Retrieved from: http://news.nationalgeographic.com/news/2013/04/life-expectancy-map/

Nave, R., (2014). HyperPhysics. Department of Physics and Astronomy, George State University.

NCI, (2010), National Cancer Institute, U.S. National Institute of Health. Retrieved from: www.cancer.gov

NCI, (2012). Antineoplastons (PDQ). National Cancer Institute, at the National Institutes of Health, 08/16/2012. Retrieved from: http://www.cancer.gov/cancertopics/pdq/cam/antineoplastons/healthprofessional/page1/AllPages

NCI, (2012). Prostate-specific antigen (PSA) Test. National Cancer Institute. Retrieved from: http://www.cancer.gov/cancertopics/factsheet/detection/PSA

NCI, (2013) Antineoplastons. National Cancer Institute. Retrieved from: http://www.cancer.gov/cancertopics/pdq/cam/antineoplastons/patient/page1/AllPages

NCI, (n.d.). Alliance of Glycobiologists for Detection of Cancer Fact Sheet. Retrieved from: http://glycomics.cancer.gov/fact-sheet

NCI, (n.d.). High-Dose Vitamin C (PDQ®). National Cancer Institute. Retrieved from: http://www.cancer.gov/about-cancer/treatment/cam/patient/vitamin-c-pdq

Newman, B., Austin, M. A., Lee, L., King, M. C., (1988). Inheritance of Human Breast Cancer: Evidence for Autosomal Dominant Transmission in High-risk Families. Proceeding of the National academy of Science. USA. Vol. 85, pp. 3044-3048

Nobelprize.org, (2012). Dr. Otto Warburg, Biography. Retrieved from: http://www.nobelprize.org/nobel_prizes/medicine/laureates/1931/warburg.html

NRDC, (n.d.). Natural Resources Defense Counsel. Retrieved from: http://www.nrdc.org/water/drinking/bw/appa.asp

Null, G., (2013). War on Health. A Gary Null Production.

Oberlies NH, Chang CJ, McLaughlin JL, (1997). Structure-activity relationships of diverse Annonaceous acetogenins against multidrug resistant human mammary adenocarcinoma (MCF-7/Adr) cells. J Med Chem. 1997 Jun 20;40(13):2102-6. PMID: 9207950 [PubMed - indexed for MEDLINE]

Oberlies NH, Jones JL, Corbett TH, Fotopoulos SS, McLaughlin JL, (1995). Tumor cell growth inhibition by several Annonaceous acetogenins in an in vitro disk diffusion assay. Cancer Lett. 1995 Sep 4;96(1):55-62. PMID: 7553608 [PubMed - indexed for MEDLINE]

Odiyo, J., & Makungo, R. (2012). Fluoride concentrations in groundwater and impact on human health in Siloam Village, Limpopo Province, South Africa. Water SA, 38(5), 731-736. doi:10.4314/wsa.v38i5.12

Ogata Y, Matono K, Tsuda H, Ushijima M, Uchida S, Akagi Y, et al. (2015) Randomized Phase II Study of 5-Fluorouracil Hepatic Arterial Infusion with or without Antineoplastons as an Adjuvant Therapy after Hepatectomy for Liver Metastases from Colorectal Cancer. PLoS ONE 10(3): e0120064. doi:10.1371/journal.pone.0120064

Ollonen, P., Lehtonen, J., & Eskelinen, M., (2005, January). Stressful and Adverse Life Experiences in Patients with Breast Symptoms; a Prospective Case-control Study in Kuopio, Finland. Anticancer Research: International Journal of Cancer Research and Treatment. Vol. 25, No. 1b, pp. 531-536.

OrganicLives, (2011). Secrets of the Hunza Valley. Organic Lives. Retrieved from: http://www.organiclives.org/_blog/OrganicLives_Blog/post/Secrets_of_the_Hunza_Valley/

Parker, V., Douglas, A., (2010). Stress in early pregnancy: maternal neuro-endocrine-immune responses and effects, Journal of Reproductive Immunology, 85, (1), 86-92, ISSN 0165-0378, http://dx.doi.org/10.1016/j.jri.2009.10.011.

http://www.sciencedirect.com/science/article/pii/S016503780900552X.

Paulson, (2003). Glycomics: The Study of Glycobiology. MIT'S Magazine on Innovation Technology, p.46, February 2003

Penn Medicine, (2011). Genetically Modified "Serial Killer" T Cells Obliterate Tumors in Patients with Chronic Lymphocytic Leukemia. Penn Researchers Report. August 10, 2011.

Pinellas County Florida Utilities, (n.d.). Fluoride. Retrieved from: http://www.pinellascounty.org/utilities/fluoridation.htm

Poisons Act 1972, (n.d.). Poisons Act 1972. Retrieved from: http://www.aberdeenshire.gov.uk/tradingstandards/business/Poisons.pdf Posnick, S., (2015). Activate Your Natural Killer Cells. Life Extension Magazine.

Provos, J., (2015). Anticancer Properties of Saffron. Life Extension Magazine.

Qadan, L., Perez-Stable, C., Schwall, R., Burnstein, K., Ostenson, R., Howard, G., & Roos, B., (2000). Hepatocyte Growth Factor and Vitamin D Cooperatively Inhibit Androgen-Unresponsive Prostate Cancer Cell Lines. Endocrinology, 141,7.

Riely, K., (2011). Childhood obesity rates on the rise in Pa. through 2011. Retrieved from: http://www.post-gazette.com/stories/news/health/childhood-obesity-rates-on-therise-in-pa-through-2011-698708/#ixzz2eNNTSH9Z

Raulet, D., & Guerra, N., (2009). Oncogenic Stress Sensed by the Immune System: Role of Natural Killer Cell Receptors. Natural Reviews Immunology, 9 (8), 568-580. Nature Publishing Group. Retrieved from: http://dx.doi.org/10.1038/nri2604

Reiche, E. M. V., Nunes, S. O. V., & Morimoto, H. K. (2004). Stress, depression, the immune system, and cancer. Lancet Oncology, 5(10), 617-25. Retrieved from http://search.proquest.com/docview/200900508?accountid=35812

Reiche, E., Morimoto1, H., & Nunes S., (2005). Stress and depression-induced immune dysfunction: Implications for the development and progression of cancer. International Review of Psychiatry, 17(6): pp. 515–527. DOI: 10.1080/02646830500382102

Reiche, E. M. V., Nunes, S. O. V., & Morimoto, H. K. (2004). Stress, depression, the immune system, and cancer. Lancet Oncology, 5(10), 617-25. Retrieved from http://search.proquest.com/docview/200900508?accountid=35812

Reinberg, S. (2007). Cancer Killed Almost 8 Million Worldwide in 2007. U.S. News & World Report. Monday, March 21, 2011. Retrieved from: http://health.usnews.com/usnews/health/healthday/071217/cancer-killed-almost-8million-worldwide-in-2007.htm

Rothermundt, C., Hayoz S., Templeton A., Winterhalder, R., Strebel, R., Bärtschi, D., Pollak, M., et al., (2014). Metformin in Chemotherapy-naive Castration-resistant Prostate Cancer: A Multicenter Phase 2 Trial (SAKK 08/09). European Urology, 66,3, pp. 468474.

Ryder, J., (2011). FDA, Texas Medical Board Fights to Kill Cancer Cure. Newswithview.com

REFERENCES

Science Magazine, (2001). Carbohydrate and Glycobiology. Science Magazine.

Seattle Cancer Care Alliance, (2012). Prostate Cancer. Retrieved from: http://www.seattlecca.org/diseases/prostate-cancer-radiation-therapy.cfm

Seidman, H., Stellman, S. D., Mushinski, M. H., (1982). A Different Perspective on Breast Cancer Risk Factors: Some Implications of the Nonattributable Risk. CA A Cancer Journal for Clinicians, Vol. 32, pp. 301-313.

Shintani, D., & DellaPenna, D., (1998). Elevating the Vitamin E Content of Plants through Metabolic Engineering. Science. 282, (5396), pp. 2098-2100.

Simha, V., (2010). More than a pinprick, the risk to India's newborns. Tehelka Magazine, 7 (24), June 19, 2010. Retrieved from: http://www.tehelka.com/story_main45.asp?filename=Ne190610coverstory.asp

Singer, S. R., Grismaijer, S., (2000). Get It Off. Understanding the Cause of…Breast Pain, Cysts, and Cancer. ISCD Press, Pahoa, Hawaii

Singer, S. R., Grismaijer, S., (2006). Dressed to Kill: The Link Between Breast Cancer and Bras. Savery Publishing Group, Garden City Park, N. Y.

Somers, S., (2009). Interviews With Doctors Who Are Curing Cancer and How to Prevent it in the First Place. Crown Publishers, N.Y.

Somers, S., (2008). Breakthrough. Crown Publishing, N.Y.

Somers, S., (n.d.). Men Vs. Women: Finding the Right Hormonal Levels. Retrieved from: http://www.sexyforever.com/public/newsletter-Finding-the-right-hormonallevels.aspx?xid=nl_SuzanneSomersSexyForeverNewsletter_20130115

Spector, R., (2010). The War on Cancer A Progress Report for Skeptics. The Committee for Skeptical Inquiry, 34.1, January/February. Retrieved from: http://www.csicop.org/si/show/war_on_cancer_a_progress_report_for_skeptics/

Spratt, D., Zhang, C., Zumsteg, Z., Pei, X., Zhang, Z., (2013). Metformin and Prostate Cancer: Reduced Development of Castration-resistant Disease and Prostate Cancer Mortality. European Urology, 4,63, pp. 709-716

Stole, V., Podoba, J., (1960). Effect of Fluoride on the Biogenesis of Thyroid Hormones," Nature, 188, (4753), pp. 855-856

Stone, G., Campbell, C., & Esselstyn, C., (2011). Forks Over Knives: The Plant-Based Way to Health. The Experiment, LLC

Seluanov, A., Hine, C., Azpurua, J., Feigenson, M., Bozzella, M., Mao, Z., Catania, K., & Gorbunova, V., (2009). Hypersensitivity to contact inhibition provides a clue to cancer resistance of naked mole-rat. Proceeding of the National Academy of Sciences of the United States of America (PNAS), 106 (46), pp. 19352-19357. Retrieved from: http://www.pnas.org/content/106/46/19352.full

Tabar, R., Nguyen-Yamamoto, L., Tavera-Mendoza, L., Quail, T., Dimitrov, V., Ann, B., Glass, L., Goltzman, G., & White, J., (2012). Vitamin D receptor as a master regulator of the c-MYC/MXD1 network, 109,46, pp. 18827 – 18832.

Temodar, (2006). Schering-Plough Research Institute. Rev. 6/06, p. 5

Texas Oncology, (n.d.). Immunotherapy. Texas Oncology. Retrieved from: http://www.texasoncology.com/media-center/fact-sheets/immunotherapy.aspx

Thomas, D. B., Karagas, M. G., (1987). Cancer in First and Second Generation Americans.

REFERENCES

Cancer Research, American Association for Cancer Research. Volume 47, pp. 5771-5776

Toniolo, P., Van Kappel, A., Akhmedkhanov, A., Ferrari, P., Kato, I., Shore, R. E., Riboli, E., (2001). Serum Carotenoids and Breast Cancer. American Journal of Epidemiology. Issue 153 Volume 12, pp. 1142-1147. doi: 10.1093/aje/153.12.1142

Trasande, L., Landrigan, P., & Schechter, C., (2005). Public Health and Economic Consequences of Methyl Mercury Toxicity to the Developing Brain. Environmental Health Perspectives, 113 (5), 590-596. Retrieved from: http://www.ncbi.nlm.nih.gov/pmc/articles/PMC1257552/

UCSD, (n.d.). Glycobiology Research and Training Center. Retrieved from: http://grtc.ucsd.edu/index.html

University of Illinois, (2013). Scientists learn how soy foods protect against colon cancer. University of Illinois. Retrieved from: http://fshn.illinois.edu/news/scientists-learn-howsoy-foods-protect-against-colon-cancer

University of Liverpool, (n.d.). Glycobiology & Glycomics. Center for Glycobiology. Retrieved from: http://www.liv.ac.uk/glyco/background.html

Venitt, (1996). Mechanisms of spontaneous human cancers. Environmental Health Perspectives, 104 (3), 633-637. Retrieved from: http://www.ncbi.nlm.nih.gov/pmc/articles/PMC1469658/

Verma, S.P., Salamone, E., Goldin, B., (1997). Curcumin and Genistein, Plant Natural Products, Show Synergistic Inhibitory Effects on the Growth of Human Breast Cancer MCF-7 Cells Induced by Estrogenic Pesticides. Biochemical and Biophysical Research Communications. Volume 233, Issue 3, April 28, pp. 692-696

Viereck, G.S., (1929). "What Life Means to Einstein," Saturday Evening Post, 26 October 1929; Schlagschatten, Sechsundzwanzig

Schicksalsfragen an Grosse der Zeit (Vogt-Schild, Solothurn, 1930), p. 60; Glimpses of the Great (Macauley, New York, 1930), pp. 373-374.

Vighi, G., Marcucci, F., Sensi, L., et al., (2008). Allergy and the Gastrointestinal System. Clinical & Experimental Immunology. Sep; 153(Suppl 1): 3–6. doi: 10.1111/j.1365-2249.2008.03713.x. Retrieved from: http://www.ncbi.nlm.nih.gov/pmc/articles/PMC2515351/

VitaNet, (2006). Lifespan of Some Cells in The Human Body! Retrieved from: http://vitanetonline.com/forums/1/Thread/1001

Wang, S. S., (2009). CT Scans Linked to Cancer. Study Warns Radiation Dose from Single Test Can Trigger Disease in Some People. The Wall Street Journal. December 15, 2009.

Warburg, (1956). On the Origin of Cancer Cells. Science. Vol. 123, No. 3191.

Warburg, (1966). The Prime Cause and Prevention of Cancer. Retrieved from: http://actualcures.com/cancer-cells-cause-prevent-cure-nutrients-nobel-prize.html

Watson, B., (2008). Are today's baby boomers burdened by toxins? Healthy Living. Retrieved from: http://www.brendawatson.com/Healthy-Living/200809/Todays-Baby-Boomers-Burdened-by-Toxins.htm.

Weil, A., (2013). Ask Dr. Weil: Is Wi-Fi Harmful to My Health? Prevention.

Wennberg, M., Stromberg, U., Bergdahl, I., Jansson, J., Kauhanen, J., Norberg, M., Salonen, J., Skerfving, S., Tuomainen, T., Vessby, B., & Virtanen, J., (2012). Myocardial infarction in relation to mercury and fatty acids from fish: a risk-benefit analysis based on pooled Finnish and Swedish data in men. The American Journal of Clinical Nutrition, 96 (4), 706-713.

REFERENCES

Westman A., Ferketich A., Kauffman R., MacEachern S., Wilkins JR 3rd, Wilcox P., Pilarski R., Nagy R., Lemeshow S., de la Chapelle A., Bloomfield C., (2010). Low cancer incidence rates in Ohio Amish. Cancer, Causes, Control, Jan;21(1):69-75. doi: 10.1007/s10552-009-9435-7. Epub 2009 Sep 25.

WHO, 2014). Electromagnetic fields and public health: mobile phones. World Health Organization. Retrieved from: http://www.who.int/mediacentre/factsheets/fs193/en/ Williams, H., (2005). Nutrition for Health, Fitness & Sport (7th Ed.). McGraw Hill Higher Education.

Williams, (2011). 'Serial Killer' Immune Cells Put Cancer in Remission. Science Now, Biology.

Williams, M., (2013). 'Vicious cycle' shields, spreads cancer cells. Rice University News & Media. Retrieved from: http://news.rice.edu/2013/09/16/vicious-cycle-shields-spreadscancer-cells-2/

World Health Organization, (2015). Cancer. Retrieved from: http://www.who.int/mediacentre/factsheets/fs297/en/

World Health Organization, (n.d.). Global cancer rates could increase by 50% to 15 million by 2020. Retrieved from: http://www.who.int/mediacentre/news/releases/2003/pr27/en/

Wright, R., Visness, C., Calatroni, A., Grayson, M., Gold, D., Sandel, M., Lee-Parritz, A., Wood, R., Kattan, M., Bloomberg, G., Burger, M., Togias, A., Witter, F., Sperling, R., Sadovsky, Y., & Gern, J., (2010). Prenatal Maternal Stress and Cord Blood Innate and Adaptive Cytokine Responses in an Inner-City Cohort. American Journal of Respiratory and Critical Care Medicine, 182:1, 25-33.

Yang, X., (2012). Study Suggests New Approach to Explain Cancer Growth: Low Oxygen Levels. UGA Today. Retrieved from: http://news.uga.edu/releases/article/study-suggestsnew-approach-to-explain-cancer-growth-low-oxygen-levels/

Zeratsky, K., (n.d.), Nutrition and healthy Living, Mayo Clinic. Retrieved from: http://www.mayoclinic.org/healthy-lifestyle/nutrition-and-healthy-eating/expertanswers/sea-salt/faq-20058512

Zhonghua Renmin Gongheguo e xing zhong liu di tu ji bian ji wei yuan hui, (1981). Atlas of Cancer Mortality in the People's Republic of China. China Map Press.

Ziegler, R. (1993). Migration Patterns and Breast Cancer Risk in Asian-American Women. Journal of the National Cancer Institute. Vol. 83, Issue 22, pp. 1819-1827

Zitvogel L, Apetoh L, Ghiringhelli F, Kroemer G, (2008). Immunological aspects of cancer

Chemotherapy. Nature Reviews Immunology. Vol. 8 (1), pp. 59-73.

ABOUT THE AUTHOR

Garry Estrada was born in Los Angeles, CA. His father was a carpenter, and his mother was an accountant for Sears & Roebuck.

The second oldest of four, Garry began working at the age of 13. His first job was cleaning cars at the local car wash. At the age of 21, Garry received a full college scholarship and completed his undergraduate degree from BIOLA University, in La Mirada, CA. He married soon thereafter and moved to Seattle, WA where he resides to this day.

Garry also received his master's degree from the University of Phoenix. Then he entered the Ph.D. program for Health & Wellness but took a leave because of illness.

Garry spent the better part of 14 years researching and writing about cancer. His documented research has resulted in his first book *"The Answers to Cancer"*.

Today, Garry finds joy as the father of four children – Jennifer, Christina, Katerina, and Michael – and four grandchildren. His current goals are to lecture on what he has discovered in the world of cancer research and to help the orphan children of "Republic Pilgrim," an orphanage located in Mariupol, Ukraine. His goal is to help them battle the AIDS virus that afflicts some of the children. He will always remember, Anatoly, a young orphan teenager who died of AIDS.

Garry maintains a love for Harley-Davidson® motorcycles, classic movies, ferry rides, and home cooking.

PLEASE RATE MY BOOK

I'd be honored if you would take a few moments to rate this book on Amazon.com.

A five-star rating and a short comment ("Great read," or "Enjoyed it!") would be much appreciated. Longer, positive comments are great as well.

If you feel like this book should be rated at three stars or fewer, please hold off posting your thoughts on Amazon. Instead, please send your feedback directly to me so that I can use it to improve the next edition. I'm committed to providing the best value to my customers and readers, and your thoughts can make that possible.

You can reach me at GarryEstradaPublishing@gmail.com.

With gratitude,

Garry

Made in the USA
Coppell, TX
17 May 2020

25961288R00167